From the Shadow of Empire

From the Shadow of Empire

Defining the Russian Nation
through Cultural Mythology,
1855–1870

Olga Maiorova

The University of Wisconsin Press

Publication of this volume has been made possible, in part, through support from the **Andrew W. Mellon Foundation** and from the **University of Michigan's Department of Slavic Languages and Literatures, Office of the Vice President for Research, and College of Literature, Science and the Arts.**

STUDIES OF THE HARRIMAN INSTITUTE

Columbia University

The Harriman Institute designates selected research conducted under its auspices as "Studies of the Harriman Institute." The Institute is pleased to publicize these works in the belief that their publication contributes to scholarly research and public understanding.

The University of Wisconsin Press
1930 Monroe Street, 3rd Floor
Madison, Wisconsin 53711-2059
uwpress.wisc.edu

3 Henrietta Street
London WCE 8LU, England
eurospanbookstore.com

1   3   5   4   2

Printed in the United States of America

Library of Congress Cataloging-in-Publication Data
Maiorova, O. E.
From the shadow of empire: defining the Russian nation through cultural mythology, 1855–1870 / Olga Maiorova.
        p.   cm.
Includes bibliographical references and index.
ISBN 978-0-299-23594-9 (pbk.: alk. paper)
ISBN 978-0-299-23593-2 (e-book)
1. Russia—History—Alexander II, 1855–1881—Historiography.
2. Nationalism—Mythology—Russia—19th century.   I. Title.
DK221.M315   2010
947.08´1072—dc22
2009046768

To my mother,

IZABELLA MAIOROVA,

and to the memory of my father,

EVGENII MAIOROV

Contents

     From Apocalyptic Battle to Beehive   128

5   The Myth of Spiritual Descent: Remapping the Empire   155

     In Place of a Conclusion: The Legacy
     of Reform-Era Nationalism   183

     Notes   193
     Bibliography   243
     Index   261

Illustrations

Acknowledgments

My book could not have been written without the assistance of several institutions that generously supported my project at its various stages. A grant from the Fulbright Program made it possible for me to spend eight productive months at the Harriman Institute at Columbia University. My preliminary research immensely benefited from the institute's intellectually stimulating atmosphere and extensive resources. I would also like to express my appreciation to the Warner Fund at the University Seminars at Columbia University for their help in publication. Material in this work was presented to the University seminar: Slavic History and Culture. The Office of the Vice President for Research at the University of Michigan provided some funding for the completion and publication of my manuscript. The Department of Slavic Languages at my home institution, the University of Michigan, not only contributed to the publication cost of this book but also granted me a much-needed semester away from teaching. I am deeply indebted to the three consecutive chairs of the department — Jindrich Toman, Bogdana

Carpenter, and Herbert Eagle—for their constant support and collegial advice over the course of my work. I also want to thank the Lithuanian State Historical Archive (LVIA) and the Fedor Tiutchev State Museum in Muranovo (the Russian Federation) for granting permission to use illustrations from their collections.

I owe a great debt of thanks to everyone who read and commented on my work in progress. I am especially grateful to Valerie Kivelson, Irina Reyfman, and Richard Wortman for having taken part in a workshop organized by the University of Michigan to discuss the nearly completed version of the manuscript: their careful reading and astute criticism guided me during the final stage of turning the manuscript into a book. The much-needed advice and persistent encouragement that Richard Wortman has offered me for many years deserve special gratitude. I have learned an immense amount from our intense conversations, formal and informal, and want to thank him for this truly exceptional intellectual experience. Ronald Suny's insightful suggestions and enthusiastic support helped me to sharpen my argument. I presented parts of this book at various seminars and conferences and benefited from each discussion that followed. I am particularly indebted to a group of American and Russian scholars who shared my interests and offered their comments both during conferences and afterward in continuing correspondence: Henryk Baran, Seymour Becker, Konstantin Bolenko, Mikhail Dolbilov, David Goldfrank, Nathaniel Knight, Laurie Manchester, Alexander Martin, Natalia Mazur, Vera Mil'china, Marina Mogil'ner, Nikita Okhotin, Donna Orwin, Alexander Ospovat, Alla Zeide, Andrei Zorin, and Ted Weeks. I want to thank Rachel Harrell, doctoral student in the Slavic department at Michigan, for her valuable editorial and translation assistance; her keen eye and linguistic sensitivity were immensely helpful. I also wish to express my gratitude to Deborah Martinsen, who provided insightful editorial comments, and to Irina Lukka for her speedy help with a number of bibliographic inquiries.

The professional expertise of Gwen Walker, acquisitions editor at the University of Wisconsin Press, made the publication process smooth and intellectually exciting. I also want to express appreciation to the anonymous reviewers for the Press. Their criticism helped me to improve my manuscript.

During all these years of engaging in research and writing, I have enjoyed the friendship of Janet and Steve Taylor, Semyon Reyfman, and Anna

Knysh; they have been exceptionally generous with their time when I have needed their support. I feel a special debt of gratitude to my daughter, Anna, who was always able to engage herself with reading and drawing, giving me time to work and gradually developing into my most precious interlocutor. And I owe my greatest thanks to my mother, Izabella Maiorova, and my late father, Yevgenii Maiorov; their love, encouragement, and understanding carried me through this project. I dedicate this book to them.

An earlier version of chapter 1 appeared in *Ab Imperio: Studies of New Imperial History and Nationalism in the Post-Soviet Space* (no. 4 [2006]: 187–224). Several sections of chapter 2 and chapter 5 were initially published in Russian in *Novoe literaturnoe obozrenie* (no. 43 [2000]: 137–65; no. 51 [2001]: 89–110) and were significantly revised for this book. A prior version of a substantial portion of chapter 3 appeared in *Kritika: Explorations in Russian and Eurasian History* (vol. 6, no. 3 [Summer 2005]: 501–34). The Amsterdam journal *Russian Literature* included a section of chapter 4 in a special issue devoted to Tiutchev (vol. 57, no. 1/2 [2005]: 103–24). I want to thank the readers and editors of these peer-reviewed journals for their insightful comments and helpful suggestions.

Note on Transliteration, Translation, and Dates

In most instances I have followed the Library of Congress system of transliteration for Slavic languages, but have retained names of well-known authors in their traditional English spelling (Tolstoy, Herzen, Gogol, Dostoevsky). Wherever possible I quote from established translations of works by major Russian writers, but modify them if necessary. All other translations are my own. All dates referring to Russia are given in accordance with the Julian (Old Style) calendar, which was used in nineteenth-century Russia.

From the Shadow of Empire

Introduction

Cultural Myth and National Self-Perception in the Turbulent Reform Era

A preoccupation with national uniqueness pervaded the intellectual landscape of nineteenth-century Russia, as it did in many European countries during the age of rising nationalism fanned by the French Revolution and the Napoleonic wars. Russia's victory over the Grande Armée (1812–15) galvanized its cultural elite, heightening their sense of national identity and sending them in search of their native roots. Although this process engaged intellectuals throughout the century, certain pivotal historical periods infused the discussions with particular passion and creativity. This book focuses on one of Russia's most turbulent and exuberant epochs—the time of social, institutional, and legal transformations known as the Great Reforms (1860s through 1870s)—and examines its contribution to national self-understanding. Precipitated by Russia's crushing defeat in the Crimean War (1853–56), the reform era produced a broad range of cultural expressions of the nation meant to salve its wounded pride and reconstitute the national community. As we shall see, new visions

3

of the nation emerged to alter national self-perception and (re)address one of the central problems of Russian national discourse: how to "find" and define the nation within an empire that overshadowed it.

Two Faces of Russianness

A telling image, reiterated in intellectual discourse throughout the century, illustrates the degree to which Russia's imperial character threatened its sense of itself as a nation. Recalling the jubilant public reception of Nikolai Karamzin's *History of the Russian State* (1818–29), Alexander Pushkin praised the author, a celebrated fiction writer, for his vivid evocation of the past and explained the book's unprecedented success with a most flattering simile: "Karamzin, it seemed, discovered ancient Rus', as Columbus discovered America."[1] Oddly, as the century progressed and memories of Rus'—the conventional name for Russia's historical heartland—came to occupy a growing place in public discourse, comparisons with pre-Columbian America persisted. In 1863 the Slavophile Ivan Aksakov described the cultural elite's emerging interest in the "obscure" parts of Rus as "something like Columbus's discovery of the New World."[2] And in 1877 Dostoevsky used the same comparison when he exhorted educated society to overcome its self-imposed alienation from the authentic values preserved in the common people: by returning to its native roots, the Westernized Russian upper class would discover the real Russia, as Europe once had discovered America.[3]

Karamzin's canonical narrative traced Russia's triumphant expansion and growing power back to the emergence of the absolutist state and thus identified Rus' with the monarchy. Yet subsequent generations of Russian writers, including Aksakov and Dostoevsky, took the notion of Rus' beyond the state, associating it with the achievements of the people and increasingly transforming it into the ultimate metaphor for the essence of the Russian nation. Oft-repeated descriptions of Rus' as terra incognita helped them emphasize the "neglected" or unknown nature of the Russian native heritage and of the people as a whole. It was this relationship between empire and nation—or, more bluntly, it was the fact that the Russian Empire overshadowed the Russian nation—that made the quest for Russianness so problematic.

As many studies of Russian history have convincingly demonstrated, the supranational policies of the monarchical Russian Empire hindered the formation of a Russian nation. The regime, whose authority was premised on the exercise of absolute power, stifled and suppressed Russia's ethnic core, as it did all subject nationalities. But for Russians, unlike other ethnic groups within the empire, it proved difficult to distinguish themselves from the imperial state, even symbolically. The empire, after all, bore the name "Russian" and its contiguous domains, not separated from the metropole by "salt water"—in contrast to Great Britain or France—made it possible to construe it as an "organic" outgrowth of Rus'.[4] The question thus inevitably arose: who are the Russians—an empire, a nation, both, or neither?

It may seem that the two names for the country—Russia and Rus'—offered a solution. They reflected the Janus-like nature of Russianness, imperial and national, and yielded two distinct terms for the Russian people (*narod*): *rossiiskii* when speaking of the multiethnic empire and *russkii* to designate its ethnic "core."[5] But these two words, and hence the two concepts of Russianness they implied, overlapped and could even be used interchangeably in many contexts. Their interweaving is visible in the political positions taken by many nationalists: disappointed at the government's supranational policy and increasingly bewailing the authorities' "betrayal" of authentic national values, they nonetheless sought to perpetuate the empire and glorify its might.

This peculiar blend of national sentiment and imperial pride—so typical of Russia in the nineteenth century—has informed the assumption, widespread in current scholarship, that Russian national identity was subsumed under that of the empire. Recently reiterated in Geoffrey Hosking's *Russia: People and Empire*, this view was further developed by Vera Tolz in her *Russia: Inventing the Nation*.[6] She argues that it was not only the policies of the autocratic regime that hampered the creation of the Russian nation. "Russians' failure to form a full-fledged nation" also stemmed, Tolz claims, from the overwhelming tendency of the majority of intellectuals to blur the line between Russia proper and the empire as a whole. As it appears from her book, the problem of nation-making was inscribed in the way the cultural elite, concerned primarily with empire, imagined the nation.[7]

Close examination of divergent expressions of nationhood calls this assumption into question. Certainly, the rise of national consciousness was in many ways constrained and impeded by the predominance of the monarchical empire. No doubt, "finding" the nation in the empire proved difficult, since the edges of Russia's core were undefined, the boundaries between the center and periphery were porous, and the state's outward growth seemed unstoppable. It is also undeniable that most visions of Russianness put forward in the nineteenth century bore an expansionist character and that the majority of Russian nationalists rejected any separation between empire and nation.[8] But these challenges did not necessarily prevent drawing a line between the two, much less imply a strict subordination of the national to the imperial.[9] The problem of distinguishing the Russian nation from the Russian Empire was very much on the minds of historians, poets, journalists—not only the few who thought coexistence between nation and empire impossible, but also the far greater number who could not conceive of Russians outside the empire. They celebrated the empire and at the same time produced a constellation of aspirations, attitudes, and impulses aimed at fostering a vivid sense of national belonging. For them, the empire was a stage where the Russian people's historical drama unfolded, and as such, it served to reinforce rather than to obliterate Russian national identity. Indeed, many expressions of Russianness symbolically plucked the nation from the shadow of empire, assigning central significance to the nation itself.

Renditions of the empire as an attribute of the nation represent, I would argue, the major legacy of nineteenth-century nationalism, one that still resonates in the minds of many Russian policy makers and intellectuals today as they seek to restore the nation's pride on the basis of its imperial potential. But what now seems old-fashioned had a different flavor a century and a half ago. It amounted to an advocacy of fundamental political changes that would alter the traditional bases of imperial allegiance. These constructs, with their implicit (and sometimes explicit) critique of the regime, could be openly articulated only during a period of relative freedom of speech like the one ushered in by the introduction of the Great Reforms. To understand how this period prompted a shift in national discourse and how it led to rethinking the empire in nationalistic terms, we need to take a closer look at the developments of the reform era.

Reimagining the Nation in a Changing Political Environment

The crushing loss in the Crimea exposed the obsolescence of Russia's military establishment and provided shocking evidence of the country's economic backwardness and the corruption of its civil administration. In response to these pressures, Emperor Alexander II—who had ascended the throne scarcely a year before the war's end—launched a series of fundamental transformations intended to avert the empire's sinking to the status of a second-rate power. The danger posed by the system of serfdom also served as a catalyst for the reforms. On March 30, 1856, soon after signing the Treaty of Paris that concluded the war, Alexander addressed the Moscow nobility with the famous words: "It is better to abolish serfdom from above than to await the day when it will begin to abolish itself from below."[10] Thus Russia embarked on a course of innovation that dramatically altered the fabric of its society.

The legislation and implementation of the reforms, as well as their collective impact on Russian life, have been analyzed at great length in the scholarly literature.[11] The sheer number of studies devoted to the period is evidence of its immense significance. While the effects of the changes on the peasantry, the landed gentry, legal culture, institutions of local governance, the military, and the revolutionary movement have been thoroughly investigated, what remains understudied is how events of the period affected the vision of Russianness itself.[12]

Initially, it was the trauma of the Crimean defeat that forced Russians to take a hard look at themselves. "Up to now," the censor A. V. Nikitenko bitterly admitted in his diary at the end of the war, "we have shown ourselves to Europe only as a huge fist, threatening its civic life, rather than a great power intent on its own perfection and development."[13] A gnawing sense of systemic failure haunted the exposé literature that emerged after the war to demand changes in many aspects of national life.[14] The introduction of the reforms lent discussions of nationhood a new urgency, further intensified by the conviction that Russia was crossing a historic threshold. Mikhail Katkov, the prime exponent of nationalist ideology at that time, captured the attitude perfectly in 1862: "There are moments in history when a nation makes an irrevocable decision and seals its fate forever. The present moment belongs among them."[15] Ivan Aksakov, another leading journalist of the day, seemed to second Katkov a year later: "There are epochs when the slow, organic pace of a nation's internal development is replaced by a general moral upheaval of the whole national organism, speeding its activity, immediately calling to the surface all its hidden and suppressed strengths. We believe that Russia is on the verge of just such an epoch . . ."[16] This sense of living through momentous times provoked heated disputes about which path Russia should take. At the dawn of the reform era, when these two sets of impulses—the crescendo of self-criticism and the search for developmental models—converged, they began to evolve into full-fledged attempts to redefine the nation.

The process was stoked by the confluence of social and political factors that marked the turbulent reform years. With the emancipation of the serfs (1861), the introduction of elective organs of local self-government, or *zemstvos* (1864), and the inauguration of Western-style judicial institutions (1864), both national cohesion and wider participation in political life seemed for the first time in Russian history to have a chance of becoming reality. Questions arose, however, as to which groups this emerging society was to encompass. Given that the reforms were to be implemented in a gradual manner (designed to become effective swiftly in Russia proper, but only after some delay in certain "backward" areas, and not at all in other regions), their introduction set in motion a mechanism of inclusion and exclusion that intensified the issue of where the borders of the nation should be drawn. Meanwhile, the acquisition of new territories—the final subjugation of the Caucasus (1864) and the enlargement of Russia's borders into Central Asia (1860s through 1880s)—gave fresh impetus to the demand to shore up the Russian people's position as the "reigning nationality," destined to shape the character of the expanding empire. Finally, the rise of nationalism throughout Europe (particularly the unifications of Italy and of Germany) and the beginning of adaptation to the challenges of modernity exhibited by the empires neighboring Russia made it urgent to rethink the supranational Romanov empire, whose cohesion relied on loyalty to the ruling dynasty.[17] As a result of these pressures, the perennial problems of Russian nationhood—relations between the people and the state, the empire-nation dichotomy, and the bases of imperial allegiance—sprang sharply into focus.

With the introduction of the reforms, an increasingly vocal corps of nationally minded intellectuals—journalists, novelists, poets, and popular historians—addressed these issues to create a spectrum of competing constructs of the nation, ranging from the romantic and religious nationalism of Ivan Aksakov and Fedor Tiutchev to the state and secular nationalism of Mikhail Katkov; from the imperial Pan-Slavism of Mikhail Pogodin to the federalism articulated by Nikolai Kostomarov; from Stepan Gedeonov's chauvinistic justification for the empire's suppression of its non-Slavic population to Lev Tolstoy's ultimate denial of Russia's imperial mission. Representing the reform era's main lines of thinking about national self-definition, these writers either shaped public opinion (Katkov, above all) or found the most felicitous expressions for views already in circulation (like Gedeonov). To fully understand their constructs, this book places them within a larger context of debates about Russia's future. It therefore features a wider group of intellectuals, including Fedor Dostoevsky, Iurii Samarin, and Konstantin Leont'ev, with whom the protagonists of this book either sparred or concurred (and frequently both, as their positions shifted over time).

All these exponents of reform-era public nationalism emerged from a broad range of intellectual and social backgrounds. Most of them were labeled either liberal or conservative by their contemporaries, and these labels have tended to stick. Scholars have observed, however, that in the case of tsarist Russia the liberal-conservative dichotomy can be misleading. This is particularly true of the opening decade of the reform era, since by the late 1870s the majority of thinkers would gravitate increasingly to the extremes of the political spectrum.[18] Thus, in the 1860s the Slavophiles Aksakov and Samarin demanded freedom of the press and freedom of speech while at the same time defending the archaic institution of the village commune and upholding the traditional notion of the unbreakable bond between tsar and people. Katkov advocated building a politically aware civil society but grounded his arguments in loyalty to an unlimited monarchy. Perhaps the most striking example of this kind of complexity is Konstantin Pobedonostsev, ober-procurator of the Holy Synod at the end of the nineteenth century, famous for his reactionary policy. During the reform period, Pobedonostsev, then a professor of civil law at Moscow University, sharply criticized all requests for broadening political rights, but in 1859 he contributed to *Golosa iz Rossii* (Voices from Russia), a periodical published abroad by the revolutionary émigré Alexander Herzen, and in subsequent years took part in the drafting of the judicial reform (1864), the most liberal of the era's transformations.[19] Given the blurry ideological map of the 1860s, I refer to the entire group under consideration here as nationalist writers or intellectuals of a nationalist persuasion.

Although these umbrella terms potentially encompass thinkers from across the political spectrum, the revolutionary intelligentsia remains marginal to my study. Their mistrust of the regime grew exponentially during the reform era—and for them this opposition to autocracy increasingly outweighed issues of nationhood. Thus, when Polish unrest and the emergence of Ukrainian separatism provoked a surge of aggressive propaganda for the "Russian cause," the leading left-wing figures—above all, Nikolai Chernyshevskii—argued that Poles, Russians, and Ukrainians should set aside their mutually conflicting claims and struggle to liberate themselves from their shared enemy, tsarist despotism.[20] A few radicals, however, managed to saturate their ideas with national sentiments; for example, Herzen incorporated some Slavophile beliefs into his socialist program. Herzen will therefore make the occasional cameo appearance in these pages.

Although reform-era thinkers of a nationalist persuasion represented conflicting ideologies, their competing constructs of the nation developed in an atmosphere of mutual influence. These constructs could be complementary (Tiutchev's belief in Russia as a universal Christian empire, for instance, overlapped with Pan-Slavism, to which he also contributed), but more often they were incompatible. While Aksakov, proceeding from Slavophile tenets, defined the Russian people as an entity separate from the state and sought resources for national renewal in pre-Petrine native institutions, Katkov—an adherent of the Hegelian model of civic development— considered the monarchy the highest manifestation of the people's spirit and ascribed to the state the main role in forging the nation.[21] Despite their fundamental disagreements on key issues of nationhood, both Katkov and Aksakov attacked (the former more scathingly) the project for Russia's future spelled out by the popular historian Kostomarov. A fervent Ukrainian separatist, he challenged the central axiom of Russian nationalism: the notion of a single all-Russian nation that included Byelorussians, Ukrainians, and Great Russians.[22] Kostomarov envisioned "the two Russian nationalities," that is, Ukrainians and Great Russians, as political equals in a future Russia and advocated a federation of independent polities, rooted, he claimed, in the political culture of Kievan Rus'.[23] Despite the striking contradictions among these three projects, the borders between them proved porous. As we shall see, in response to political pressures, sporadic affinities emerged between divergent groups of thinkers and contentious issues sometimes receded, allowing them to find common ground, if only temporarily.

What occasionally brought these individuals together was the fact that, though generally loyal to the regime, they nonetheless opposed imperial policies from a national standpoint. They criticized the government for its unwillingness to elevate "the Russian people" (however this category was understood) to the status of "reigning nationality" within the empire and excoriated Nicholas I for neglecting Russian interests while supporting autocratic regimes in Europe.[24] The doctrine of official nationality encapsulated in Count Sergei Uvarov's slogan, "Orthodoxy, Autocracy, and Nationality," also failed to satisfy reform-era intellectuals. While proponents of the doctrine articulated the concept of the monarchical nation and promoted loyalty to the ruler as the basis of imperial patriotism, writers of a nationalist persuasion proposed "the Russian people" as the primary object of allegiance, usually alongside the ruling house.[25] The majority of independent thinkers also shared a general mistrust of the empire's bureaucracy, which they claimed exceeded its proper role, arbitrarily controlled the state machinery, and thus impeded the development of the entire nation.[26] United by these attitudes, the protagonists of this book grappled with a common set of issues as they worked to redefine the nation in a changing political environment.

The first of these issues stemmed from anticipation of the rapid modernization that the reforms were expected to effect. In the late 1850s and early 1860s the majority of nationally minded writers welcomed reform but took pains to show that no transformation could shake the steadfast character of the Russian people. Nationalism always seeks to highlight a national community's uniqueness and continuity. In an era of fundamental change under the obvious influence of Western European models, this impulse ran rampant, forcing Russian thinkers to confront the inescapable questions: How could their ideal of an unchanging people be reconciled with the urgent need for social and political innovations? Could the sense of national distinctiveness be linked, if only rhetorically, to the impending modernization?

An unprecedented relaxation of censorship and sudden increase in the number of newly permitted periodicals allowed public opinion to flourish.[27] In the 1860s, discussions of Russian national identity escaped the bounds of elite salons to spread through meeting halls and onto the pages of novels, poems, "thick journals," and the daily press. Yet this broadening of the audience brought with it another problem. It precipitated a search for a new language capable of appealing to a wider cross section of society. What would be the source of the discursive strategies to resolve this issue? In their unadulterated form, neither the refined philosophical lexicon elaborated by the Slavophiles and the Westernizers in the 1840s nor the doctrine of official nationality—discredited in the eyes of many intellectuals—could provide a new language of nation.

Russian thinkers of a nationalist persuasion faced one more potentially fatal question. The expansion of the discursive space of nationalism did not entail an expansion of its political space. Although the reforms at first appeared to have opened the floodgates for wider political participation, these hopes proved illusory. Not only did the regime deny society access to the decision-making process, but many intellectuals also approached the idea of including the masses in political life with utmost wariness.[28] Nonetheless, they presented themselves not merely as advocates of the national interest but as spokesmen for the people, touting their own views as a distillation of the spirit and indeed the will of the nation. Yet how could they claim to speak with the voice of the nation when political conditions deprived the people of institutionalized ways to express their desires?

Defining Russia's future by means of historical myths and legends offered one way out. It allowed intellectuals to rhetorically link the perception of the people's uniqueness with hopes for, or fears of, the modernizing impetus of the reforms—and thus to absorb innovations while maintaining a sense of national continuity. Since historical myth is a democratic commodity, consumable at every level of society, it also facilitated the development of a rhetoric capable of reaching out to various social strata. Moreover, it could be taken to represent the voice of the people, since the common folk were perceived as inheritors of the legendary past and a living repository of pure national ideals, perpetuated in myth. Finally, by invoking stirring narratives of the past, writers could justify programs of national transformation as restorations of deeply ingrained native institutions. The broad power of historical myth explains its pervasive presence in the various expressions of nationhood. The chapters that follow trace how fictional prose, poetry, popular historiography, and the daily press harnessed the tale of the founding of Rus', legends of Cossack independence, war narratives, and the story of the nation's birth to rhetorically (re)constitute the Russian nation.

Reform-Era Mythmaking as Justification
of Nation-Building Projects

In the past two decades, with the "cultural turn" in nationalism studies, scholars have intensively examined the role of historical myths and collective memories—shared visions of the past—in nationalist discourses. Most historians agree that nations, as opposed to ethnic communities, are relatively late historical developments that began to emerge in Western Europe in the late eighteenth century, when social, technological, and political conditions converged to make it possible for them to come into being. If nations are to be forged, they must first be "imagined," as Benedict Anderson put it in his groundbreaking book, *Imagined Communities*. It is the intellectual elite who project the nation in literature, theater, painting, and other forms of cultural production, by evoking or manufacturing collective memories and shared beliefs. As Anthony Smith has argued, preexisting culture plays a formative role in this process by defining the limits and determining the nature of the national imagination: nations are envisioned within parameters established by previous cultural traditions.[29] In Russia it was predominantly the old historical myths that set these parameters and provided a flexible framework to support the sense of national belonging.[30]

From the perspective of collective memory, nationhood might be understood as a complex process of appropriation, negotiation, and contestation over the past, involving a broad range of actors.[31] With the beginning of the reform era, as the government loosened its control over the public interpretation of history, new renditions of the basic myths multiplied. By embracing some memories and repudiating others, Russian intellectuals reshaped the most appealing narratives to turn them into sites for the inculcation of ethnic sentiments and thus compete with the political mythology generated by the state, which tended to downplay ethnic motifs. This book traces how independent thinkers refashioned collective memories to construct an ethnic basis for the empire—or, to use their own language, to "discover" Rus' in Russia. Their attempts exemplify what Étienne Balibar has called "fictive ethnicity," that is, an idealized representation of the people that makes it possible for expressions of the past to be seen as a model to emulate.[32] Nineteenth-century writers "invented" a Rus' whose qualities would be discernible in the Russia of their day as a way to justify their projects for the empire's transformation.

Viewed from this perspective, mythmaking takes on a profound significance in the dialogue concerning Russia's future that unfolded between the authorities and leaders of public opinion as the reforms progressed. Of course the different groups of nationalists diverged in their political views, but many of them shared a vision of Russia as a national empire that would develop over time in the direction of the European nation-states, which appeared more successful in their dealings with multiethnic subjects. Several Russian writers therefore used mythmaking in their attempts to press the government, with varying degrees of assertiveness, to embark on a new nation-building process.

Scholars have previously noted that the Russian case does not fully correspond to either of the two types of nation-building prevalent in nineteenth-century Europe. In the first model, exemplified by England, France, and Sweden, a monarchy supported the high culture of its ethnic core and used administrative measures to incorporate subject peoples into the state and its dominant culture. These countries evolved, initially under the aegis of the monarchy, into culturally uniform nation-states with a single set of literary traditions and historical memories dispersed throughout the populace. In the second model, ethnic communities lacking their own statehood, native ruling class, and uninterrupted literary traditions (like the Czechs, the Serbs, and the Irish) acquired the attributes of nationhood through struggle against alien rule. As Miroslav Hroch has shown, in this second model of nation-making the intelligentsia—scholars, priests, and journalists— discovered (or invented) cultural distinctiveness and constructed a national identity for their people in order to win recognition from the dominant nation and later to pursue autonomy or political independence.[33]

The Russian monarchy would appear to fit the first type of nation-making, since it possessed a Russian ruling class and institutionalized Russian high culture. As in countries of the first group, the Romanovs made some efforts to bureaucratically and culturally integrate subject nationalities, especially their elites. Yet the imperial authorities, fearing political instability and facing a host of other pressures that varied from region to region, often found it prudent, if not imperative, to maintain institutional differences among subaltern populations.[34] With the rise of national movements across the empire, the government sometimes even increased Russia's heterogeneity by supporting or encouraging the national consciousness of nontitular nationalities (such as the Latvians or the Chuvash) in order to counterbalance the expansionist nation-building projects of non-Russian regional elites (in this case, the Poles and the Tatars) that vied for the "minor" peoples' cultural—and potentially political—loyalty.[35] This inclination to perpetuate, at least in part, the linguistic, religious, economic, and administrative disparities within the empire kept the Romanovs from implementing the first kind of nation-making. To the extent that Russia followed the first pattern, it did so inconsistently, sporadically, and ambivalently.[36]

What the Russian Empire managed to do more consistently was to stifle and partially suppress its own ethnic core. It was primarily Russian peasants who were subjected to serfdom and therefore lived under more restrictive social, legal, and economic conditions than did the non-Russian rural population. Moreover, the nobilities of some subject nationalities—Tatars, Poles, Baltic Germans—enjoyed membership in the empire's ruling elite and often controlled regional life, exercising authority over the local Russian peasants in both legal and economic terms.[37] Russians thus dominated the empire in quantitative terms (if, in line with the practice of the day, all East Slavs were counted as "Russians"), but they could not be considered dominant when it came to civil rights.[38] As a result, Russian national discourse often sounded oddly like that of peoples deprived of political independence. Though the analogy with, say, the Czechs or the Ukrainians should not be pressed too far, nonetheless the Russians, like nondominant ethnic groups, often struggled against elites that were ethnically alien to them. In clashes between the Polish landowners and the "Russian"—actually Ukrainian or Byelorussian—peasants in the Western provinces of the empire, social conflicts tended to align with ethnic tensions.[39] This fusion of social and national motives, typical for peoples suffering under foreign rule, makes clear how Russia diverged from the French and English pattern.[40]

Since the Romanovs favored a supranational imperial model, the Russian people often lacked support from their own state. If a state does not forge the nation, the cultural elite takes that role upon itself, developing a discourse that inevitably runs to some degree counter to the regime. In Russia, intellectuals assumed this function. As in nation-making of the second type, the inspiration for Russian nationalism came largely from independent thinkers who sought to define the nation on the basis of its ethnic memories. Like any intelligentsia shaping a national community through contestation with a regime, they harnessed centuries-old symbols and stirring narratives of the past to foster a belief in the uniqueness of their people and reconnect educated society with the authentic values from which it had become estranged. But as in nationalism of the first type, spokesmen for the Russian nation envisioned the centralizing power of the state as the primary agent of nation-building. They called not for popular political activism but for action from above, appealing to the government to place itself in the service of the empire's "ruling nationality."

With the dawn of the reform era, these demands became increasingly vocal, seeming to fall on fertile ground. Not only did the unfolding transformations inspire hopes of strengthening and consolidating the Russian people, but official rhetoric itself appeared to promise a fundamental shift in national policy. As Richard Wortman has shown, Alexander II took on the role of "leader of the people" and instigator of a broad process of renewal, emulating the model of a national monarch exemplified at that time by Napoleon III.[41] In 1859 Iakov Rostovtsev, chair of the Editing Commission, which had been established to work out provisional conditions for the abolition of serfdom, attributed broad nation-building significance to the reform. He declared that by liberating the serfs, the emperor "creates in Russia such a nation as has never before existed in our fatherland."[42] Heartened by this encouraging attitude, the press began to propagate the idea that, with the peasant emancipation, Alexander II was poised to accomplish the historical mission of freeing and empowering the Russian people. "Having put an end to legalized slavery and thus called the entire nation to civic life," stated Katkov, "the monarch could not help but initiate a policy that defends the interests of the Russian people, for the two things are, in essence, one and the same."[43] Not only for Katkov but also for many of his contemporaries, abandoning the non-national imperial model and affirming the Russian people's status as the "ruling nationality" would be a natural outgrowth of the reform process.

These expectations assumed that developments in Russia would come increasingly to resemble the nation-building processes of France or England—and some writers discussed in the following chapters (Katkov and Gedeonov, in particular) explicitly measured the reforms' impact against these Western European patterns. Nonetheless, all these thinkers chose to frame the creation of the nation as a re-creation: they celebrated the ongoing transformations as a chance to revitalize native institutions and return to an authentic self. The Slavophiles articulated such views most consistently. "Russia is called," pronounced Aksakov in 1863, "to develop its original local and state order [*zemskoe i gosudarstvennoe ustroistvo*], cultivating it organically from its own stock."[44] Even some Westernizers understood the reforms as a unique opportunity for Russia to restore patterns of national life deeply embedded in the past. Comparing the innovations of the 1860s with the reforms of Peter I, Catherine II, and Alexander I, Katkov pointedly sidestepped the language of analogy: "We are embarking now on the fourth and, of course, most important epoch of transformation, for now, clearly, the legislator does not and cannot limit himself to the task set forth in all previous epochs: the invention and imposition of rules. Now he must derive law from the root elements of the people's traditions and of life itself."[45] While the actual architects of the reforms, like Rostovtsev, envisioned the emergence of an entirely new national community, intellectuals of a nationalist persuasion drew on historical myths to legitimate their visions of Russia's future. They used ethnic memories to increase the prominence of the Russian people and to domesticate the French and English model of nation-building. It would simply be restoring deeply ingrained traditions, they contended, if the monarchy were to abandon its ambiguous stance, tip the scale in favor of the Russian people, and unify the heterogeneous population of the empire on the basis of allegiance to its ethnic core.

Alexander II, however, made little effort to change national policy. Although proclaiming his commitment to strengthening the Russian people, he maintained the privileged position of non-Russian ethnic elites and was reluctant to undertake aggressive assimilation practices.[46] Thus not only did the regime thwart the formation of a Russian nation by shrinking from the first type of nation-building, but it also deprived independent thinkers of the possibilities inherent in the second model of nation-making: Alexander forestalled the development of a nationalist movement of the sort that emerges from struggle with an unambiguously hostile government by creating the impression that he, too, was committed to building the Russian nation. This situation heightened the significance of cultural mythology in Russian national discourse and led it to assume a peculiar function. Not only did mythmaking set the terms for discussions of nationhood and justify political transformations; still more important, it symbolically resolved political problems that the government could not—or did not wish to—address. As we shall see, the tale of the founding of the Russian state, the

story of the Russian people's spiritual birth, and narratives of the monarchy's restoration at the beginning of the seventeenth century helped to
recast the monarchical supranational empire as a national one. When Alexander II's policies frustrated the expectations aroused by his reforms, these
myths emerged as symbolic substitutes for political change and captured
the imagination of scholars, poets, novelists, and journalists. As a result,
though Russian nationalism languished as a political force, it thrived as a
rhetorical power present in all spheres of cultural production.

How mythmaking came to serve as a substitute for real change may be
seen in intellectuals' attempts to adopt certain elements of civic nationalism. Though these reform-era thinkers did not call for popular activism,
some of them nonetheless articulated demands for wider participation in
public life as part of their nation-building projects. A large segment of the
press expressed hopes that Alexander II would "crown the edifice [of the
reforms]," a phrase widely used at the time to mean granting a constitution
and representative institutions.

As with the government's putative nation-building project, it was the
emperor himself who initially encouraged these aspirations and so contributed to the atmosphere of political yearning. In times of crisis, when
the regime found it necessary to solicit public support, Alexander seemed
to signal a readiness to make political concessions. As he set out to abolish
serfdom, the government allowed open discussion of the reform and en-
trusted the landed gentry with the task of assisting in its preparation. Although this unprecedented decision arose from the tactical necessity of
winning gentry support for abolition—and the emperor quickly retreated
from the policy—many of the cultural elite perceived the move as a sign
of an official plan to foster independent action among the most educated
stratum of society, to be followed in the near future by the wider population.[47] During the next critical period, after emancipation was proclaimed,
Alexander tried a more conciliatory posture, seeking to alleviate growing
tensions and discontent, particularly among the landowners. To defuse the
increasingly oppositional mood, he found opportunities to ally himself
with educated society, which Nicholas I had always regarded with suspicion,
and for the first time allowed representatives of the low-ranking nobility
and the peasantry to join the ruling elite in imperial ceremonies.[48] When
the Polish uprising of 1863—yet another wave of political unrest—broke
out, Alexander again resorted to the tactic of making vague promises to

devolve some power to the public. In a manifesto issued on March 31, 1863, he sought to pacify the rebels and spoke of a "new era" in civic life, hinting at a broadening of political rights in Russia. Katkov took advantage of the moment to advocate the creation of a new institution that would channel public opinion to the tsar—without, however, subverting the principles of absolutism. He called it the people's advisory representative [*soveshchatel'noe predstavitel'stvo*] to the supreme power and envisioned it as a way of giving society a voice (though not a vote) in the decision-making process.[49] Throughout the 1860s, the Slavophiles also articulated their demand for a national *zemstvo* assembly to give a voice to the "land"—a synonym, in their language, for the people.[50]

As we know, Alexander refused to relinquish any political initiative and ultimately dashed all hopes for broader political participation. No constitutional projects met with his approval, no matter how modest they were or who voiced them—the gentry assemblies, independent writers, Interior Minister P. A. Valuev, or Grand Duke Konstantin Nikolaevich (the emperor's own brother).[51] Yet his unwillingness to introduce representative institutions competed with—and was at times outweighed by—his reluctance to reject them outright. Among the protagonists of this book, such ambiguity fed the belief that autocracy need not be a bar to popular involvement in political life.

None of these thinkers, however, understood the people's empowerment in terms of imposing Western institutions on Russian soil. Instead, they inscribed it within authentic historical models, conjuring epic scenes from past wars. As many historians have observed, memories of war figure prominently in processes of national self-definition.[52] In Russian national discourse, they occupied an even more crucial position. Although the autocracy rejected the civic aspects of nationhood during peacetime, it could not do without the active participation of the populace in times of crisis. Capitalizing on this situation, a vocal group of writers came to employ the cult of military victories as a justification for—and indeed a Russian incarnation of—popular sovereignty. As a result, war memories performed a vital function. They could virtually transform the people, deprived of political breathing space, into a key political player; turn the fragmented Russian populace into a cohesive community; and present the Russian core as the politically dominant group within the empire. This transformative power of the symbol of war became even more significant when the period of ambiguity with regard to popular participation ended. With Alexander's harsh response to the Moscow gentry assembly's demand for wider political rights (1865) and Dmitrii Karakozov's attempt to assassinate the emperor (1866),[53] hopes for public involvement in decision making gradually faded—and memories of popular war came to function as a symbolic substitute.

This vital role of the war cult in Russian national discourse reveals the aggression inherent in Russian nationalism. If war provides the only arena for mass participation in political life, then demands for popular empowerment inevitably lead to bellicose propaganda and even to violence itself. Although nineteenth-century Russian nationalism was more a rhetorical than a political force, in the long run cultural expressions do enter the political scene. The aggressive character of Russian twentieth-century nationalism, with its support of pogroms and wars, was thus encoded in the reform era's national mythmaking. And so long as war memories serve as a substitute for popular participation in political life—a substitution that has become a trademark of Putin's Russia, where civil society is underdeveloped and the cult of war grows steadily—nationalistic sentiments will continue to find their primary outlet in military action, just as they did in the nineteenth century.

Nationalizing the Empire through Historical Mythology

Although exponents of reform-era public nationalism represented conflicting ideologies, they developed certain points of concurrence. My focus on historical mythology—the common denominator of all constructs of the national self—makes it possible to examine rival expressions of nation in comparative perspective and trace how they interacted, competed, and occasionally converged.[54] Building on Prasenjit Duara's contention that nationalism "marks the site where different representations of the nation contest and negotiate with each other," this approach helps to reveal both the attitudes that divided rival groups of intellectuals and those that narrowed the distance or even transcended the ideological barriers between them.[55]

A collective commitment to "finding" the nation apart from the empire united various reform-era thinkers. It was not only the Slavophiles who drew sharp contrasts between the people and the state. Katkov, who conceived of the nation as centered on the state, also allowed some symbolic distance between the two. He distinguished between the Russian heartland and the vast imperial space in order to articulate a program for strengthening the Russian nation within the empire.[56] Katkov's attitude exemplifies how "the nationalists' desire to see the state as the embodiment of the nation"[57] did not presuppose a blurring of boundaries between nation and empire. On the contrary, this conviction often required that they be sharply, though symbolically, demarcated in order to make visible the very nation the state was expected to embody.

Katkov's newspaper *Moskovskie vedomosti* (Moscow news) forcefully articulated and disseminated programs for unifying the heterogeneous state on the basis of, and for the benefit of, the "ruling nationality." And the journalist's exceptional influence, Andreas Renner has shown, contributed significantly to the emerging vision of the empire-nation.[58] But Katkov was not alone, during these years, in this attempt to single out the Russian people as the culturally and politically dominant group within the empire. The idea emerged across the intellectual spectrum and pervaded various fields of cultural endeavor, ultimately taking on a life of its own. Such constructs were sometimes eclectic, often ambiguous, and always incompatible with the regime, but they governed reform-era national discourse. Though mutually contradictory, many of them converged in rendering the empire an attribute of the Russian people, inscribed in their historical mythology.

Focusing on the transformation of national self-perception in the aftermath of the Crimean disaster, chapter 1 traces how novelists and journalists holding various views came to see the nation as an evolving entity in urgent need of (re)construction. They began to employ collective memories in a radically new way—not only to celebrate the national community's uniqueness but also to suggest how it should be changed and how its authentic institutions might be revived. Thus a new mode of national mythmaking took shape. The growing understanding of the nation as a political construct and the use of myths as blueprints for its transformation became reciprocal, mutually enhancing processes. Cultural heritage assumed a developmental character and helped to domesticate changes based on Western European models.[59]

With this new approach to the nation, it became natural to ask who would be responsible for the task of (re-)creation. In official ideology, historical myths clustered around the dynasty: the ruler represented the fundamental source of all Russian achievement. Public nationalism, on the contrary, refashioned collective memories to promote the people (often together with the dynasty) as the primary agent of change. The monarchical myth of imperial conquest and usurpation as justifications for absolutism gave way to narratives of the "organic" expansion of the Russian people, who were seen as protectors of the "weaker tribes" and bearers of a powerful assimilative force.[60] To demonstrate this shift, chapter 2 focuses on the ancient tale of the invitation of Varangian princes to rule over Rus', canonized in Nicholas I's time as the Russian foundation myth.[61] It is striking that this legend, which had traditionally celebrated a monarch as the prime mover of national history and glorified submissiveness to rulers as a unique national trait, came in the reform era to portray the people as a collective protagonist in history, capable of building a powerful state and of nationalizing the dynasty they once had summoned from the West. Moreover, the Varangian legend now defined the Russian people not only through their relations to the ruler but also through their encounter with, and assimilation of, the diverse non-Russian population of the empire. Thus new renditions of the foundation narrative made it possible to rethink the monarchical empire in nationalistic terms, as a product of the activity of the entire nation under the dynasty's leadership.

Yet how could the Russian people build the state and russify the subject population, if they themselves were stifled by the regime and deeply fragmented along social divides? Chapter 3 argues that reform-era thinkers adopted memories of popular wars as the dominant form of national myth-making in order to symbolically consolidate the nation and imagine it as a decisive political player. These rhetorical efforts drew predominantly on a long-standing construct of the Patriotic War (1812–15) as a struggle undertaken by the entire nation, rather than the regular army: the victory was believed to show unity across social strata, the people's devotion to the regime, and the superiority of pious Russia to corrupt Europe.[62] During the reform era, writers reappropriated this familiar myth for new ends. The nationalist press of the 1860s enshrined Russia's resistance to Napoleon as a moment of truth when the ruler assumed the role of national leader and the Russian people demonstrated their capacity to determine their future. In this way, journalists of the period made memories of 1812 into the pattern for enlisting the ruler in the national cause, building a renewed monarchy, and transforming Russians into the politically dominant group within the empire.

The two final chapters explore the complex interplay between the ethnic, imperial, and religious dimensions of Russian national identity. Juxtaposing two very different texts, chapter 4 analyzes Tiutchev's five-stanza poem, "A horrid dream has been burdening us" (1863), and Tolstoy's four-volume novel, *War and Peace* (1863–69), in the context of the reform-era cult of military victories. Both writers found the nation at war but perceived it in completely different ways. Tiutchev endowed the Russian people with a universal mission and used it to justify violent expansionism: as the exclusive bearers of Orthodox truth, he avowed, Russians were destined to build a universal Christian empire. The poem identifies distinctive Russian ethnic features with religious ones, imagines Rus' as a worldwide Christian empire, and replaces historical time with the apocalyptic end of days. For Tiutchev, the meaning of Russian nationhood comes from the interweaving of religious mission and imperial impulse that defines the historical destiny of the people. Tolstoy's construct of the nation is the antithesis of Tiutchev's. *War and Peace* tells an ethnocentric story of the nation at war, defying the imperial dimension of Russianness and situating the nation in historical time. The author condemns expansionism and sees the power to consolidate the nation not in military victories but in collective suffering. Although for Tolstoy memories of war mobilize ethnic sentiments and unite the Russian community across generational divides, he finally proclaims the superiority of the Christian over the national and arrives ultimately at a denial of nationalism. The poem and the novel, despite their fundamentally different visions of Russianness, reveal how persistent tensions within Russian nationalist discourse—between ethnic and religious aspects of national identity—intensified during the reform era and undermined attempts to build a coherent expression of the nation on both principles at once.

Chapter 5 further explores these tensions, focusing on the myth of the Russian people's spiritual birth that underpinned the Pan-Slavist project for the Russian Empire's future. The myth traced the nation's spiritual descent back to the Slavs' conversion to Christianity and Cyril and Methodius's missions, particularly their translation of the Gospels, which, as the Pan-Slavists believed, added religious bonds to the blood ties connecting the Slavs. The chapter examines the ways in which participants in the Slavic Congress in Moscow (1867) utilized this myth to justify Russia's imperial destiny, while tightly interweaving ethnicity and faith. But, again, the synthesis of these two aspects of Russianness proved fragile: it could survive only as long as the doctrine remained untested by national realities. When the press began to discuss the rise of independence movements in the Balkans, contradictions between the religious and the secular emerged, polarized the Russian Pan-Slavists, and led to attempts to decouple these two forces. Orthodoxy had long been the key to Russian identity, but in the imperial context it acquired a more fundamental significance: Orthodox rituals, traditions, and other religious expressions provided one of the most tangible means of distinguishing what was then perceived as the Russian nation—that is, all East Slavs—from the rest of the Romanovs' subjects, who were predominantly non-Orthodox. The increasing difficulty of reconciling ethnicity and faith during the reform era made even more challenging the task of redefining the monarchical empire as a national one.[63]

The public discourse examined in the following five chapters took shape in the first decade and a half of the reign of Alexander II—from the mid-1850s through the late 1860s—when hopes of profound political change opened the floodgates for a wide array of nation-building projects. During the 1870s, the concluding period of the reform era, the debates on Russian nationhood persisted and even briefly intensified in the atmosphere of public agitation that led to the Russo-Turkish War (1877–78). But it was the expressions of nation worked out in the 1850s and 1860s that set the ground rules for those debates. On the eve of the war, a wide segment of the press voiced hopes for enlisting the emperor in the national cause, promoted the people as a decisive political actor, and envisioned Russia as a growing Slavic empire charged with the mission of safeguarding Orthodoxy. In the 1870s these views garnered unprecedented support across the political spectrum, though the propagandists for the war had merely fine-tuned the constructs of the previous decade, adapting them to a new political climate, where hopes for public participation in political life had faded and left war the only arena of popular involvement. The nationalist legacy of the 1860s outlasted the reign of Alexander II and was revitalized in the concluding decades of the nineteenth century, when the regime began to identify itself more closely with the Russian nationality. It was the "Russian party," led by some of the protagonists of this book, that inspired these developments. Back at the beginning of the reform era, this "party"—Katkov, Aksakov, Pobedonostsev—elaborated the national mythology that Alexander III would later resort to in fashioning himself as the leader of the national cause and embarking on policies of aggressive Russification.[64] Since the constructs of the 1850s and 1860s played such a profound role in Russian national discourse, this book focuses primarily on the opening decade and a half of the reform era. Although the chapters that follow touch on the 1870s, they do so only in passing, and I therefore exclude this decade from the chronological span indicated in the subtitle of the book.

By analyzing the national discourse of the reform era, this study uncovers the cultural roots of the nationalist rhetoric still being deployed in modern Russia. Myth-based visions of the nation have enjoyed a striking resurgence since the disintegration of the Soviet Union. In today's Russia, all the writers examined in this book are being republished on a large scale, and the collective memories they helped shape have become common currency in discussions of the nation's future. In an age when a putatively democratic regime limits press freedom and the public sphere, policy makers and a large segment of the cultural elite have begun once again to cultivate popular myths and memories of wars instead of working to build civil society.

1

A Shifting Vision
of the Nation

*Constructs of Russianness in the Aftermath
of the Crimean War*

The Crimean War (1853–56) began as yet another round in the pro-
tracted struggle between the Romanov and the Ottoman Empire
that spanned the eighteenth and nineteenth centuries. Russians
initially called the conflict the Eastern War, but it soon took on a European
dimension as, driven by strategic interests, England and France joined
forces with Turkey. With the escalation of the war, Austria also threatened
to attack Russia, while Prussia posed at best a latent hazard.[1] Facing enemies
on all sides, Russian authorities and public alike drew on two sets of heroic
memories—of Russia's centuries-old antagonism with the East, and of its
conflicted relationship with the West—to inflame and channel Russian patriotism.[2] How, then, did this rich arsenal of historical narratives come to
be understood, once the Russians lost the war? Scholars have thoroughly
examined how the Crimean defeat compromised Russia's geopolitical
status and provoked sharp public criticism of the government. What remains understudied is how Russians reconfigured the patriotic language

the war had elicited. Which visions of nationhood came to dominate and which were marginalized?

The evolution of two persistent symbols of Russia is revealing in this respect. Throughout the reign of Nicholas I, both official propaganda and public opinion commemorated the Patriotic War (1812–15), cherishing it particularly in times of crisis. Thus, in response to the November rebellion in the Kingdom of Poland (1830–31), poets, independent thinkers, and partisans of official ideology all alluded to the 1812 triumph as confirmation of Russia's capacity for collective sacrifice, of the brotherhood supposedly prevalent across social strata, and of the country's messianic role in world history.[3] Although memories of 1812 constituted one of the central tropes of the "invincible nation" during the Crimean campaign, by war's end and immediately thereafter intellectuals of a nationalist persuasion had not only grown skeptical of such exploitation of the victory over Napoleon but transformed it from a source of national aggrandizement to an instrument of self-critique and redefinition.

Another national symbol underwent a similar evolution. From the eighteenth century onward, numerous thinkers, working from different ideological perspectives, encoded Russia's vast, flat, open space as a metaphor for its greatness, as well as for its people's inexhaustible potential.[4] It was the rhetorical blurring of the line between Russia proper and the empire as a whole that made this image central to imperial discourse before and during the Crimean War. Yet after the defeat, as we shall see, the most distinguished Russian writers either dramatically transformed those "boundless" expanses into sucking swamps and snowy wastes or severed the conventional link between wide-open spaces and national virtues. Rather than invoke Russia's vastness as a means of articulating imperial vision, postwar representations of the homeland reflected the need to "find" the nation within the empire and symbolically separate the two.

That both symbols should have been challenged at once is far from coincidental. In rhetorical practice, the two were often intertwined, illustrating and supporting each other. Indeed, nothing so convincingly cast the native landscape as proof of the people's might and repository of their glorious memories as the story of Napoleon's army being expelled and, according to the recurrent cliché, bogged down in Russia's endless snowy fields.[5] Reinterpretation of one symbol required that of the other, since both stemmed from a conventional approach that defined the nation by reference to historical achievements, nature, or Providence. The loss of the Crimean War precipitated attempts to break out of this conceptual framework and led to fundamental changes in patterns of national self-perception.

To grasp the innovative character of the postwar rhetoric, it is important to distinguish between two sets of concepts: "patriotism," or the "patriotic," on the one hand, and "nationalism"—the "national" or "nationalist"—on the other. Although various interpretations of the relationship between these two concepts exist in the scholarly literature, in this book "patriotic" denotes imperial patriotism, that is, sentiments and rhetorical clichés focused on loyalty to the tsar, the absolutist regime, and the imperial state, while "national" and its derivatives designate those beliefs and discursive practices that take the Russian people as their primary object of devotion and concern. Since the majority of reform-era nationalists never challenged the monarchy and supported the empire's integrity, these two concepts frequently overlapped and were at times interchangeable.[6] The distinction between the two is a matter of emphasis: whether priority is given to the Russian people or to the monarchical empire. Analyzing how nationalism in nineteenth-century Western Europe absorbed and ultimately marginalized republican patriotism, which was built on the ideal of human freedom across national barriers, Maurizio Viroli has called the process "the nationalization of patriotism."[7] To be sure, Russian patriotic language had nothing to do with the liberal rhetoric of citizenship, equality, and political rights. Yet Russian postwar intellectuals also sought to "nationalize" traditional patriotic discourse, with its predominant focus on monarchical empire—a discourse that, just like the rhetoric of civic solidarity in the West, encompassed supranational overtones and could serve as an antidote to nationalism. With the loss of the Crimean War, Russian thinkers began to reinterpret patriotic symbols to envision Russia's future in terms of national primacy. To examine this shift, we will first explore the wartime discourse of patriotism that served as a point of departure for many intellectuals in their postwar nationalist rhetoric.

The Crimean War as Commemoration of the 1812 Victory

Even before it began, the Crimean War was poetically interpreted through the prism of Russia's struggle with Napoleon. In the first days of September

1853—more than a month before the start of military action against the Ottoman Empire and almost half a year before the Western powers' entry into the war—Fedor Tiutchev composed the poem "Nieman," in which he covertly predicted that Russia stood on the brink of another triumphant war with the West.[8] Depicting the Grande Armée's picturesque entry into Russian territory in 1812, "Nieman" celebrates Napoleon as the "wondrous warrior" (*voitel' divnyi*) who controls the fates of humanity. Yet as the poem unfolds, the portrait of a victor gives way to the image of a doomed commander leading his army to defeat:

> I mimo prokhodila rat'—
> Vse grozno-boevye litsa,
> I neizbezhnaia Desnitsa
> Klala na nikh svoiu pechat' . . .
>
> [And the troops marched past—
> With stern, battle-ready faces,
> And the inexorable Hand of Fate
> Set its seal upon them . . .][9]

"Nieman" offers a remarkable example of how the romantic cult of Napoleon, enormously popular in Russia, and the vision of the Patriotic War as confirmation of Russia's greatness could coexist within a single text. The more Tiutchev elevates the "man of genius," the more Russia's triumph over him proves the nation's unique role in world history.

Events themselves offered fertile ground for historical parallels with Napoleon's invasion of Russia. Military and diplomatic maneuvers leading up to the war were conducted against a backdrop of fundamental political change in France. In 1852 the Second Empire was proclaimed, and Louis Napoleon, French president and nephew of the great emperor Napoleon, declared himself Napoleon III. Despite the Russian court's opposition, the Napoleonic dynasty thus sat again on the throne of France, undermining the Holy Alliance's decisions and symbolically restoring the First Empire.[10] When the war started, Tiutchev confidently proclaimed it "the recurrence of 1812" and the victorious resolution of "the thousand-year dispute of East and West."[11] Yet these expectations proved prophetic only insofar as they anticipated the essential pattern that was to govern Russian perceptions of the war.

At the outset of the "Eastern campaign," some thinkers conflated memories of the Patriotic War with the history of the Crusades, in which Russia had never participated, to symbolically justify its right to control Jerusalem's holy sites and protect the Orthodox peoples who were subjects of the Ottoman Empire. Indeed, it was the Russian-French rivalry over the right to maintain the holy places in Ottoman-ruled Palestine that marked the beginning of the conflict. In his letter to the Pan-Slavist M. P. Pogodin on Christmas Day of 1853, the history professor S. P. Shevyrev, a supporter of official nationality, observed: "From all of Russia there is sympathy for the war. . . . It is a crusade. . . . Everyone is ready to sacrifice. The movements remind me of 1812."[12] Pogodin's articles and G. Titov's brochure *The Crusades and the Eastern Question* (1854) forged a still more explicit link between the Patriotic War and the centuries-long confrontation between Christians and Muslims: only the country that had defeated Napoleon could fulfill the high mission to which "exhausted Western Europe" had proven itself unequal.[13] The perception of the Crimean War as an extension of the successful Patriotic War, ridicule of the "nephew" (Napoleon III) as the direct inheritor of his "uncle's" (Napoleon I) disgrace, interpretation of coincidences in the chronology of the 1812 and current campaigns as providential signs—all these themes permeated the press, popular verse, and personal correspondence in the early days of the war.[14]

At first glance, the view of the "Eastern campaign" refracted through the memory of the 1812 triumph is nothing short of astonishing. One might have expected the interpretation of military events to hinge on Russia's previous victories in the Crimea and the Caucasus—the main theaters of the present war—and to rely on historical narratives invoking Russia's age-old struggle with the "barbaric" East. Or else one might have expected patriotic symbolism to focus on Russia's traditional role as defender of oppressed Orthodox peoples. Yet while such imagery did play a role in wartime rhetoric, the projection of current events onto the Patriotic War overshadowed and absorbed all other historical analogies—and not only for poets and historians. The government elevated the glories of 1812 over all other military accomplishments as well. Nicholas I made this parallel explicit in an imperial decree that announced the severing of diplomatic relations with England and France (February 9, 1854): "If the enemies attack Russia's borders, we will be ready to meet them with the severity bequeathed us by our ancestors. Are we not now the same Russian people whose valor is attested by the memorable events of 1812!"[15] At the beginning of the war, the authorities reissued popular prints (*lubki*) depicting the heroic events of the Patriotic War, while graphic artists who were creating images of the Crimean conflict frequently compared the two wars—with the full approval of the imperial censors.[16]

In its coverage of the campaign, the official newspaper *Russkii invalid* (Russian veteran) promoted the memory of the triumph over Napoleon as the apotheosis of the true Russian spirit, visibly emerging across the country's divergent regions and uniting them in time of crisis. Praising the bravery of Odessa's inhabitants when their town was under siege (in 1854), the author of one account ecstatically observed that "merry souls sang the native legends of the year twelve" and in this fashion "under the thunder of enemy fire" Odessa took on an authentic Russian character.[17] It was Sevastopol, the fortress defended by Russian troops for several months and finally surrendered, that emerged as the most famous locus of the Russian spirit during the Crimean War and thus fit ideally with the official image of Russia as a national empire. Parallels between the defense of Sevastopol and the heroic battles in Russia's core during the Patriotic War circulated widely to support this claim.[18]

Russkii invalid utilized the glories of 1812 to incorporate non-Russian ethnic groups, including the Tatars, into the struggle against the Turks.[19] In its report on a speech made by a Nizhnii Novgorod imam serving as army chaplain, the newspaper emphasized that the imam called on his coreligionists to follow the feats of 1812 and defend their homeland "in whose depths repose[d] . . . the bones of [their] fathers."[20] The sermons of Innokentii (I. A. Borisov), archbishop of the Kherson-Tauride diocese, clearly demonstrate the power of memories of 1812 both to symbolically unify and to russify the empire. As though following Tiutchev's poetic logic, Innokentii interpreted the Anglo-French landing on the Crimean coast as an echo of the successful entry of Napoleon's troops in 1812—and thus the first step toward their inevitable downfall: "In time of battle, does the enemy intrude first into the Russian land? To invade it, with its vast expanses, is always possible; what is hard—as experience shows—is to extricate oneself without falling prey to the birds of the air and the beasts of the earth . . ."[21] Directly contradicting customary representations of the Crimea as temperate, picturesque, and ultimately exotic,[22] Innokentii extends the fearsome features of Russia's heartland—the endless expanses, harsh climate, and wild

animals—to the southern corner of the empire. The preacher thus paradoxically endows a territory that came under Russian control relatively recently (in 1783) with the attributes of Russianness, portraying the ethnically
diverse empire as a single entity bound together by the Russian spirit.[23]

Popular verse also disseminated this official image of the empire, utiliz-
ing the symbolic currency of 1812 in a similar way. Celebrating the Russian
victory over the Ottoman fleet in the battle of Sinop (1854), *Russkii invalid*
published a poem, "On the current war," that begins with conventional
praise of late eighteenth-century triumphs on the Black Sea. As the stanzas
unfold, however, the focus shifts from naval victories won at the empire's
frontier to the Patriotic War, which took place in the historical heartland:

> Ne dvenadtsatogo-l' goda
> Vy khotite, gospoda?
> My gotovy. Rus' rodnaia
> I mogucha i sil'na.
>
> [Gentlemen, do you seek
> The year twelve?
> We are ready. Native Rus'
> Is powerful and strong.][24]

Presenting the 1812 campaign as an achievement of Rus' and setting it
atop the hierarchy of Russia's victories, the poem symbolically enshrines
the state's ethnic core as the defining spirit and dominant force of the diverse empire. To elaborate this vision, the unknown author of the poem re-
iterates Pushkin's use of 1812, alluding to his missive "To the Slanderers of
Russia" (1831). Written in response to Europe's condemnation of Russia's
brutal suppression of the November uprising in Poland, Pushkin's poem
ends with an invitation to the Western instigators of anti-Russian propaganda to send their troops to experience the defeat of 1812 one more time:

> Tak vysylaite zh k nam, vitii,
> Svoikh ozloblennykh synov:
> Est' mesto im v poliakh Rossii
> Sredi nechuzhdykh im grobov.
>
> [So, bards, send along to us
> Your enraged sons:

> There's room for them in Russian fields
> Among the graves of their kinsmen.]

The concluding stanza of "On the current war" threatens foreigners with a similar prediction:

> Prikhodite zhe k nam v gosti!
> Chestno vstretim my gostei.
> I ulozhim vashi kosti,
> Sred' nechuzhdykh vam kostei! . . .
>
> [Come, then, be our guests!
> We know how to treat guests.
> We will lay your bones to rest
> Among the bones of your kinsmen! . . .]

The use of vocabulary and syntactic constructions that echo Pushkin's "invitation" to the hostile foreigners make these lines a recognizable reference to "To the Slanderers of Russia," a poem that, in harmony with official ideology, presented the Russian Empire as a united nation.[25] Written in the somewhat anachronistic style of a victory ode, Pushkin's missive projects the Polish rebellion onto Russia's struggle with Napoleon, emphasizing two dimensions of each conflict. On the one hand, he presents both conflicts as holy wars of ethnic resistance, feats of Russian nationality. Lines about the ancient "quarrel among the Slavs" refer to the people's war of the early seventeenth century, when a Russian popular militia liberated Moscow from Polish intruders. Allusions to that earlier Polish incursion, calling the Russians a Slavic "tribe," veneration of the Moscow Kremlin, and evocations of the national epic hero (*bogatyr'*) all inscribe the suppression of the Polish rebellion of 1830 and the memory of 1812 into a paradigm of ethnic heroism. On the other hand, Pushkin invokes imperial victories (the taking of Izmail, Suvorov's victory in Warsaw) and envisions the diverse parts of the imperial realm—"from Perm' to Tauride, from the cold Finnish cliffs to burning Colchis"—joining together to oppose the enemy. Pushkin thus not only inserts the destruction of Napoleon's army into the triumphal imperial narrative but fuses the ethnic and imperial dimensions of the events of 1812 to portray Russia as a national empire—and it is precisely this pattern that jingoistic poetry and official propaganda of the 1850s sought to emulate.

Though references to the Patriotic War pervaded the official rhetoric of the Crimean War, Nicholas was well aware of the dangers inherent in 1812 as a symbol of unconstrained popular movements potentially hostile to the regime. To erase such implications, official ideology, well before the launch of the Crimean campaign, styled the fight against Napoleon's army as the people's struggle not so much for their own freedom as for legitimate order.[26] During the Crimean War, in his imperial manifestos, Nicholas pointedly employed parallels with 1812 to reassert the union of the monarch and the common people and reinforce the image of the ruler as an embodiment of the nation's will: "When necessary we all, tsar and subjects— to repeat the words Emperor Alexander spoke in a time of trial similar to this—stand before the ranks of our enemies *with sword in hand and the cross in our hearts* to defend the most precious blessings in this world: the safety and honor of the Fatherland."[27] The very date chosen for promulgation of this manifesto demonstrates that Nicholas missed no opportunity to link the current war with the memory of the 1812 victory. It was read from the pulpits on December 25, the first day of Christmas, when from 1812 onward all of Russia's churches held a thanksgiving service to commemorate the expulsion of Napoleon's army.[28]

The more tragically events on the battlefield unfolded, the more ingeniously the authorities exploited the memory of the Patriotic War. Once one chose to see the Crimean events through the prism of the Patriotic War, any military failure could be interpreted as a sign of Providence's special design and a token of inevitable future success, since the Russian army of 1812 had also withstood many losses.[29] This is why Alexander II, upon his ascent to the throne after Nicholas's death (in 1855), frequently resorted to the symbol of 1812. On receiving word of Sevastopol's surrender, the young tsar encouraged Prince M. N. Gorchakov, chief commander of forces in the Crimea: "Do not lose heart, but remember 1812 and trust in God. . . . Two years after the burning of Moscow, our triumphant troops entered Paris. We are the same Russians and God is with us!"[30] Informing the Russian armies and the navy of Sevastopol's collapse, Alexander compared its defense to the greatest feats of Russian arms, among them the Battle of Borodino.[31] Even after the government signed the humiliating Treaty of Paris (1856), the emperor visibly entwined the narratives of the two wars in public ceremonies. His coronation (1856), set to coincide with the anniversary of the Battle of Borodino (August 26), was intended to symbolically overcome the painful loss of the war and to reassert the deep bond between the monarch and his subjects.[32]

Wartime Representations of National Character

In its catalog of national virtues, official rhetoric entwined the people's humility, selflessness, and devotion to the throne with their martial valor and strengths, physical and spiritual. What supposedly distinguished Russians from others was this amalgam of submissiveness and epic heroism, embodied in brave individual soldiers and symbolized above all by Ivan Susanin, whose legendary self-sacrifice in saving the life of Mikhail Romanov, the founder of the ruling dynasty, had placed him during Nicholas's reign at the center of mythmaking about the unbreakable union of dynasty and people.[33] "His blood has soaked into the heart of every Russian"; thus *Russkii invalid* explained the mass heroism of Russian soldiers.[34] Physical strength and courage were also evoked through the feats of the ancient Greeks and Romans. This strategy persisted from 1812 through the Crimean War, enriched along the way by the theme of Orthodox faith, which became more prominent toward midcentury, reflecting the growing significance of the first pillar of official nationality.[35] In 1854 Pogodin, who contributed to the formation of this doctrine, claimed that the heroes of the current war had surpassed the *Iliad*. The source of their superiority was, of course, Russian Orthodoxy with its spirit of humility.[36] *Russkii invalid* extolled the Russian warrior, graced equally by Spartan and Christian qualities and distinguished by a readiness to sacrifice himself "at the tsar's first word."[37]

This conflation of bellicosity with self-sacrifice and of Homeric heroes with the Russian Christ-figure constituted common ground for both official rhetoric and wartime literary representations of the national character. In the missive "To the Don Cossacks" ("Dontsam," 1854), written by the self-taught provincial poet I. S. Nikitin, the stock motifs of official propaganda all appear: the dominance of the Russian spirit over the entire empire, Russia's harsh climate and endless steppe as proof of the country's greatness, epic military feats culminating in the victory over Napoleon, and the ability of the people to sacrifice themselves.[38] To top it off, the poem portrays the Cossacks as the embodiment of Russianness, a staple of official propaganda since the 1812 war.[39]

During the Crimean War, even Lev Tolstoy, despite the skeptical nature that made him, in B. M. Eikhenbaum's words, incapable of writing "anything crudely tendentious,"[40] drew on these widespread imperial idioms, though he did so ambivalently. In the beginning of 1855, depressed by the military losses, the young artillery officer Count Tolstoy sharply criticized the Russian army, seeing in it the corrupt and repressive regime in miniature. Like the majority of intellectuals, he blamed military failures on serfdom, which official rhetoric had completely excised from its portrayal of the campaign. In an unfinished tract that reads like part of the period's flood of exposé literature, Tolstoy declared: "We have not an army, but a rabble of oppressed yet disciplined slaves, taking orders from thieves and mercenaries."[41] Yet, as Donna Orwin has observed, the article's dismal description of Russian soldiers—"oppressed, oppressive, and despairing"— finds its optimistic mirror image in the story "The Woodfelling" (1855), completed after the author arrived in Sevastopol and felt a strong surge of patriotism.[42] Here Tolstoy divides soldiers into "the submissive, the commanding, and the despairing," endowing the "commanding" with noble traits and declaring the "submissive" to be the most widespread type, embodying the people's propensity to obey.[43] In the sketch "Sevastopol in December" (1855), written immediately thereafter, Tolstoy more explicitly excludes the theme of oppression from his picture of the army. Now he claims that neither the hope of reward nor the fear of authority could inspire such feats as those accomplished by Sevastopol's defenders.[44]

One idealized national trait begets another. The unbreakable union of humility and heroism constitutes the underlying motif of "Sevastopol in December" and fits tidily into official war rhetoric. Moreover, by accentuating the epic strength of the Russian warrior, Tolstoy clothes him in antique dress, again echoing official propaganda. In the sort of hackneyed phrase that he will later deride in *War and Peace*, the writer calls Vice Admiral V. A. Kornilov "a hero worthy of ancient Greece."[45] If in *War and Peace* Tolstoy aims to reveal the truth hidden behind the mythical accretions (and turns a particularly ironic eye on the parallels drawn between classical antiquity and the Russian soldiers of 1812), in this Sevastopol sketch he claims that in the besieged city a "glorious historical legend comes to life" (*stanovitsia dostovernostiiu*).[46] Most significantly, Tolstoy in his work—like Archbishop Innokentii in his sermons—symbolically anoints the Crimean peninsula with Russianness. While depicting southern landscapes as markedly exotic, he nonetheless asserts that the fearlessness of Sevastopol's inhabitants gives the town a thoroughly Russian character.[47] The motifs of Russians' unique bravery (in details developed in "The Raid" and "Sevastopol in December") and of national unity across social barriers ("Sevastopol in December") also constitute points of commonality between Tolstoy and official propaganda. It comes as no surprise that *Russkii invalid* excerpted "Sevastopol in December" from *Sovremennik* (The Contemporary), where the story first appeared, and Alexander II ordered the sketch translated into French.[48]

This is not to downplay Tolstoy's iconoclastic attitude toward conventional literary representations of war or to overlook the serious limitations on his willingness to subscribe to imperial patriotism. Like Nikitin and many others, Tolstoy welded elements of official rhetoric together with a definition of the Russian self expressed through the customs of the common people.[49] Like no one else, he enriched his battle prose with fine psychological portraits that grabbed his contemporaries' attention. The censor's numerous changes to the journal version of the Sevastopol sketches testify to Tolstoy's unusual use of existing idioms. The dialectic of fear and courage, pacifism coupled with delight at military feats, the portrayal of blood and mud as a background for heroism, and, finally, the absence of jingoistic slogans—all these the censor's pen and scissors sought to correct.[50] Though Tolstoy overturned many conventional assumptions about war, this should not prevent us from seeing that he exploited extant patriotic clichés and praised the same national traits idealized in *Russkii invalid*. The war made it possible for the commonplaces of imperial patriotism to function in literature and official propaganda.

1812 as Contested Symbol

The Crimean War brought out a complex mixture of emotions and attitudes in educated society—from ecstatic expectations of the impending fulfillment of Russia's imperial destiny (as in the cases of Tiutchev, Pogodin, and Shevyrev) to a bitter defeatism tempered by the hope that military loss might lead to a relaxation of the repressive regime.[51] This is not to say that all critics of the government dreamed of defeat and all enthusiasts of the war blindly supported the authorities. Though Aleksei Khomiakov, like other Slavophiles, welcomed the Eastern campaign, his approval of the war went hand in hand with distress over Nicholas's regime. In "Russia" (1854), a poem popular in its day, he imbued the war with the paradoxical potential to cleanse the country of its sins—"the yoke of slavery" and "black injustice" in the courts—and thereby realize Russia's high mission, the liberation of the Slavs. This paradox inspired him to address Russia: "O, unworthy chosen one, / You are chosen!"[52] With the regime blocking all open advocacy of political change, militarist schemes appeared the only accessible cure for the country's ills.

For opposition-minded circles, the real value of the 1812 victory lay in its ability to symbolize unconstrained popular movements—a memory Nicholas I prudently avoided triggering. Hoping that the Crimean campaign would turn into a Russian people's war, Pogodin—now a critic of Nicholas's policies—urged the tsar to "sound the call" and raise up "all the land," as in the days of Poltava and Borodino.[53] The diary of V. S. Aksakova, a member of a famous Slavophile family, records how the growing oppositional mood among Moscow intellectuals coalesced around the image of the Patriotic War as a military accomplishment of the common folk. She compared the militias of 1812 and 1855 to reveal, on the one hand, the people's capacity for deciding Russia's fate and, on the other, the government's underlying fear of popular participation in military action.[54] Some Westernizers demonstrated a similar attitude to the 1812 symbol. In the 1850s Herzen used references to the glory of 1812 to prove the historical energy of the Russian people and their ability to free themselves from absolutism and bring socialism to a "decaying" Europe, thus once again liberating it (this time not from Napoleon but from the tyranny of bourgeois values).[55] In this way, the memory of the Patriotic War promoted by the intelligentsia sounded an altogether different note than that of government propaganda.

Many years later Dostoevsky parodied this contestation over 1812 in his novel *The Idiot* (1868–69). The author devotes an entire chapter to the mentally disturbed General Ivolgin's fantastic account of how as a boy he stayed behind in French-held Moscow and served as a page to Napoleon. The general has his child persona utter fiery patriotic phrases, impressing the great conqueror with the indomitable Russian spirit. A man of ruined reputation, Ivolgin appropriates the sacred national symbol to rehabilitate himself in the eyes of his fellows.[56] To make clear the mockery behind Ivolgin's "memoirs," Dostoevsky introduces a second wild story on exactly the same subject: the tale of Lebedev's leg, blown off by a bomb and buried with pomp and circumstance in French-held Moscow. Lebedev concocts this story, despite being in possession of two perfectly good legs, in order to ridicule and provoke the general. Both absurd anecdotes represent Dostoevsky's covert sarcasm at the exploitation of the Patriotic War. It is no coincidence—though it seems strange at first glance—that Prince Myshkin, the novel's protagonist, should compare Ivolgin's mad fictions to the opening chapter of Herzen's *Past and Thoughts*, where the memoirist recounts how he (a newborn baby) and his parents stayed behind in the surrendered Moscow of 1812. His father chanced to meet Napoleon, who sent him to the Russian emperor with an offer of peace.[57] Despite their utter dissimilarity in tone and content, the thematic echoes between Ivolgin's and Herzen's stories—a child as the natural intermediary between warring sides, Napoleon's search for a Russian emissary to send to Alexander—justify the odd comparison of the mad general's fantasies with Herzen's recollection. By juxtaposing these two stories, Dostoevsky not only sheds ironic light on Herzen's use of memories of the Patriotic War but also parodies the polarization of conceptions of the 1812 victory as an indicator of ideological divisions within society. It is significant that both of Dostoevsky's characters, Ivolgin and Lebedev, who recount the events of 1812 differently, represent competing political outlooks. While the mad general sees himself as an inheritor of the noble tradition and gives voice to the tenets of official nationalism, Lebedev aligns himself with the nihilists, who openly debunk patriotic symbols.

The discursive practices that Dostoevsky ridiculed in *The Idiot* unfolded fully at the end of the Crimean War, when intellectuals transformed the 1812 memories into a means of criticizing the government. On learning of the surrender of Sevastopol, Prince Dmitrii Obolenskii, a reform-minded jurist and an ally of the Slavophiles, disputed the official equation ("we" are the same, "of Borodino and Paris"): "Now, in consolation over the fall of Sevastopol, many say: 'It's nothing. The enemy was also in Moscow.' I don't know if 1812 can serve as a guarantor of the current war's being concluded successfully—not only were the character and purpose of that war . . . completely different, but Russian society was also incomparably more whole, more moral, and the government more reasonable."[58] As though challenging both Archbishop Innokentii's sermons and the imperial manifestoes, E. A. Shtakenshneider recorded in her memoirs the opinion of the Petersburg liberal circle to which she belonged: "Without railroads, without telegraphs, what made Russia so frightening? Surely not just its size and un-familiarity? Or was it still 1812 and the glory of 1814? We had grown so used to appearing strong that we came to believe in our own strength, although we should have known very well what strength a decaying organism pos-sesses."[59] Comparison of the Crimean and the Patriotic Wars now served as a measure of how far the country had deviated from its authentic self.

In postwar rhetorical practice, two series of metaphors reflecting the need for reforms gained wide currency. On the one hand, the end of the Crimean campaign saw the proliferation of metaphors of spoilage, sick-ness, decay, torpor, and the sleep of a "great nation." On the other, with Alexander II's ascent to the throne and the awakening of new hopes for public life, metaphors of rebirth, recovery, and revival appeared. Thus the idea of the national community as an evolving entity entered the public discourse. If official wartime propaganda postulated Russia's might as the product of exclusive, immutable, and eternal national features (piety and devotion to the monarch above all), then the defeat brought into question not only the protective power of these virtues but their very existence. In a homily delivered in February 1855, Filaret (V. M. Drozdov), the metropoli-tan of Moscow, directly linked the military failures to Russia's deviation from the path of righteousness and, flatly contradicting official rhetoric, accentuated the rupture between generations: "Sons of Russia! The God of Vladimir, the God of Alexander Nevskii, the God of Peter . . . from genera-tion to generation down through the centuries has bequeathed and pre-served for us the pure, holy Orthodox faith in Christ and through this faith has sowed and propagated in the lives of our ancestors good seeds. . . . Are we using this inheritance wisely? . . . It would be hard to stop if we set out to name how many of the pious, good, innocent, humble traditions and habits of our fathers are neglected and lost."[60] While Filaret, the most au-thoritative church leader, considered Orthodoxy compromised and thus questioned the first tenet of Uvarov's triad, the intellectual elite challenged another underlying principle of official nationality—loyalty to the mon-arch. The war, wrote the young Moscow University professor B. N. Chiche-rin, "had shattered the union of tsar and people."[61] P. A. Valuev, future min-ister of internal affairs, claimed that antagonism to the government now permeated society.[62] To be sure, Filaret, Chicherin, and Valuev criticized the regime from differing political standpoints, but all their observations pointed in the same direction.

The Crimean defeat forced many intellectuals to seek new strategies for defining the nation. The works of L. N. Tolstoy, I. S. Turgenev, and M. E. Saltykov-Shchedrin demonstrate that literature dramatically contributed to this process. The following section, focusing primarily on Tolstoy's novella *The Cossacks*, explores their writings in the context of postwar criticism of the regime. Expressive of Tolstoy's personal views, which differed substantially from any of the ideological movements of that time, *The Cossacks* nevertheless fits within the broader attempts to redefine Russia and thus marks a major shift in national self-perception.

Tolstoy's *Cossacks* and the Postwar Shift in the Vision of the Nation

In the years immediately following Tolstoy's return from Sevastopol, his attitude toward wartime rhetoric took a sharply skeptical turn, due in part to the influence of the opposition-minded circle around the journal *Sovremennik*, where all his early writings appeared. By the beginning of the 1860s, however, Tolstoy had developed a no less critical view of the proreform movement, with its Westernism, advocacy of modernization, propagandizing for women's emancipation, and reliance on the bureaucratic state as a major agent of the impending reforms. In *The Decembrists* (1860–61), an unfinished novel set in the 1850s that laid the groundwork for *War and Peace*, he offered a sarcastic portrait of post-Crimean society's exaltation at the prospect of fundamental change: "The victorious Russian troops returned from surrendering Sevastopol to the enemy. . . . Russia celebrated the destruction of the Black Sea fleet, and Moscow of the White Stones met and congratulated the remainder of the fleet's crews on this happy event."[63] Tolstoy highlighted the absurdity of the triumphal spirit that reigned at the end of the war in order to lampoon the proreform atmosphere precipitated by the defeat.

In the novella *The Cossacks* (1853–63), he takes one further step toward addressing certain key issues of national development brought to light by the Crimean War. Like the literature of the preceding decades, *The Cossacks* approached the question of the authentic Russian self by juxtaposing the Europeanized cultural elite with the simple folk who embody the national spirit. The aristocrat Olenin, the story's protagonist and the author's alter ego, finds his ideal in a Cossack village, but his attempt to fit in there proves unsuccessful. There is nothing new in the conflict itself, except the piercing sense of personal tragedy that Olenin experiences over his estrangement from the Cossacks. What is new is that the novella signaled a move away from simple veneration of the common people as the repository of true Russian virtues. Tolstoy elevates the Cossack community to epic heights, drawing comparisons with "biblical legends," in order to set new goals for the entire national community.[64]

Throughout the nineteenth century, various forms of artistic and political expression—both mass and high culture, official ideology and literature—used the figure of the Cossack to represent the distinctive Russian spirit.[65] In his depiction of the Cossack community, Tolstoy follows this tradition but reconfigures it dramatically. First and foremost, his image of the Cossack subverts the official stereotypes disseminated during the Crimean War. *The Cossacks* undermines the equation of Russianness with an amalgam of strength and submissiveness—a combination that, as we have seen, played a central role during the war. Among the Cossack traits foregrounded in the novella there is no mention of either humility or obedience; instead, independence, initiative, adventurousness, and daring appear in abundance, often to excess. Although Olenin observes problematic ethical areas in the life of the community, such as theft, debauchery, and sexual license, he admires the Cossacks for their self-reliance, creative potential, and primordial energy. What particularly captivates him in the Cossack community is the spirit of independence, inherent not only in the men but also in the women. Descendants of fugitives from Russia, living "from time immemorial" along the Terek River under the *Greben* (the Ridge)— "the first crest of forested mountains" in Chechnya—this Old Believer community, which has never experienced serfdom and has to a large extent escaped both church control and state pressure, symbolizes for Tolstoy a double freedom, religious and personal.[66] The independent spirit of the Greben Cossacks holds deep political implications in the novella.

While Tolstoy served as a military officer in the Caucasus (1851–54), the "wild country" attracted him with its mixture of "two utterly wholly incompatible things—war and freedom."[67] These "incompatible things" coalesce in the novella's underlying theme, making it possible for Tolstoy to explicitly position these inhabitants of the empire's dangerous frontier as separate from the state. Drawn into war with the Chechens, they do not enter the regular standing army, which subjected soldiers to brutal treatment at the hands of their commanders while forcing them to commit corresponding violence against civilians. Moreover, Tolstoy stresses the spirit of enmity that separates the army and the Cossacks. The Greben settlers look with hatred on the infantry regiment quartered in their village. Cossack women curse the regiment and call it the "horde"; Cossack men "disdain . . . the oppressor-soldier." In an 1857 draft of the novella, the author even compares the Russian troops in the Cossack village to an enemy army "in captured territory."[68] At the center of the story, Tolstoy places an emblematic scene in which the daring Lukashka, the embodiment of the Cossack spirit, meets a group of soldiers marching toward him and, seeking to provoke them, intentionally refuses to give way.[69] Presenting the Greben community as neither stifled by the regime (like the mass of Russian peasants) nor serving as its coercive instrument (like the regular army), Tolstoy marginalizes his Cossacks and symbolically separates them from the Russian state.

To make their unique status even more apparent, Tolstoy emphasizes how different the Cossacks are from the rest of the Russian population. Mutual alienation divides them not only from the army and the cultural elite but also from the rest of the Russian common people. While the Cossacks think that "the Russian *muzhik* is something strange, a wild and contemptible creature," the soldiers—former peasants—do not recognize the Greben settlers as Russian and ridicule their language and customs.[70] Thus Tolstoy calls into question the ethnic homogeneity of the Russian people. The novella raises high cultural and linguistic barriers between different groups of Russians, even as it blurs the lines between the Cossacks and their Muslim counterparts. Thanks to their centuries of contact and intermarriage, the Russian inhabitants of the Greben show some similarities to the Chechens. Smuggling and horse-stealing as parts of everyday life; a common ethos with respect to war; the cult of weapons, bravery, and freedom— all these common features create a dynamic of mutual attraction on the frontier.[71] If during the Crimean War, in "The Woodfelling" (1855), Tolstoy tended to attribute true courage only to Russians, contrasting them with peoples of the East, he is now inclined to liken the Greben community to the Chechens, with their martial spirit as the point of convergence.[72]

It is possible to identify two seemingly contradictory impulses in Tolstoy's depiction of the Cossacks. On the one hand, he emphasizes their otherness and educates his readers, explaining in detail the ethnographic and linguistic differences between the Greben's inhabitants and the peasants of Russia's heartland. On the other hand, Tolstoy claims that the Cossacks "held onto . . . the Russian language and faith in all their former purity," ascribes to them elements of central Russian dialects, and makes them the bearers of a common Russian folk tradition.[73] As a result, the Greben community simultaneously represents both the Russian self and its other.[74] In these militant Old Believers pushed to the frontier, Tolstoy finds a free community unconstrained by the state, close to the "barbaric" East, and embodying Russianness.[75]

With this interpretation of the Greben settlers, Tolstoy addresses at least three issues that came to occupy a central place in public discussions after the Crimean defeat. First, he overturns the myth of a national empire, portraying the Greben Cossacks as Chechenized, whereas official ideology considered the Cossacks indomitable propagators of the Russian spirit and prime movers of the imperial mission on the frontiers. Second, he questions the unity of the Russian nation, emphasizing the fragmented nature of the "ruling nationality" and the elusiveness of its body, which is obscured and divided by the state. Finally, Tolstoy raises the issue of national character, demonstrating that initiative and energy do constitute distinctive Russian traits but are preserved intact only in a marginalized segment of the population.

One of the most painful aspects of post-Crimean discourse was the question of who lost the war: the government or the people? Although the heroism of the rank-and-file defenders of Sevastopol seemed to give a clear answer to that question, doubts inevitably arose: Were the authorities alone guilty? Did they alone bring about the defeat? The belletrist and political thinker N. A. Mel'gunov, in his pamphlet exposing the shortcomings of Nicholas's Russia, concisely expressed these doubts: "Courage and composure in military affairs are the defining traits of the Russian; but are these qualities sufficient . . . when it comes not to obeying an order, but using one's head!"[76] The sentence ends not with a question mark but with an exclamation point. For many of his contemporaries, the defeat had provided a dismal answer, revealing all too clearly how the regime had diminished the nation's creative potential.

The passivity of the common people came to occupy a central place in the political tracts that circulated in manuscript in Russia or were published abroad at the end of the war and immediately thereafter. The jurists and historians B. N. Chicherin and K. D. Kavelin—two eminent Westernizers—saw the Russian *muzhik* as "a miserable sufferer" not yet awakened "to independent and rational action."[77] The Slavophile Iu. F. Samarin included the nation's "mental somnolence" and the "stagnation of its creative forces" in his list of Russia's most blatant maladies.[78] Mel'gunov, who occupied an intermediate position between the Slavophiles and the Westernizers, surpassed them all, calling the lack of initiative Russians' "original sin."[79] Criticism of the national character seeped into fiction as well. I. S. Turgenev focused on passivity among the educated segments of society. Elena, the main character of his novel *On the Eve* (1859), falls in love with the energetic Bulgarian Insarov, spurning her compatriots on account of their shiftlessness. For Turgenev the erotic, matrimonial, and creative debacles of Insarov's Russian rivals resulted not simply from their own personal weaknesses but from the suffocating political system that had rendered them inert. Lingering oppression damaged all levels of society, plunging it into lethargy—on this point intellectuals from across the political spectrum could agree.[80]

Although Tolstoy, unlike many critics of the existing order, saw the Crimean War and the defense of Sevastopol as confirmations of the might and heroism of the Russian people, he believed that the bureaucracy in general and Nicholas's regime in particular had suppressed the nation. *The Cossacks* differs from Turgenev's novel—and from the pieces of journalism cited earlier in this discussion—in that it expresses this attitude not negatively, by pointing out what is lacking, but positively, by celebrating the spirit of independence and creativity that still survives, if only at the edge of the empire, in a marginalized community of untamed warriors. In other words, Tolstoy's claims about the great potential of the Russian people rest on a group that has kept its Russian values intact only by removing itself far from the coercive grasp of the state.

To reinforce the potency of this construct, Tolstoy singles out the Greben community in two distinct ways. First, without a hint of skepticism, the author recounts the Greben Cossacks' legend of how Ivan the Terrible recognized them as an Old Believer community and guaranteed them religious tolerance.[81] Tolstoy ignores the fact that in the sixteenth century the Caucasian exiles could not have been considered Old Believers, since the church schism occurred some hundred years after Ivan the Terrible's death. This aura of dissidence, projected back to a time before the schism took place, symbolically widens the distance between the Greben community and the state. Second, the story undermines the customary association of Cossacks with Holy Rus'—the mythic image of the Russian native land that, according to literary convention, Cossacks not only defend but epitomize. As Judith Kornblatt has demonstrated, this staple of the Cossack myth evolved gradually in Russian literature from the seventeenth century to culminate in Gogol's *Taras Bulba* (1842), in which the freedom and expanse of the steppe were equated with "the all-encompassing Russian soul," and the Cossacks embodied both parts of the equation.[82] To subvert this stock image, Tolstoy portrays the exotic Caucasian landscape, with its mountains and vineyards, as the Greben Cossacks' beloved home. His refusal to highlight the Cossacks' ties with Rus' is all the more eloquent given that this motif figured prominently in the press while Tolstoy was at work on the novella.[83] This deviation from the conventional depiction of the Cossacks entailed a reconfiguration of other aspects of their traditional representations as well. Tolstoy utilizes the essential feature of the Cossack myth—that they live at the border of alien worlds, temporal (primordial and modern), spatial (West and East), and cultural (civilization and savagery).[84] But, capitalizing on the Cossacks' duality, Tolstoy goes on to imbue it with sharp antistate connotations. If the Greben community represents Russia's true self, then not only foreign enemies or alien cultures serve as Russia's other but also the bureaucratic state. Tolstoy's anarchistic views made it possible for him to introduce this innovation into the Cossack myth and thus radically, albeit symbolically, lift the Russian people from the shadow of the empire.

Tolstoy also departed from the literary convention that located the Cossack community either in a chronologically distant era or in a timeless mythic past.[85] Though he surrounds his Cossacks with the epic aura, the novella's subtitle, "A Caucasian Story of 1852," sets the action on the eve of the Crimean War. To understand Tolstoy's decision, one should recall that the Russian army's victory in the Caucasus—the only truly successful theater of the Crimean campaign—led to the region's final subjection to the Russian Empire. Although *The Cossacks* appeared in 1863, the subtitle indicates that its characters live in a prewar Caucasus, not yet fully absorbed into the empire. In the novella, the Greben community still sits on a dangerous frontier and therefore represents the spirit of independence. This is not to say that Tolstoy condemned the expansion of the empire; only later would he develop such an attitude. At this point, his primary concern was to redefine the Russian nation, and setting the story in 1852 made it possible for him to construct the Greben community as an embodiment of Russia's true self by contrasting it with the state.

Two types of violence, depicted in completely different ways, graphically reinforce this juxtaposition of the Cossacks and the state. At the outset of the story, Lukashka shoots a Chechen *abrek* who intrudes into Russian territory (*abrek* was the word for those Chechens who did not recognize the Russian government in the Caucasus). Tolstoy describes this incident twice, initially in an objective manner, through the voice of an omniscient narrator, and then in first person, in the words of Lukashka himself, who boasts of his deed. Surprisingly, in both accounts Tolstoy downplays the moral aspects of the killing—a central theme in his battle prose before and after *The Cossacks*. Instead, he indirectly justifies the act, associating it with instinctual struggle through parallels with hunting and the life of animals. Olenin's qualms over the incident only illustrate the futility of his efforts to fit into the Greben world. Among the Cossacks, it is the old man Eroshka— an intermediary between the aristocratic protagonist and the Greben community—who broaches the ethics of the killing. But Eroshka keeps his comments on Lukashka's deed to a minimum. When violence is done to the Chechens by regular army soldiers, however, Tolstoy has Eroshka speak out repeatedly about the senselessness of the violence inflicted on the mountain folk (at one point even breaking into song).[86] The divergence in these assessments stems from the differing nature of the violence in question. When Lukashka kills the *abrek*, he is defending his people. When the regular army destroys a Chechen village, it is merely obeying an order. Unlike the soldiers, Lukashka not only commits violence but voluntarily exposes himself to danger. In the final clash with the Chechens, no one orders him forward, but he rushes into the fray of his own accord and receives a potentially fatal wound (the reader is left in doubt about the hero's fate).

The Cossacks' relation to violence constitutes their principal similarity to the Chechens: both sides are defending their land and their community. Significantly, Lukashka is wounded by the brother of the *abrek* he had killed. The two are not anonymous combatants but mortal enemies. This lends the entire conflict the quality of a clash between two nationalities, equals in battle. Tolstoy establishes thorough parallels between Lukashka and the *abrek* he kills at the beginning of the story. Although we see

Lukashka's victim only after his death, the author emphasizes that both men possessed the qualities of leadership. Tolstoy also depicts each man's physical beauty and uses their racial differences as a backdrop against which to reveal their similarities (strong, muscular, beautiful bodies).[87] By setting the narrative in 1852, Tolstoy puts the Cossacks in the same position of fighting for their independence as the Chechens.

Given that the Greben settlers epitomize the Russian nation's true self, this juxtaposition of the two equally matched rival communities entails symbolic consequences. *The Cossacks* dramatizes an ideal situation where Russians fight only for their land and their people — not on behalf of a regime that stifles the Russian nation. In the real world, of course, struggle for the Russian people inevitably meant defense of the state and of the government. This vicious circle tormented many writers of the time. Setting *On the Eve* in the summer of 1853, Turgenev highlights that, with the Russian army's successes on the Danube at the very beginning of the Crimean War, movements for the independence of the Balkan peoples begin to emerge. While the war brings the Bulgarians hope, the Russians remain oppressed by their own government and, Turgenev emphasizes, are losing their love of country.[88] In the novel, resurgent Bulgaria and still-uniting Italy represent two different patterns of struggle for national rebirth, equally attractive to the author and equally inapplicable to Russia.[89]

The Cossacks addresses precisely this conundrum: how to fight for the Russian people without fighting for the Russian state. A note Tolstoy made in his diary while at work on the novella concisely encapsulates the author's intent: "The future of Russia lies in Cossackdom [*kazachestvo*]: freedom, equality, and compulsory military service for all."[90] Lukashka in his clashes with the Chechens is the prototype of the citizen-volunteer defending his community, the antithesis of the standing army that lost the Crimean War. Still, though for Tolstoy the Greben settlers held the key to a Russian national revival, his vision of Russia's future was not a fully developed political blueprint. Moreover, in subsequent decades Tolstoy would abandon the view expressed in the note cited here. By the time the government introduced universal military service (1874) and thus started down the path toward nationalizing the army — a path long before taken by many Western countries — Tolstoy's beliefs had evolved in a way that subsequently would place him at the forefront of protests against compulsory military service. Conscription contradicted his teaching of nonresistance to violence, which he elaborated during the 1880s. In the late 1850s to early 1860s, however, Tolstoy held up the embattled Greben community as a possible source for national reconstruction.

During the reform era Tolstoy was not alone in seeking an epitome of the nation's true self in the frontier societies of Cossacks or Old Believers. The historian N. I. Kostomarov wrote a series of works on the Ukrainian Cossacks, seeking to cast them as the last redoubt of ancient popular sovereignty stifled in the East Slavs by the Russian monarchy. In 1855 Herzen also envisioned a "return to Cossackdom" as an authentic means of building the nation, precisely because Cossacks, he emphasized, had developed "far from the grasp of the state."[91] Mel'gunov celebrated the Old Believers exiled to the Caucasus as "the distillation of everything independent that lies hidden in the simple Russian."[92] Many writers held up the Old Believers as an active, economically successful, and purposeful segment of the population, although representatives of various ideological trends tended to construct them differently.[93] It was their search for a model of national development that drew these thinkers to such marginalized communities.

A Turning Point in National Mythmaking

In the aftermath of the Crimean War, the idea of improving and perfecting the national community gained ascendancy. The historian S. M. Solov'ev recalled that at that time almost all his contemporaries saw transformation as the only means of "recovering the people's energies."[94] Even some Slavophiles articulated plans for re-creating the nation, although, in keeping with romantic nationalism, they saw it as a primordial entity—not something in need of "building." In 1858 Iu. F. Samarin, one of the leading Slavophile thinkers, published a detailed account of the reforms undertaken in Prussia at the beginning of the nineteenth century, in the wake of its crushing military defeat by Napoleon. He not only prescribed a similar path for his own country but asserted that the changes, enacted by the "strong will" and "free mind" of the Prussian politicians, had awakened the people "from drunken slumber" and "united them as a nation."[95] This invocation of an intellectual force capable of transforming the national community is very characteristic of postwar rhetoric. It signals a major shift in national self-perception: the nation is no longer taken for granted but understood as an entity to be (re)constructed.

Identifying the awareness of a need to (re-)create the nation as the distinctive feature of nationalist ideologies, David Bell traces how this idea, propelled by institutional crisis, emerged with particular strength in late eighteenth-century France.[96] Although the political concept of nation remained underdeveloped in Russia, the post–Crimean War era witnessed a similar tendency among Russian thinkers to subject the existing concept of nationhood to fundamental criticism and thus foster a vision of the nation as a damaged entity in need of reconstruction. In the late 1850s the weakening of censorship made it possible to publicly articulate plans for improvement. The fortunate coincidence of these two fundamental shifts—the shift in national self-perception and the beginning of a "thaw"—allowed the notion of the nation as a political construct to enter public discourse.

Although various ideological groups envisioned the development of the nation in different ways, after the humiliating defeat the majority of intellectuals conceded the necessity of modernizing Russia, which meant that they appealed to Western models, albeit cautiously. The need to free the serfs, expand the educational system, reform the courts and the army, and develop technologies and means of communication all forced Russians to consider Western practices. Yet whatever they borrowed from the West, almost all conceptions sought to sustain a sense of national continuity by rhetorically linking foreign ideas with native traditions. In articulating their program of change, even such Westernizers as Chicherin and Kavelin asserted: "We are a nation overwhelmingly attached to our legends and customs."[97] Recovering a virtuous national past came to be understood as a means of introducing changes that would nurture the nation's true self.

Tolstoy's position took shape in this atmosphere. His motto cited earlier—"freedom, equality, and compulsory military service for all"—reveals him as a spiritual heir of the Enlightenment, well acquainted with such Western instruments of national consolidation as universal military service. Tolstoy, however, never applied such patterns directly to Russian soil. As an opponent of Westernization, modernization, and political efforts to alter social life, he looked to Russia's native institutions for authentic ways to address urgent national issues. Like many European intellectuals, he saw in the extension of military duties to the entire populace a means of forging the nation. Like many Russian intellectuals, he inscribed his vision for the nation's transformations—even those developed under the obvious influence of Western European blueprints—within an authentic historical patrimony (in this case, *kazachestvo*). Intellectuals rediscovered or manu-factured Russian cultural distinctiveness not only to celebrate the nation or to foster a belief in its uniqueness, but also to suggest authentic ways of transforming it. National self-image expressed through cultural myths thus served as a means of rhetorically perfecting the nation.

The new approach to the nation as a political construct dramatically altered the functions of existing patriotic clichés. We have seen that after the Crimean defeat critics of the regime utilized the memory of the Patriotic War to gauge the extent of the nation's deviation from its true self. At that time, the perception of Russia's boundless spaces also underwent signifi-cant transformation. During the Crimean War, Innokentii's sermons, Niki-tin's verses, and *Russkii invalid*'s articles all imagined Russia's vast expanses as the epitome of the people's might, a repository of the country's heroic past, and a divinely appointed means of defense. Directly disputing this convention, Tolstoy severed the link between Russia's native landscape and the Cossacks, who represent for him the nation's essence. Tolstoy's novella thus not only contradicts the equation of Russianness with unbounded space, but it undermines definitions of the nation through reference to conventional native landscapes.

M. E. Saltykov-Shchedrin called the metaphor into question from a dif-ferent direction. He finds the traditional landscape positively treacherous, full of peril not for the invading enemy but for Russians themselves. In *Pro-vincial Sketches* (1856–57), he first paints magnificent "fields as far as the eye can see," seeming to offer this image as a powerful antidote to the empty life of bureaucrats, the author's main target. But then the peaceful village idyll morphs into endless sleep, the picturesque peasant becomes an obtuse slave, and the inscrutable expanse turns bloodthirsty: you "drown in the swamp of provincial life, which on the surface is so green that from a distance you could, perhaps, imagine it to be a lush meadow."[98] Recasting the celebration of the Russian landscape as a funeral for its inhabitants, Saltykov-Shchedrin marked the path many writers would later take.[99] Mel'gunov proposed the most radical reinterpretation of the spatial meta-phor by refusing to acknowledge Russia's vast territory at all. Without proper means of communication, he wrote, the Russian expanses were a fic-tion, because a person simply could not comprehend them. An advocate of railroad development, Mel'gunov compared railroads to the blood vessels of an organism, asserting that the Russian Empire would remain fragmented until it was united by a modern means of transport.[100] As this last example shows, attempts to undermine the conventional understanding of national space stemmed from the sense that the nation needed to be reconstructed, not praised.

This shift in the function of a stable national symbol reflected a new approach to nationhood. Before the Crimean War, intellectuals defined it by reference to something preexisting—something "eternal" or long since established, be it the physical environment, divine ordinance, or the mythic past. Within this conceptual framework, the nation was a given and the agent of its fate was understood to be something independent of human will. After the war, Russians looked at themselves through a new lens. They came to see the national community as an evolving entity that might deviate or be resurrected as a result of the people's activity and that therefore should be treated as an object of care and construction. While the former approach fell entirely within the paradigm of romantic nationalism, with its tendency to extrapolate a country's fate from its presumed national character, the latter cautiously adopted a vision of the nation as political construct, with its premise that nations are not given but made. When a nation is to be (re-)created, the agent of its fate is man—be it the state, the intelligentsia, or a particular class. This shift brought with it a new way of using inherited patriotic idioms. The physical environment, Providence, and historical achievements now became grist for discussions of social transformation, tools for rhetorical redefinition of the nation.

Questions remained about who would undertake the national community's reconstruction and how it would evolve. We will now explore how different responses to these questions emerged and how Russian intellectuals struggled to redefine the nation by means of its most popular cultural myths.

2

The Varangian Legend

Defining the Nation
through the Foundation Myth

Throughout the imperial period of Russian history, the tale of the summoning of the Varangian princes occupied center stage in the national mythology. Appearing in the *Primary Chronicle* (compiled in the twelfth century) under the title "Whence the Land of the Rus' Came into Being," the story tells how in the year 862 diverse native peoples in the vicinity of Novgorod, exhausted from mutual warfare, sent an envoy "over the sea" to invite foreign military leaders to serve as a neutral intermediary force, saying: "Our land is great and abundant, but there is no order in it: come rule and govern us." In response to this invitation, the story goes, Prince Riurik, his brothers, and their retinue—the Varangians, whom the chronicle also refers to as "Rus'"—came to Novgorod to bring peace to the people, confer their own name on their new home, and establish its first dynasty.[1] Early in the eighteenth century, when systematic study of the ancient sources first began, scholars identified the Varangians with Scandinavian Vikings and credited them with the founding of the state, the

introduction of autocracy, and the imposition of other institutions that
gave rise to Kievan Rus'.[2]

Known as the Norman theory of Russia's origins, this interpretation of
the tale became a magnet for controversy soon after it emerged. Initially
propounded by eighteenth-century historians of Germanic descent (Th. S.
Bayer, G. F. Müller, and A. L. Schlözer), it presented the life of the Russian
people prior to the Varangians' appearance on the scene as a period of savagery unworthy of study. This approach drew vigorous protests from scholars of Russian descent. The astronomer N. I. Popov and the renowned scientist and writer M. V. Lomonosov accused the "Normanists" of harboring
a desire to humiliate the Russians by depicting them as intrinsically inferior
to Scandinavians. The first salvos of the controversy over the tale were thus
couched in the language of ethnic sentiment, revealing the insecurity and
resentment that the Norman theory elicited in the patriotic mind.[3]

One would think such reservations would have compromised the
Norman theory and hindered the legend from playing a significant role in
Russian political discourse, let alone the quest for Russianness. Yet just the
opposite occurred. For educated Russians, products of the Petrine cultural
revolution, the tale of a ruler "from over the sea" made it possible to claim
Russia's kinship with the Western world while at the same time leaving room
for constructing the country's identity in contrast to it.[4] V. N. Tatishchev,
the prominent historian and intellectual supporter of the reforms of Peter
the Great, embraced this theory, as did many others after him.[5] At the end
of the eighteenth century, court historiographer Mikhail Shcherbatov took
the story of the summoning of the Varangians to mean that Russia's authentic political order relied on harmonious relations between rulers and
aristocracy.[6] The opposition-minded writers of the Enlightenment also utilized the tale but viewed it from a different angle. Seeking to undermine the
legitimacy of the regime, A. N. Radishchev employed it as evidence that
Russia's ancient political system was based on a social contract that Riurik
subsequently broke, thus prefiguring the despotic character of Russian
autocracy.[7]

In the nineteenth century the large group of intellectuals who subscribed to the Norman theory was increasingly challenged by a growing
cohort of anti-Normanists, who, like Lomonosov before them, vehemently
denied the Scandinavian origin of the ethnonym Rus' and of the Varangians
themselves. Yet even the most vocal anti-Normanists tended to refashion the

tale rather than reject it outright.[8] For all these thinkers, regardless of their
views, the story of how the dynasty came into being and how the monarchy
was founded served as an apt metaphor for the state-nation nexus. The
legend was utilized by those who viewed the nation as centered on the state
(typically, they identified the birth of the nation with the founding of the
state) and by those who viewed the nation as centered on the people (they
distinguished between the appearance of the nation and the state). Normanists and anti-Normanists were to be found among both camps of nationalists, and these overlapping allegiances resulted in an astonishing profusion
of rival readings of the tale.

Though the majority of intellectuals accepted as almost axiomatic that
the legend had some basis in fact, all the thematic components of the story
constituted contested terrain and proved highly debatable. What was the
Varangians' cultural and ethnic background? When and why did they ar-
rive? Did they not come as conquerors, only to be transformed into invited
leaders by the compilers of the *Primary Chronicle*, anxious to salve Russian
pride? On what terms and with what consequences did they interact with
the indigenous population? Finally, what was the role of the non-Russian
ethnic groups, the Chud and the Ves, who, according to the chronicle, participated in inviting the foreign rulers? The inventiveness of the myriad an-
swers given to these questions, the length and scope of the discussion, the
large number of people who took part in it (including exponents of official
ideology)—all these factors helped transform the Varangian legend into a
remarkably resilient core cultural symbol that underpinned competing
concepts of Russianness.

Remaining on the ideological agenda throughout the nineteenth century, the tale gained such popularity in the 1860s that Mikhail Katkov found
it necessary to remind his readers that the question of Russia's origins was
not to be decided by a general vote.[9] In this chapter we shall examine how the
reform era refashioned the tale and altered its content and functions. But to
address this issue, we must first briefly trace its evolution prior to the 1860s.

The Dynastic Myth Becomes a Tale
of the Nation's Uniqueness

Just like the origin myths of England, France, and other monarchic states,
the story of Riurik's arrival first spoke to the emergence of the dynasty and

state power and only later came to express the spirit of the people.[10] This shift took place as the quest for national identity started to develop. Nikolai Karamzin's popular *History of the Russian State* (1818–29) represents the beginning of this process.

Karamzin defined Riurik's arrival as the foundation of Russia's "history and greatness"; this statement fit perfectly with the Normanist view that Russia's history began with the appearance of the Varangians.[11] Yet his version was a radical reconsideration of the previous renditions of the tale. While the eighteenth-century scholars had presented pre-Norman Russians as barbarians,[12] Karamzin portrayed the summoning of the rulers as a conscious and voluntary decision on the part of the Russian people that proved their inherent wisdom. He glorified the calling for the Varangians as "an astonishing event, practically unparalleled in the chronicles" of other countries: "Everywhere the sword of the strong or the wiles of the ambitious introduced absolute monarchy [*samovlastie*]. . . . In Russia, however, it was established by the mutual consent of the citizens." Karamzin emphasized: "The Slavs voluntarily abolish[ed] their ancient popular government and ask[ed] for a sovereign from the Varangians."[13] This construct of absolutism "by consent" dramatically recast the foundation of the monarchy as an expression of the people's will and their instinctive predisposition to autocracy. Karamzin did not forget to list the Chud and the Ves (the "Finnish tribes") among the participants in the act of summoning, but he assigned them the role of silent witnesses to a uniquely Slavic action and treated them as attributes of the empire's grandeur. This vision of the monarchy's birth buttressed Karamzin's state-centered concept of the nation and shaped the historical imagination of subsequent generations of Russian thinkers.

During the 1830s and 1840s, when the debates over national identity were reinvigorated by the rise of nationalism across Europe and the emergence of Russian historicist philosophy, the foundation myth helped articulate a new wave of constructs of the nation. Accepting Karamzin's concept of a voluntary invitation, M. P. Pogodin further expanded its symbolic potential and transformed the story into a metaphor for the love and mutual devotion between the tsar and the people. First propounded in 1832, his reading of the Varangian tale derived from a broader formula for the essence of Russian history, elaborated under the influence of and in polemic with the French historical school. In his book *The General History of Civilization in Europe* (1828–30), François Guizot asserted that it was the spirit of personal independence, pluralism, and the ethos of struggle by individuals and social strata against one another and against coercive governments that moved the Western world forward. Pogodin not only admitted that Russia lacked these features, but he also claimed that their absence accorded Russia a unique status. The supremacy of the collectivist ethos over individualism, the absence of social conflict, the spirit of submissiveness and pacifism and, finally, the devotion of the people to their ruler—all these defined the distinctiveness of Russian history. The fundamental differences between the two civilizations stemmed, he argued, from the difference in their founding. European kingdoms arose from conquest by alien forces, but the Russian monarchy grew out of the invitation of and voluntary submission to foreign princes: "Our ruler was a peaceful, invited guest, a desired *protector*, while the Western ruler has been a hated usurper, the chief *enemy* from whom the people vainly seek protection."[14]

Pogodin treated the summoning of the Varangians as the formative event of Russian history and saw it repeat itself time and again across the Russian past. He claimed that Prince Oleg's "settlement in Kiev was as peaceful as Riurik's in Novgorod."[15] Even more paradoxically, he presented the growth of Kievan Rus' and of the Petrine Empire within the same framework: "Kiev subjugated the Drevliane or Radimichi even less [forcefully] than Moscow subjugated Tver', or Russia Finland."[16] As that last quotation shows, Pogodin tended to blur the lines between the invitation of foreign leaders and Russia's "subjugation" of outlying regions. He lumped them all together under the general category of "amicable bargain" (*poliubovnaia sdelka*): "Just as in the West everything proceeded from conquest, so for us everything proceeds from the summoning, the unopposed occupation, and the amicable bargain [between the ruler and the people]."[17] Regarding Riurik's arrival, Pogodin admitted that "in those harsh, wild times invitation and conquest were . . . very close, similar to each other, a very fine line divided them—but they were distinct!"[18] To make that distinction more evident, Pogodin resorted to subject inversion, judging the founding act by its distant results and centuries-long repercussions: "Fine differences between seeds are seen plainly in their flowers and fruits."[19] The "subjugation" of Tver' by the Muscovite princes or Finland by the Russian Empire came to represent "fruits" and thus to prove the peaceful starting point of Russian history. By equating voluntary invitation with military domination, Pogodin justified coercive absolutist power as an expression of the people's spirit. By blurring the line between Russia's ancestral land and its conquered territories, he tended to erase the divide between the country's ethnic core and its non-Slavic population, thereby asserting the national character of the empire.

While Pogodin used the foundation myth to symbolically legitimate the regime, his contemporaries the Slavophiles did just the opposite. They also subscribed to the concept of voluntary summoning, but, unlike Pogodin, they denied that it bore even superficial or sporadic similarity to conquest. P. V. Kireevskii took issue with Pogodin: "Invitation and conquest not only were not *close* to each other; they were complete opposites."[20] The Slavophiles highlighted the difference between the two not only because they sought to emphasize Russia's crucial difference from the West, but also because it helped them define the nation apart from the state—even as the state's opposite. According to the Slavophiles, the Vikings founded the state not to impose alien ways on the indigenous populace (as the Norman theory held) but to protect the people and free them from the need to commit violence. Riurik and his successors, Kireevskii believed, never introduced personal ownership of land and thus did not infringe on such native Russian institutions as the village commune (*obshchina*), one of the essential features of all Slavic peoples: "The land's belonging to the *entire commune* . . . is completely incompatible with conquest; it [communal ownership] not only was not abolished after the summoning of the Varangian princes, but, as we know, it exists to this day."[21] The preservation of authentic social and economic patterns served to confirm the fact that the state established by the Varangians did not alter the Russians' native traditions but remained merely an external guarantor of their well-being. Thus, for the Slavophiles, the calling of the Varangians led to the establishment of ideal relations between the state and the people—relations that the autocratic regime subsequently undermined.[22]

Despite all the differences between Pogodin's and the Slavophiles' versions of the Varangian legend, both renditions of the myth rested on romantic assumptions about the nation's unchangeable nature—a nature either manifested in the monarchy (Pogodin's view) or protected by a monarchy that did not intrude into the inner fabric of national life (as the Slavophiles believed). Pogodin and the Slavophiles were also similar in their emphasis on the moral impulse behind the summoning and the Christian virtues the people exhibited in submitting voluntarily to their ruler.

Though Riurik arrived more than a hundred years before Rus' was converted to Orthodoxy, Pogodin declared proudly, "Our people submitted peacefully to the first comer," because they were endowed with "patience" and "humility," the "lofty Christian virtues that adorn our history."[23] Conscious of the anachronism, Pogodin and the Slavophiles wove Christian motifs into the legend to emphasize the religion as an inalienable component of Russian identity. For them, Russians accommodated themselves to Christian values even prior to their conversion due to the "harmonious accord" between Christianity and the primordial Slavic spirit.[24]

While both these constructs put forward concepts of the nation centered on the people, the Westernizers used the myth to highlight the role of the state as creator of the nation. The most articulate contributions to this discussion came from adherents to the "state school" of history: K. D. Kavelin, B. N. Chicherin, and another member of the group, S. M. Solov'ev, who elaborated a version of the legend that dominated school textbooks in the second half of the nineteenth century. In 1851, in the opening volume of his *History of Russia from Ancient Times*, Solov'ev acknowledges the "great import" of the Varangians as state builders, managing, unlike many of his predecessors, to reconcile the theory of the Norman conquest with that of the invitation. He claims that the former simply preceded and paved the way for the latter. The contentious Slavic tribes invited the foreign princes because, having earlier been under their control, they had already benefited from their consolidating power. Following a Hegelian scheme of state-promoted civic development, Solov'ev replaces the romantic myth of a submissive and peace-loving people with a rational explanation of the summoning: Riurik's arrival reconciled, united, and elevated the quarrelsome tribes to a higher level of social progress. Solov'ev terms the summoning of the Varangians an "all-Russian event" (*vserossiiskoe sobytie*), as opposed to a Russian (*russkoe*) one, to emphasize that it led to the creation of a centralized state—the highest form of national life, according to Hegel.[25] He mentions that "the Finnish tribes" participated in the summoning, but, like Karamzin, Solov'ev does not assign them any particular role other than providing clear evidence of the state's grandeur and multiethnic character.

These three divergent versions of the foundation myth derived from and provided a testing ground for three competing visions of the state-nation nexus. While Pogodin viewed the state as an incarnation of the people's distinctive spirit, and the Slavophiles defined the nation apart from the state and viewed the latter as merely a shield for the former, for Solov'ev the nation did not exist "before," outside of, or apart from the state. It was, he believed, forged by the state. Despite these differences, the three narratives of how the state was founded operated within a framework of shared assumptions. First, they all assigned the Russian people a submissive role, even though the motivation they attributed to people's submission varied in each case. For Pogodin, it was their limitless loyalty to and love for their ruler; for the Slavophiles, it was their inborn revulsion at wielding power; and for Solov'ev, it was simply their realization of the benefits of having a strong leader. Significantly, none of these constructs invoked Karamzin's thesis that by calling for the Varangians the Slavs "voluntarily destroyed their ancient popular government," since such a belief contradicted the picture of the people's apolitical nature. Second, all three conceptions defined the Russians through comparison with European peoples, while basically ignoring their encounter with other ethnic groups within the empire. The "Finnish tribes," although they figured among the participants in the summoning, lacked any distinguishing features and were thus of no use in defining the Russians, other than to serve as confirmation of the empire's greatness.

During the reform era, both of these motifs were to undergo dramatic revision. New renditions of the myth would infuse the image of the people with activism and shift the focus of discussion to the problem of a multinational empire. To refashion the tale in this way, reform-era thinkers reconsidered not only the constructs presented thus far but also the official version of the Varangian myth put forward during the 1830s and 1840s.

Sacralization of the Myth
in Official Propaganda

Pogodin's story of the "amicable bargain" attracted Nicholas I's approval and saturated the precepts of official nationality with historical memories. As Richard Wortman has shown, Nicholas defined the people's devotion to the Westernized monarch as a distinguishing Russian pattern, one that could be traced back to the calling of the Scandinavian princes.[26] The emperor firmly imposed this interpretation of the myth. In 1852 he even issued an order to the minister of education establishing the state teaching institutions as the sole guardians of the memory of Russia's sacred origin.

This directive came as a reaction to what had seemed merely academic debates. In 1851, in reexamining the *Primary Chronicle*, Solov'ev uncovered some inconsistencies in the way it counted years and, rather than dating the summoning to 862—the conventional year of Riurik's arrival—moved it back a decade.[27] Proponents of official ideology hastened to rebuff this change in chronology as blasphemy against deeply ingrained popular beliefs: "There are in History holy dates, holy names, holy convictions, which must be approached with the greatest of care," admonished Pogodin.[28] The foundation of the Russian state was laid, he averred, in 862: "So we were taught; so our fathers believed; so repeats the entire Russian people."[29] Shifting the date of Russia's founding might open the floodgates, Pogodin feared, for revising the entire body of collective memories.[30] Presented with a detailed report on this matter, Nicholas reiterated Pogodin's arguments, making comments in his own hand on the original paper: "I am of the same opinion, for so I was taught in my youth, and I am now too old to believe otherwise."[31] Then he decided the question with nothing less than an imperial command, issuing an order "to hold firm" the conventional date of the event and "be guided by it completely in all educational institutions of the Ministry of Public Education."[32] Nicholas I's safeguarding of the date and, more broadly, his appropriation of the legend paid unmistakable tribute to its growing appeal.

Alexander II was also keen to take advantage of the myth. In keeping with the conventional date of the summoning, in 1862 he held a lavish celebration of the Millennium of Rus'. It was intended to confirm Alexander's adherence to official nationality, while injecting new attitudes and dynamics into the doctrine. Wortman's insightful interpretation of the festivities has demonstrated how Alexander II redefined Nicholas's legacy, adapting a Western form of popular leadership to the Russian mythical tradition and thus producing an ambiguous concept of the nation.[33] Next we will further explore how the commemoration harnessed the foundation myth to inspire hope that crucial transformations were under way to reconstitute the nation.

Staging the "Amicable Bargain"

The celebration consisted of a series of ceremonies clustered around the unveiling and consecration of a monument to the Millennium of Russia, erected in Novgorod, on its central Sophia Square. Originally, it had been proposed simply to dedicate a monument to Riurik. Yet, after discussing the matter in 1857, the Committee of Ministers issued a decree that radically broadened the scope of the project: "The invitation to Riurik represents, without a doubt, one of the most significant epochs of our state, but we, his descendants, should not and cannot disregard the achievements of our other autocrats."[34] To celebrate Russia's triumphal progress over the past millennium, the government called for "a national monument" (*narodnyi pamiatnik*), where "the greatest events of the history of our fatherland shall be depicted."[35] In 1859, after a competition with more than fifty designs, the young artist M. O. Mikeshin's project was recognized as being "most in accord with the government's intentions."[36]

By the time the commemoration took place in September 1862, the emancipation of the serfs was in full swing. On the very first day of 1862, two other major projects—the introduction of elective organs of local self-government (*zemstvos*) and the inauguration of Western-style judicial institutions—had been officially announced in all the newspapers as already in preparation (both began to be implemented in 1864). Though the cultural elite greeted them enthusiastically, these transformations produced feelings of uncertainty, fear, and anxiety, which only intensified the sense of resentment engendered by the lost Crimean War. The alarming events of 1862—peasant uprisings, student unrest, the gentry's opposition movement, the attempts on the life of two successive governors of the Kingdom of Poland (Count A. N. Liders and Grand Duke Konstantin Nikolaevich), a rash of fires in St. Petersburg, the dissemination of revolutionary leaflets, which penetrated even into the Winter Palace—all these created an atmosphere of foreboding. As preparations for the millennium celebration unfolded against this dismal backdrop, it evoked mixed feelings even among those directly involved in the project. After one of the commemoration committee's meetings, P. A. Valuev, the minister of internal affairs, lamented in his diary: "It's a bad idea to erect a monument to the living. And Russia is alive. Will that same Russia we now revere as our mother still be alive after the millennium?"[37] As the day of the celebration drew closer, he asked himself in even more dramatic fashion: "Is it possible to avert the Fatherland's falling to pieces?"[38] Many members of the ruling elite shared this morose outlook and feared that the commemoration could become a lightning rod for popular disaffection.[39] As one observer recalled, "There was a rumor going around in those days that the monument had been mined and was supposedly going to be blown up at the very moment of its unveiling."[40] Given the risk of terrorist acts, Alexander decided to limit the festivities to a parade of troops and a church service consecrating the monument, but he did not cancel the jubilee ceremonies altogether.[41] They were designed to instill a vision of the reform era that offered an antidote to the crisis of insecurity and inspired hopes for the nation's further development.

The celebration opened with the imperial family sailing along the river Volkhov to Novgorod, where a lavish reception awaited them. The tsar's arrival at the ancient capital was staged as a symbolic reenactment of Riurik's advent. First, the direction of both journeys was similar. Departing from St. Petersburg, Alexander and his retinue approached Novgorod from the Baltic Sea, as the Varangians were said to have done. Second, the water route taken by Alexander recapitulated the *Primary Chronicle*'s account of the Varangians' coming "from over the sea." Since railways had not yet reached Novgorod, it might seem that purely pragmatic considerations had dictated the choice of the river route had not Alexander on the next day undertaken another journey by ship. He sailed on a launch from Novgorod to Riurikovo Gorodishche—the legendary dwelling place of the first Russian ruler—thus reaching by stages Riurik's final destination. On both river trips, Alexander was met by rejoicing throngs, thus playing out the drama *the ruler comes to the people*.

Official and semiofficial press accounts promoted this interpretation of the festivities. They portrayed jubilant Novgorod as a richly decorated stage on which the people's voluntary submission to the Varangian prince was reenacted. "Novgorod as it were became the capital once again," reported a correspondent for *Syn Otechestva* (Son of the Fatherland), "and our thoughts instinctively returned to those times when Prince Riurik came to this land to rule the people."[42] In his memoirs, Valuev, chief organizer of the spectacle, put it even more succinctly: "The past was resurrected before the eyes of the present."[43] Most newspapers presented the reunion of ruler with ruled in the traditional mode—as a symbolic recapitulation of the people's love for the ruler—and highlighted their rapture at the emancipation of the serfs.[44] By dramatizing the sacred moment of Russia's birth and at the same time by making the reforms a central theme of the ceremonies, the commemoration joined the starting point of national history with the present day and thus portrayed the reforms as a restoration of the nation's authentic patterns, rather than a break in its development. As we have seen, this was exactly how thinkers of a nationalist persuasion chose to understand Alexander II's innovations, and in this way the commemoration could only reinforce their hopes that the government would embark on policies that would strengthen the Russian nation.

The monument visibly placed the current transformations along a continuum of Russia's progress, spurred at each step by series of reforms "from above." While the structure's upper part—a kneeling woman and an angel beside a cross resting on a hemisphere—represented Orthodoxy, the sculptural groups of its main tier portrayed, as the Committee of Ministers had prescribed, "the six remarkable epochs in the history of the Russian state," each epoch centered on a ruler-reformer (fig. 1). Here the drama of Russia's growth unfolds, with Riurik symbolizing the birth of the state; Vladimir, the conversion to Christianity; Dmitrii Donskoi, the beginning of liberation from the Tatar yoke; Ivan III, the introduction of absolute tsardom; Mikhail Romanov, the restoration of autocracy after the Time of Troubles; and Peter I, the foundation of the empire.[45] The concept of *transformation* governed the selection of these "remarkable epochs." The monument drew a straight line of descent from Riurik to Alexander by means of an inscription encircling the structure on a level with the six sculptural groups: "Dedicated in the year 1862, during the successful reign of the emperor Alexander II, to the past millennium of the Russian state." A medal coined in 1862 to celebrate the monument's unveiling also visualized the link between Riurik and Alexander II, depicting the two rulers side by side.[46]

Peter the Great dominates the composition: his sculpted figure is placed on its main, north side, facing Sophia Cathedral and opening onto Novgorod's central square.[47] All official accounts began with descriptions of this image, thus sacrificing chronology for the sake of foregrounding transformation as the dominant pattern of Russian history.[48] In contrast to his conventional representations, Peter here symbolizes not a rupture in Russia's development but its continuity, since the preceding rulers presented on the monument are also reformers. The link between Peter and his predecessors was further strengthened by the fact that three of them also brought innovations from foreign lands: Riurik himself came from overseas, Vladimir adopted Christianity from "the Greeks," and Ivan III united Russia on the model of Byzantium (for this reason his sculpted figure carries the Byzantine attributes of power). The monument's design blended

Figure 1. Millennium of Russia Monument, Novgorod. Design by M. O. Mikeshin, 1862. View from the north side. (Drawing from *Semenovskii, Pamiatnik tysiacheletiiu Rossii*, title page)

Peter's customary martial image with the theme of his civic achievements. Though the titanic ruler appears striding energetically forward and
trampling a defeated Swede, behind him the sculptor has placed an angel
who, as official accounts claimed, "shows the path Russia . . . must take in
order to fulfill its first emperor's command and achieve a level of education
and greatness equal to the Western powers."[49] While Nicholas I admired
Peter the Great as "the high point of absolutism," an emblem of domination and authority,[50] Alexander II humanized the first emperor in the spirit
of his own reign, presenting the reforms of the 1860s as the fulfillment of
Peter's legacy. Thus the monument depicted transformations carried out
under the influence of Western models as an authentic way of moving Russia forward.

Inscribing Alexander's reign within the sequence of pivotal epochs, the
jubilee propaganda underscored its focus on internal problems. A popular
brochure published for the anniversary portrayed the emancipation of the
peasants as the removal of the final obstacle to the success of the nation-
building process: "We have liberated ourselves from enslavement by the
Tatars, fought off the foreigners, and now we are free from domestic slavery, as well. Our score with the previous millennium—through which we
struggled for our freedom against internal and external enemies—is settled.
The Russian land has now attained its freedom, and embarks on a new life
with the new millennium. Forward, brothers, to a new life, to new, peaceful
civic triumphs!"[51] On the day of the Novgorod celebration, the lead article
of *Syn otechestva* even went so far as to define the current reforms as a shift
from state-building to nation-building: "A thousand years ago Riurik laid
the foundations of the Russian monarchy. . . . A thousand years later Alexander II laid the foundations of all-national [*obshchenarodnaia*] life by
destroying the yoke of slavery."[52] While such pronouncements outlined
Russia's future in ecstatic but vague terms, the symbolism of the commemoration seemed to suggest a more precise vision of how the nation
should develop.

The millennium monument's lower section is girded by a continuous
bas-relief frieze of 109 figures, a clear attempt to incorporate new actors
into the national pantheon. An "edifying chronicle in faces," the frieze con-
sists of four thematic groups: "enlighteners" (the term referred to saints
and leaders of the church), "statesmen," "warriors and heroes," "writers and
artists."[53] The last group is of particular interest. Although by this time

almost everywhere in Europe, the great poets and philosophers of the past had achieved the status of patrons of the nation,[54] in Russia they were included in the national pantheon for the very first time. By repudiating Nicholas's alienation of the educated elite as contaminated with anti-Russian spirit, the monument put writers and scholars on the same level as generals, church hierarchs, statesmen, and even some rulers who appeared in the frieze. Among writers, apart from Lomonosov, Derzhavin, Karamzin, Zhukovskii, and Pushkin, all at various times loyal to official ideology (although Pushkin's is a more ambiguous case than the others), the monument also depicts Lermontov, Gogol, and Griboedov (fig. 2), some of whose works were removed from the censor's list only with Alexander II's ascent to the throne.[55] In his memoirs, Mikeshin credited himself with inspiring this unprecedented decision. When in private conversation with Alexander II he suggested including in the monument "all the worthy people who have contributed to Russia's greatness in the various branches of learning, intellect, science, etc.," the tsar supposedly responded with enthusiasm: "I'll allow you to implement it as my idea."[56] The main ceremonies of the Novgorod festivities reveal the same intent. At the time of the kneeling service, which followed the unveiling of the monument, a deacon read proclamations in prayer written by Filaret, the metropolitan of Moscow, at Alexander II's request. The emperor ordered that not only rulers be remembered in these prayers. After the eternal memory (*vechnaia pamiat'*) of the princes and

Figure 2. Millennium of Russia Monument, Novgorod. Design by M. O. Mikeshin, 1862. Part of the bas-relief depicting writers and artists. From left to right: M. V. Lomonosov, D. I. Fonvizin, G. R. Derzhavin, A. F. Kokorinov, F. G. Volkov, I. A. Krylov, N. M. Karamzin, V. A. Zhukovskii, N. I. Gnedich, A. S. Griboedov. M. Iu. Lermontov, A. S. Pushkin, N. V. Gogol, M. I. Glinka. K. P. Briulov, D. S. Bortnianskii. (Drawing from Semenovskii, *Pamiatnik tysiacheletiiu Rossii*, appendix)

tsars of the past, an almost identical prayer was pronounced for "all the chosen sons of Russia who over the centuries [had] faithfully worked for its unity, benefit, and glory."[57] Both the frieze and the church service signaled Alexander II's readiness to broaden his understanding of who embodies the nation and who might serve as agents of nation-building.

The same inclusive impulse is evident in the organizers' effort—cautious though it was—to incorporate into the festivities historical memories associated with resistance to the centralized state. The jubilee symbolism combined two rival images of Novgorod—reflections of competing versions of Russia's past—into a locus of identity for the entire nation. While the myth of the summoning of the Varangians celebrated the ancient capital as the cradle of the monarchy and an emblem of the people's humble devotion to their rulers, in literature (initially in Radishchev's writings, followed by romantic and Decembrist poetry), Novgorod was featured as the symbol of native seeds of popular sovereignty and of resistance to coercive Muscovite absolutism. During the reform era, memories of the *veche* (popular assembly) and of Novgorod's ancient independence had a profound ideological resonance. On the eve of the jubilee, the renowned historian N. I. Kostomarov published an article, "On the Significance of Great Novgorod in Russian History," in which he glorified both Novgorod and Pskov as antagonists to autocracy and prototypes of republican freedom.[58] In March 1862, at a benefit evening for the Literary Fund, P. V. Pavlov, a professor at St. Petersburg University, gave a speech about the Millennium of Russia, in which he also presented ancient Novgorod as the main counterweight to the "coarse Tatarism and half-dead Byzantinism" of the Russian monarchy.[59] To reconcile these disparate, if not mutually exclusive, historical memories, the organizers of the festivities masterfully manipulated the emblems of freedom, beginning with the most famous—the *veche* bell.[60]

As many observers remarked, the monument's general shape, "especially when seen from a distance, resembles a bell with an extended mouth," evoking associations with both the Tsar Bell, symbol of absolutist power, and the *veche* bell, symbol of Novgorod's self-governance.[61] For many journalists, the monument's location on the site where the *veche* had once gathered (within the walls of the Novgorod Kremlin and in front of the Sophia Cathedral) resonated strongly with the tradition of popular sovereignty.[62] On the day of the celebration, *Sankt-Peterburgskie vedomosti* (Saint Petersburg news) proclaimed: "On the heels of our recollections of Riurik, memories of the *veche* and its bell, of Novgorod's freedom and pride . . . all pass before our eyes."[63] The popular brochure "A Conversation beside the Monument to the Millennium of Russia" also reminded readers that "the will of the people" had ruled Novgorod. Having avoided the Mongol yoke, the city remained a reservoir of indigenous civic institutions: "Only in this corner," the brochure asserted, "did free, independent Rus' survive," preserving "native law," "truth in judgment, and excellent administration."[64] Veneration of the ancient capital as a treasury of authentic traditions was accompanied by strikingly favorable references to Novgorod's resistance to Muscovite absolutism. Marfa Posadnitsa—the heroine of Novgorod's fifteenth-century struggle for independence from Moscow—made her way onto the monument. Placed within the group of "warriors and heroes," she stands alongside Minin, Pozharskii, and Susanin, who traditionally symbolized unbounded devotion to the throne.[65] Given that the monument included only four women, and all of them except Marfa belonged to the ruling house (Princess Olga, Tsarina Anastasia Romanovna [Ivan the IV's first wife], and Catherine II), her great significance for the creators of the monument is unmistakable. True, the bas-relief shows her in the moment of defeat: "Tears flow down her cheeks, at her feet lies the broken *veche* bell," observed the correspondent for *Sankt-Peterburgskie vedomosti*. "Marfa cries over this bell for her dead lord Great Novgorod."[66] The tragic figure of the Novgorod heroine and the broken *veche* bell at her feet (fig. 3) served to show the

Figure 3. Millennium of Russia Monument, Novgorod. Design by M. O. Mikeshin, 1862. Part of the bas-relief depicting warriors and heroes. In the center is Marfa Posadnitsa, crying over the broken bell of Novgorod. (Drawing from Semenovskii, *Pamiatnik tysiacheletiiu Rossii*, appendix)

triumph of monarchical power over regional interests. Nonetheless, both the sculptural figure of Marfa and official accounts portrayed her as a manifestation of national values, praising her "proud bearing," "proud face," self-reliance, and majesty.[67] Together with evocations of the *veche*, her figure conveys the conciliatory and inclusive spirit of the commemoration. Fusing rival historical narratives into the shared collective memory, the monument demonstrated the monarchy's capacity to combine disparate elements, even oppositional ones. On the eve of the *zemstvo* reform, elevation of the Novgorod tradition of self-government to the status of common heritage served, once again, to instill a perception of the current transformations as a restoration of authentic institutions.

The list of historical figures excluded from the national pantheon conveys the festivities' conciliatory ethos no less eloquently than do the names of those included. The commemoration's organizers found no room for Ivan the Terrible in the monument and did not mention him in any of the ceremonies celebrating past monarchs. Banished from the millennium jubilee, he represented a silent antithesis to Alexander's "scenario of love," as Wortman has defined the ideology of the reign.[68] Newspaper accounts gave voice to this contrast. After revisiting the gloomy sites of Novgorod's past violence—the ruins of Marfa Posadnitsa's house and the bridge over the Volkhov from which people were thrown at Ivan's orders—the correspondent for *Syn Otechestva* concluded in a triumphant tone: "But today these places, full of horror, are fated to witness the rebirth of a new era of rational freedom and to see scenes filled with sincere, unfeigned feelings of devotion to the Restorer of that freedom."[69] Valuev, too, noted the inclusive spirit of the commemoration (in this case referring to Ivan III): "That first Russian tsar, who bears the historical appellation of *gatherer* of the Russian lands and who in his reign broke the ancient freedom of Novgorod, did not foresee that the celebration of the millennium of the Russian state would occur precisely there, in Novgorod."[70] Nothing revealed the conciliatory ethos of the event more eloquently than the initial decision to exclude Nicholas I from the monument. Only in the final stage of the project, with the list of figures to be represented already published in the official calendar, *Mesiatseslov na 1862 god*, was Nicholas hurriedly "rehabilitated" and inserted into the bas-relief (a change that required partial reconstruction of the nearly completed monument).[71]

Despite all these innovations, commemorative symbolism was dominated by a historical narrative that identified the nation with the absolutist
state and the autocracy. The achievements of the rulers presented on the
main tier of the monument visually outweighed (and literally overshadowed) the pantheon of Russia's "chosen sons" on the lower section. The idea
of the nation as an ethnic entity with distinctive traits other than devotion
to the throne was absent from the millennial rhetoric. Nor did it convey any
sense of the nation as a collective protagonist in history. The jubilee symbolism managed to suggest a broadening of the nation while still identifying it with the autocracy—a position that perfectly captures the ambiguous
nature of official ideology at the beginning of Alexander II's reign. As discussed earlier, the reform era dawned with high hopes that the impending
transformations would eventually bring the peasantry into society, broaden
civil rights for all strata, and ultimately diminish the social and cultural
divides within the population. Although fostering a sense of public involvement in civic life and seemingly preparing to bridge the gap between state
and people, the government nonetheless precluded political participation
and maintained obstacles to the growth of national cohesion. The complex
interplay between these mutually contradictory trends pervaded the millennium celebration: it seemed to chart a new nation-building project, but
at the same time remained within the old framework of official nationality.
These ambiguities explain why the commemoration evoked highly divergent responses from the public.

The Protean Legend

A full ten years after the millennium celebration, the monument made a
cameo appearance in Dostoevsky's *Demons* (1872), which mimics vividly, if
in caricature form, the commemoration's divisive effects on society. One of
the novel's most dramatic scenes relates a "catastrophe" that unfolds at a literary reading to benefit impoverished governesses. While the first two readers, Karmazinov and Verkhovensky, a couple of over-the-hill writers, leave
the audience perplexed and dissatisfied, a third orator—a walking grab-bag
of clichés of 1860s radicalism, whom the narrator calls "insane"—literally
polarizes the crowd. Hearing him "publicly defame Russia," some in the audience are on the verge of walking out in outrage, while almost half the hall

"bellows its thunderous delight." These contrasting reactions come to a head when the "maniac," calling for the destruction of the regime, mentions the "colossal bronze ball" erected in Novgorod "in memory of the millennium of disorder and idiocy already gone by." At this point, some spectators rush the stage to silence him; others leap to his defense. Here the scene breaks off, and we never learn who wins the impending fight.[72] Dostoevsky is alluding not only to the actual scandal that arose during the millennium preparations—Pavlov's speech, mentioned earlier, for which he was exiled from Petersburg—but also, more broadly, to society's conflicting reactions to the official celebration.

The wide range of responses to the commemoration exhibited by journalists, poets, and scholars reflects the pool of competing visions of Russia's future. M. N. Katkov, editor of *Moskovskie vedomosti*, enthusiastically reproduced the jubilee rhetoric about the peasants' emancipation, placing the ongoing changes within the Hegelian framework of civic development, to which he had long adhered: over the preceding millennium "the Russian state had achieved its material development" and must now "fulfill its higher calling" to forge "an independent and fruitful national life." Katkov looked eagerly toward the reforms as a transition from state-building to nation-building and a step toward a progressive future, when Russians would overtake the nations of Europe.[73] Slavophiles, on the contrary, condemned the commemoration as a glorification of the imperial state and its Westernized culture, both alien to the common people. "It has occurred to me many times when I visited the Novgorod Kremlin," P. Polevoi wrote in the Slavophile newspaper *Den'* (The Day), a few days before the celebration, "that instead of the notorious monument to Russia's millennium, it would have been much better to take care of the ancient Kremlin walls and towers, living monuments of past centuries, to protect them from both administrative abuse and desecration by ignoramuses. Would not this brand-new monument look ridiculous among majestic walls covered with the moss of centuries?"[74] Only a church, insisted the Slavophiles, could be a real monument to the preceding millennium, since they viewed Orthodoxy as the defining aspect of Russianness.[75]

The ceremony drew open criticism from many witnesses who, like the Slavophiles, saw the nation as centered on the people, rather than on the state. In the atmosphere of *muzhik* worship that colored the 1860s, a celebration that ignored the nation as a cultural entity was naturally greeted with sarcasm and became a lightening rod for antigovernment sentiment. Many publications drowned out the jubilee rhetoric with a steady buzz of ridicule and grousing. The funereal associations that the monument conjured for Valuev on the eve of the festivities resurfaced in a more playful form in several satirical articles. Thus an anonymous feuilletonist for *Otechestvennye zapiski* (Notes of the Fatherland) appealed to his readers to erect a tombstone for him in the town of his birth, whose made-up name mocked the name of Novgorod: "Do not forget to raise a monument to me in the place of my birth, namely, Myshgorod [Mouse-town]." Envisioning this monument to himself, the anonymous author grotesquely intertwined the miserable—indeed the mousy—with the grandiose: "This monument should be shaped like a little bell to show that my life has been full of naught but empty chatter. Put a cross on top of this bell. . . . The cross is to rest on a hemisphere to symbolize that I have done much good to half the world."[76] A blatant parody of the millennium monument, the passage turns revered national symbols—the Tsar Bell and the *veche* bell—into tinkling cymbals, and the monument's very conception into the ravings of a megalomaniac. If for Dostoevsky, the nihilist who denounces the Novgorod commemoration is "insane," for *Otechestvennye zapiski* the sculpture makes visible the sick mentality of the regime itself.

Two famous works of satire reflect the sense of frustration produced by the official commemoration. While previous generations had inscribed national virtues in the foundation myth, for these two writers it was a compendium of national flaws. A. K. Tolstoi's poem "A History of the Russian State from Gostomysl to Timashev" (1868) takes in the entire sweep of Russian history, opening (as custom demands) with the summoning of the Varangians and the shopworn formula: "Our land is great and abundant, but there is no order in it."[77] As with Pogodin, this initial event points to the governing principle of Russian history, but for Tolstoi, the recurrent imperative is prompted by endless chaos: no matter who rules, no matter where they come from, nothing has changed in Russia for a thousand years—"there's *still* no order in it" (*poriadka net kak net*).[78] The poet repeats this formula—the main motivation for the summoning of the Varangians—in his account of each reign, giving the whole millennium an absurd cast.

Absurdity also lies at the heart of a satirical sketch by M. E. Saltykov-Shchedrin: in the sixth chapter of his *Contemporary Idyll* (1878), he places the legend in the mouth of an antihero, Gadiuk (the name derives from the verb *gadit'*, to play dirty tricks, to shit on), who proudly claims that his ancestor was responsible for inviting the Varangians.[79] By incorporating the fictional Gadiuk—an ordinary man—into a sacred legend, the chapter mocks previous interpretations of the tale, which had sought to turn the dynastic myth into a common past for the entire community. Gadiuk's Novgorodian forebear proposes to his compatriots that they rid themselves of the burdens of freedom by sending emissaries to the Varangians, who used to raid them mercilessly, with the suggestion that they come and take over in order to "loot, burn, kill and rape according to the law." This mission scares even hardened brigands like the Varangians. On his arrival in Novgorod, Riurik has a prophetic dream, foretelling the tragic fate of a nation that will humbly endure violence from its own rulers. He considers running off, but Gadiuk's clever ancestor persuades him that a thousand years hence the people will gratefully erect a monument to him "on this very spot."[80] Saltykov-Shchedrin and Tolstoi held different political views, but they both rendered the Varangian legend in most sarcastic terms, as an absurd story of the state's growing hostility to the people.

Although in the wake of the millennium celebration it became an easy target for satirists, the foundation myth continued to fuel nationalists' imagination, enabling them to recast the nation-state nexus. Like the generation of the 1840s, the new group of writers was certain that the roots of a unique Russian identity resided in the Varangian tale, but they reconfigured it dramatically to display different national virtues. The reform-era intellectuals differed all the more sharply from their predecessors in that they lived in a period when nationalism as a political force was remapping Europe. They watched, enthralled and frightened, as both Italy and Germany unified. And they kept a wary eye on the growth of separatist movements in the Ottoman and Hapsburg empires. With the Polish rebellion (1863–64), the rise of Ukrainian nationalist ambitions, the "pacification" of the Caucasus (1864), and the thrust into Central Asia (1860 through the 1880s), the Russian Empire was facing profound challenges. Reform-era versions of the foundation myth increasingly addressed the pressing problems of empire. In the following discussion, I explore three divergent readings of the legend, each of which implied—and at times explicitly proposed—a distinct project of nation-building. In spite of the differences between them, these three projects represent a new mode of national mythmaking that utilized historical memories as a charter and justification for the political transformation they proposed.

Multiplied and Relocated Summoning: Kostomarov's Federalist Project

In his writings the historian N. I. Kostomarov subverted many of the cultural myths that symbolically legitimated the centralized state and the concept of a single all-Russian nation encompassing Byelorussians, Ukrainians, and Russians.[81] Much of his innovation stemmed from the belief that the Ukrainians (the Little Russians, to use nineteenth-century terminology) had a future apart from the Russian people (at that time often called the Great Russians). This conviction brought with it a commitment to forging a Ukrainian national identity, a task that inevitably entailed recasting Russian identity, since the two constructs competed for the same ancestors, heartlands, and historical events.[82] In this context, the Varangian legend, recounting as it did the birth of the state, could not help but become a target for his attacks. Yet, although Kostomarov raised doubts about the tale's essential elements, the kernel of the story seemed to haunt his imagination, supplying him with a malleable framework for rhetorically recasting Russia as a political community.

Kostomarov articulated his novel rendering of the foundation myth in the pages of *Sovremennik*, the influential left-wing journal, in an article titled "The Origin of Rus'" (1860). Its opening statements are indicative of the audacity of the construct he propounds. Kostomarov links Russia's birth not to the summoning but to the expulsion of the Varangians, an event that, according to the *Primary Chronicle*, preceded the invitation of Riurik and his brothers. Though previous scholars had not ignored this event, none seemed to feel it held any great significance for the subsequent course of history. Kostomarov, on the contrary, elevates the act of casting off the "Norman yoke" to epic heights and posits it as a defining historical moment. Several times he emphatically repeats a line from the chronicle— "[The Slavs] chased out the Varangians and did not pay them tribute!" (*Izgnasha variagi za more i ne dasha im dani!*)—and concludes his article with this ringing phrase. For Kostomarov, rejection of alien authority, not submission to it, marked the origin of Russia. Love of liberty, combative spirit, and the struggle for independence thus became the salient national qualities, rather than the Slavic passivity, submissiveness, and lack of political initiative that had been underscored in the 1840s.

Kostomarov's second proposition was even more provocative. The article asserts that in ancient times the word "Varangians" had designated not one particular ethnic group but any foreign military retinue—and thus did not necessarily refer to the recently expelled Normans at all. He then presents various linguistic and ethnographic "facts" to assert that the eviction of the "Norman Varangians" was followed by the summoning of the "Lithuanian Varangians." The choice of a new ethnic identity for the invited rulers, at first glance a strange move, made it possible for him to declare that they had no lasting impact on Russian life. While the powerful Normans had left an indelible mark on many peoples of Europe, the Lithuanian princes could claim no comparable role—indeed, Kostomarov argues, they soon sank without a trace into the Slavic milieu. Though scholars had disputed the Norman theory long before Kostomarov, his effort to dismiss it stemmed from a desire to demonstrate that the East Slavs had remained essentially unaffected by foreign influence.[83]

The article met with immediate approval from the radical press, especially after Pogodin, enraged by its conclusions, challenged his colleague to an academic duel: a public debate on the origins of Rus'. This event took place on March 19, 1860, at Petersburg University, in an enormous room that nonetheless could not begin to hold all the potential spectators.[84] As observers noted, the students who constituted the bulk of the gathering far preferred Kostomarov's vision of combative self-reliant Slavs.[85] The editors of *Sovremennik* also enthusiastically endorsed his construct, since it defused the ideologically charged beliefs imposed by the regime.[86] As the senator K. N. Lebedev, Pogodin's supporter, disapprovingly observed, "Kostomarov has shifted the matter from the field of scholarship to the field of nationalities."[87] Discussion of the Varangian legend had in reality never left the "field of nationalities": what annoyed the senator was the increasing stridency of its political implications.

The political subtext of Kostomarov's rendition of the tale definitely contributed to its success, but a sense of bewilderment and disorientation came to dominate discussions of his theory. The satirical journal *Iskra* (Spark) ran a caricature that depicted the dispute: in the foreground Kostomarov and Pogodin make their arguments to each other, while in the background Varangians "of uncertain parentage" (*ne pomniashchie rodstva*) "sit

Figure 4. "Dispute Over Who Were the First Varangians Summoned to Our Shores—the Lithuanians or the Normans." Foreground: N. I. Kostomarov (*left*) and M. P. Pogodin (*right*). Background: On the left are the "Knights of Bedlam," a jocular name for supporters of the radical journal *Sovremennik* and its satirical supplement, *Svistok*. As the caricature indicates, they side with Kostomarov. In the center, Prince Riurik, his brothers, and their retinue are in the dock. On the right stand "the ghosts of Th. S. Bayer, A. L. Schlözer, and F. I. Krug," the creators of the Norman theory, who support Pogodin. The text of the caricature drew on Pogodin's letter to Kostomarov, published prior to the dispute: "I am throwing down the gauntlet and calling you to a duel. I need no seconds but the shades of Bayer, Schlözer, and Krug . . . you may invite as your second any of the Knights of Bedlam" (*Sovremennik*, no. 1 [1860]: 1–32). (Caricature from *Iskra*, no. 13 [April 8, 1860])

in the dock awaiting a verdict." The caption explains that after a "long and fruitless" investigation, the judges could not determine where the Varangians came from, so the trial was postponed for a thousand years (fig. 4). Saltykov-Shchedrin also mocked the duel with a sketch about the town of Glupov [Foolsville], a metaphor for Russia, whose academy sponsored an

essay contest on the theme "Where Ivanushki Come From." The winning
entry, "Ivanushki Grow under Rocks," showed that Glupov had no past and
was highly unlikely to have a future.[88] As he was leaving the Pogodin-
Kostomarov debate, the poet P. A. Viazemskii said: "We used not to know
where we were going; now we don't even know where we're coming *from*."[89]
The *Iskra* caricature, Saltykov-Shchedrin's sketch, and Viazemskii's bon
mot show how public opinion linked questions of Russia's origins with
thoughts about its future—and remained confused on both counts.[90]

As though in answer to the confusion engendered by the duel, in his
subsequent writings Kostomarov dropped the theory of the Varangians'
Lithuanian roots to elaborate a counternarrative of Russia's beginning that
would better fit his vision of the country's future. In his study "Legends of
the Russian Primary Chronicle in Light of the Oral Epic" (1873), Kostomarov sharply divorces the birth of the nation from that of the state. Folk tales
and songs about the mass migration of various Slavic groups from the
Danube River area to the "Russian continent" constitute, he claims, the most
reliable source of information about "the origins and destiny of the nation." On the basis of folklore, he draws a picture of the migration of the
Slavic tribes and their mixing with—or at times only settling alongside—
the original Slavic population of the region. Compared with the Varangian
myth, this alternate story holds considerable advantages for imagining the
nation. It shifts Russia's birth to a more remote past, thus yielding a much
longer and richer national history. It also lends more convincing support to
the idea that indomitability and love of liberty were distinctive traits of the
Slavs of ancient Rus'. Under pressure from their Roman conquerors, only
the most strong-minded, argues Kostomarov, left the Danube to regain
their freedom. Finally, this myth proposes and symbolically bolsters a new
vision of national genealogy. Since "each branch of the Russo-Slavic people"
came to this land separately, each possessed of its own distinct past and
its own heroes, this new narrative of descent recognizes many forefathers
who could be regarded as founders of their communities, instead of Riurik,
the lone founder of the state.[91] Kostomarov highlights Russia's diversity and
presents its history as the responsibility of a group of collective actors: the
Slavic peoples of Rus', once numerous but reduced over time until only the
Great Russians and Little Russians remained (for him the Byelorussians did
not constitute a separate "nationality"). Furthermore, Kostomarov believes
that since pre-Mongol Rus' was a union of independent principalities,

recovery of regional identities would provide insight into the original political order and thus chart a possible future for the country on the basis of its authentic culture. His works are filled with hints—given the censorship, he could say nothing more directly—that for Russia the road to nation-building lay through federalism, which would offer both "Russian nationalities" freedom to develop in an autonomous manner.

Within this new construct, Kostomarov treats the calling of the Varangians as the turning point in the formation of the pre-Mongol polity, mining the tale for the shared memories of the "Russian nationalities." "The summoning can be called a great, a universal event," he pronounces in 1862, "since it determined the historical trajectory of the many tribes that would come to constitute the Russian people."[92] In contrast to the official version of the myth, he equates the summoning not with the founding of an autocratic state but with the introduction of a unique combination of two types of authority: "The prince and the *veche*, two entities of differing origins, agreed to cooperate with each other." Kostomarov here revives Karamzin's thesis of the existence of popular government in pre-Varangian Rus'. Unlike Karamzin, however, he interprets the invitation of the foreign leaders not as a repudiation of popular sovereignty but as its pragmatic fusion with princely power. The Varangians, he concludes, brought to Rus' a unifying impulse that led to the later strengthening of the state, but they curtailed neither the independence of the separate tribes nor the principle of popular sovereignty: "The Russian lands existed each unto itself [*samobytno*]," and all together acknowledged their common bonds in language, religion, and the ruling house.[93]

In his article "The Origin of Autocracy in Ancient Rus'" (1870), Kostomarov finds creative ways of inserting the summoning into the history of each constituent community of the Russian polity. He argues that the story of Riurik's invitation, improbable in 862, reflects, albeit in embellished form, the political practice of a later period: the time when the *Primary Chronicle* was composed. In his opinion, the institution of princely rule changed substantially with the adoption of Orthodoxy in the tenth century. In pre-Christian times, all princes, including those of Riurik's dynasty, defended the populace from enemy incursions but also exacted high tributes and wielded brutal power over their subjects. Kostomarov calls such princes "raiders" and "robbers"—something like pirates for hire—who served as a protective cover to the land without impinging on the local culture.

Even more than the Slavophiles, Kostomarov thus divorces the state from the people at this stage of Russian history. In the eleventh and twelfth centuries, however, Kostomarov recognizes moral bonds emerging between the princes and the people—a result of the influence exerted by Christian teachings: when "the pagan egotism of base desires" began to give way to "the idea of service to the community," the prince was transformed into "a ruler, a judge, and a defender" of the people, "at home with their customs and laws."[94] He believes that at this point the *veche* reigned supreme, in perfect harmony with the prince, who now was elected by the assembly and whose role was to execute its will. For Kostomarov, the chronicle's account of Riurik's summoning reflects these harmonious relations between rulers and people, but with two important reservations. First, the chronicle had arbitrarily transplanted the story to the ninth century in order to confer an aura of antiquity upon these trusting relations between prince and *veche*. Second, no less arbitrarily, from his point of view, the chronicle rechristened the "election" of the prince an "invitation" and located the event exclusively in Novgorod, thus inaccurately portraying Riurik's arrival as a unique occurrence.[95] Kostomarov claims that such stories—even the sacramental formula "Our land is great and abundant . . . come rule and govern us"— "in fact were repeated in every land, every time a prince assumed power."[96] Thus, in place of a single Novgorodian summoning—a historical myth that symbolically legitimated autocracy as an ancient institution and served the ideal of the unitary state—Kostomarov proposes a multiplicity of summoning elections, which instead justify the principle of federalism as the native political order and serve as the embodiment of an authentic version of popular sovereignty.

Kostomarov maintains that Muscovite despotism—the direct descendent of the Mongol yoke—had destroyed these ancient freedoms. Whereas the Ukrainians managed to preserve elements of their popular sovereignty longer, Russians felt the corrupting and oppressive influence of autocracy earlier and with greater intensity. If one wanted to revive the national ideal manifested in the Riurik legend, therefore, the place to look for it was Ukraine. Thus the summoning, multiplied and relocated in time and space, made it possible to imagine Russia as a political union of Slavic nationalities and to single out the Ukrainians as guardians of a pure national identity for all East Slavs.

Kostomarov's reading of the legend indicates a growing imperial consciousness among the cultural elite. To judge by his federalist views, it would seem that he viewed Russia as a multiethnic state. Yet not only does he narrow its Slavic core to only two "nationalities"; he also emphatically denies the empire's non-Slavic population any role in history other than purely destructive. Following their move from the Danube, he argues, "the warlike colonies" of Slavs had defeated and forever enslaved the non-Slavic aboriginal population of the "Russian continent." He utilizes the Varangian legend once again to dramatize this belief. Only representatives of the "ruling people," Kostomarov postulates, participated in the summoning(s). Having staked out this position in "The Origin of Rus," Kostomarov never abandons it. "Do not be misled," he warns, by the fact that the chronicle names "the Finnish tribes" among those who took part in the decision to invite the Varangians—and Schlözer, Karamzin, and Solov'ev all took this vague assertion on faith. Such a claim, Kostomarov asserts, contradicted the entire march of history. He depicts the "subject foreigners" (*podvlastnye inorodtsy*) as completely "subordinated to the Russo-Slavic population" and incapable of participating in the summoning.[97] If "these trifling peoples" (*narodtsy*) had contributed to the decision and consequently preserved some shred of independent agency, they would "somewhere, somehow have put up some resistance" to the Russians. Kostomarov even goes so far as to reformulate the cause of the summoning in an imperial spirit: it was not, as the chronicle reports, clashes between tribes that inspired the Slavs to call in the Varangians, but rather "the need to restrain and subdue the subject *inorodtsy*."[98] This thesis—though it blatantly contradicted his claim that the peoples in question were already subdued—turns non-Slavic groups into opponents of, and indeed the prime motivation for, the summoning of the Varangians.

Although the majority of Russian nationalists rejected Kostomarov's federalist agenda and, a fortiori, the separatist ambitions of the Ukrainians, a growing number of writers addressed the issues he raised. Their nation-building projects grew out of completely different conceptual frameworks, but as we will see, their readings of the legend also made the people into agents of their own fate, recast relations between ruler and nation, and emphasized Russians' supremacy over the diverse inhabitants of the empire.

Gedeonov's Varangians and Rus':
The Rise of Exclusive Nationalism

The interpretation of the Varangian legend advanced by S. A. Gedeonov, the most influential nineteenth-century contributor to anti-Normanism, gave rise to a new wave of debates about the beginning of Rus'. An amateur historian, a man of vast erudition and wide-ranging intellectual interests, Gedeonov occupied a series of prominent government positions, including director of the Hermitage Museum (from 1863 to 1878) and director of the imperial theaters (from 1867 to 1875). For about thirty years, he worked on his seminal two-volume monograph, *The Varangians and Rus'*. The book as a whole was published in 1876, but in 1862 he hurried the most provocative sections into print in time to challenge the underlying concept of the millennium celebration.[99] He rejected the Norman theory for the very reason that official ideology embraced it: because it portrayed the people's peaceful subordination to a Westernized ruler as a distinctive national trait. Like Kostomarov, Gedeonov found this model insulting and did not shy from declaring that a wounded "sense of nationality lay at the foundation" of his study.[100] Though he did not hide behind the mantle of impartial scholarship, Gedeonov's statements were no more biased than those of other popular historians of the nineteenth century, and his methods were by no means those of a dilettante. He adhered to the academic standards of his day, demonstrated an acquaintance with then-current theoretical paradigms, and mobilized vast quantities of data from different fields: linguistics, archeology, numismatics, and ethnography. Although his contemporaries were quick to make light of his nationalistic zeal—and rightly so—the scholarly community treated his book with respect, and even Pogodin, who vigorously defended the Norman theory in his debates with Kostomarov, found some of Gedeonov's conclusions plausible.[101]

While Kostomarov concocts a Lithuanian identity for the Varangians, Gedeonov, like many other anti-Normanists before and after him, insists on their Slavic origins. He claims that Riurik came to Rus' from the Baltic Wends, a branch of the Western Slavs whose fate he depicts in the most tragic terms: over four centuries the "Germano-Scandinavian peoples" deliberately destroyed the "handful" of courageous Wends—"a once proud and wealthy lineage" settled on the banks of the Elba and the Oder— and after much "bloody struggle" managed to obliterate all traces of their existence.[102] His thesis of the Varangians' Wendish origin gave rise to a series of conclusions that addressed the central problems of Russian nationalism during the 1860s by once again renewing the protean potential of the legend.

First, Gedeonov persistently conflates the East and West Slavs, even calling the vanished Wends "our Varangian ancestors."[103] He thus makes Russia the repository of a common Slavic identity, symbolically expands its territory, and provides historical justification for the Pan-Slavic project. Second, in highlighting the tragic fate of the Wends and their ties with the Russians, Gedeonov insinuates in his readers' minds a sense of the Slavs' vulnerability to their bellicose German neighbors. In the 1860s—a period marked by German unification and the rise of an independence movement among Slavs settled in the Hapsburg Empire—the motif of German aggression became a major preoccupation of the nationalist press in Moscow and in Petersburg. Gedeonov's book is shot through with attacks on the Germans, reflecting the growth of anti-German propaganda and the increasingly defensive character of Russian nationalism, always ready to cast Russia as the victim of dangerously overbearing European states.[104] Third, the image of a Slavic Riurik allows Gedeonov to transform the legend of the summoning of a foreign ruler into a symbol of the nation's ethnic purity. The Russians invited Wendish princes to rule them, Gedeonov argues, because they recognized kinship ties and cultural affinity with the newcomers.[105] Thus, the arrival of the Varangians did not bring "any alien ethnic stock . . . into the Slavic-Russian [*sloveno-russkoe*] community."[106] It is not entirely clear whether he is speaking here of racial or cultural homogeneity, or indeed of both at once. Yet in any case, the language of ethnic exclusivity dominates the book. Fourth, and most importantly, the idea of Slavic roots for the house of Riurik simultaneously hints at a source of nationalization for the Romanov dynasty and upends the idiom of the people's subservience to a Westernized autocrat. Like Kostomarov, Gedeonov considers the Slavs' distinctive traits to be an "unconquerable love of liberty" and an utter unwillingness to submit themselves to foreigners. Already sharing the Russians' customs and values, the Wendish newcomers not only did not interfere with the "essential laws" of the Russian community, but they willingly accepted these "laws."[107] In this way, Gedeonov reverses the familiar idiom: under his pen, the voluntary submission of people to ruler becomes a voluntary submission of ruler to people, or more precisely, to the Russian people's authentic values, habits, ethics, and institutions.

Gedeonov places the monarchy—which existed, he insists, long before Riurik's arrival—first among these institutions.[108] In ancient times, Gedeonov observes, the life of every Slavic clan (*rod*), tribe, and religious community had been defined by the patriarchal principle that conferred on elders an uncontested right to power. The unlimited authority of princes, arising out of a recognition of the seniority of their *rod*, was an expression of this deeply ingrained pattern. When, however, the internecine strife described in the chronicle around 862 had brought Novgorod to a state of chaos, "the order of seniority was lost and along with it, the very notion of the leaders' legitimacy." The only way out of this crisis was "to hand over princely rule to a new dynasty," to Wendish princes "highly placed in Slavdom" due to the seniority of their princely lineage. This patriarchal model makes it possible for Gedeonov to explain the phenomenon of the summoning in terms of native customs and thus to claim that the autocratic principle is an "organic feature" of Slavic culture.[109] He agrees with Karamzin that the invitation to the Varangians demonstrated the Novgorodians' wisdom and maturity, but for him that maturity is manifested not in a sudden leap from popular government to autocracy (he views popular government as a product of Karamzin's and Kostomarov's imaginations) but rather in the fact that the native principle of respect of a senior clan found its natural expression in the establishment of the new dynasty.

This construct presented Gedeonov with a conundrum: how had Rus' developed so rapidly into a powerful state—already by the eleventh century—if not through external influence? Even "moderate" Normanists, who, unlike the "immoderate" Schlözer, did not label pre-Varangian Rus' a backwater of ignorance and savagery, credited the Scandinavians with the construction of a powerful state. For Gedeonov, on the contrary, the rapid development of Rus' was a natural outgrowth of the high level of pre-Varangian Slavic civilization. He bluntly asserts that, by many indices, in the ninth century the Slavs were the most "advanced" and "civilized" peoples in Europe. At a time when the "half-savage Normans" lived by pillage and the Germans were mostly hunters (thus Gedeonov relegates them to the lowest rungs of the "civilizational" ladder), the Slavs had already become master craftsmen and "experienced farmers," with "agricultural implements unknown to the Germans." The Russian language of the ninth century already exceeded "all other tongues of the day" in the richness of its vocabulary and "in its development of grammatical forms." In their level of education, the

Russians surpassed not only the Germans but all other peoples as well. The Slavs' "natural inclination toward civic life" (*grazhdanstvennost'*) blossomed in Rus' and gave rise to a strong state that was the envy of foreigners. Only prejudiced historians, Gedeonov concludes, could suggest that such an advanced people would agree to "voluntary submission to the hostile yoke of half-savage Normans."[110] If the Russians had not enjoyed cultural preeminence over others before the summoning, "no outside influence, especially that of Varangian pirates, could have created in just a few years the Rus' of Vladimir and Iaroslav."[111]

This argument about the Slavs' superiority to their European counterparts had previously been peripheral to the national discourse. Romantic nationalism, as we have seen, constructed the summoning in terms of an absence of the qualities that defined Western history—an absence of competition, aggressiveness, political ambition, and conquest by a foreign ruling house. In this way, both the Slavophiles and Pogodin had praised hidden national virtues that could promise Russia a possible leadership role in the future. Gedeonov, on the contrary, resorted to the crude language of national superiority. Just as the second half of the nineteenth century saw the spread of racism in Europe, Russia experienced a similar turn to chauvinism. *The Varangians and Rus'* dramatically reflects this shift.

Unlike its Western counterparts, however, Russian exclusive nationalism was not rooted in social Darwinism. Loyal to the regime, reform-era nationalists did not embrace positivism, with its underlying liberal attitudes, as a complete system. In this respect, they reacted to positivist philosophy very much like other European right-wing intellectuals. Nevertheless, one may define some Russian thinkers of the nationalist persuasion—including Gedeonov—as men of the positivist era, who appropriated the creed selectively, if not eclectically.

Herbert Spencer's theory, which applied the Darwinian struggle for existence to the social sphere, using it to justify violence, was not completely out of tune with Gedeonov's construct. Like Kostomarov, Gedeonov emphasized the Russians' unlimited domination over the non-Slavic population of Rus' and singled out the role of the "ruling nationality" in the summoning. No historical facts, he argued, could support the notion of Russians and Finns cooperating as equal partners in this act; the summoning—"the essential fact of Russian history"—was "an exclusively Slavic fact" as well as a clear indication that in the struggle with other tribes the Russians "were destined to dominate and meld all extraneous people and tongues into a single Russian whole."[112] Like Spencer, Gedeonov justified the Russians' right to inflict violence on their subject peoples on the grounds that they were more advanced and civilized. This type of argument, however, circulated widely in the imperial discourse of nineteenth-century Europe and need not have come directly from Spencer. In *The Varangians and Rus'*, one senses more strongly the presence of another positivist current: Auguste Comte and especially Henry Thomas Buckle, two thinkers, immensely popular in Russia, who saw education, knowledge, and intelligence as the prime forces for progress.

Buckle's *History of Civilization in England* (1856–61), with its focus on national development, offered Gedeonov a congenial explanatory paradigm. Following Buckle, he saw the growth of knowledge and the spread of education as the source of the rapid advancement of Kievan Rus'. As with Buckle, for Gedeonov material circumstances determined cultural and intellectual success, and the latter, in turn, became the prime engine of national progress.[113] In Buckle's system, intellectual development governs human progress and determines the direction each nation takes, while religion most often acts as a brake. Gedeonov was close to Buckle in his attitude toward Christianity. Orthodoxy did give fresh impetus to Russian culture — Gedeonov did not deny that — but he tended to downplay religious conversion as a threshold event and emphasized the cultural continuity between pagan and Christian Rus'. In his book, Prince Vladimir is not remembered as the Baptizer of Rus', nor is Iaroslav the Wise a virtuous Christian; instead, Gedeonov finds both rulers appealing as instigators of intellectual and cultural achievements. He directs his readers' attention to the growth of knowledge, the spread of education, and the cultivation of crafts and trade as the distinctive accomplishments of Kievan Rus', thus shifting his focus away from the more conventional national virtues: piety and heroic feats in defense of the native land.

Nonetheless, Gedeonov did not subscribe to the scientism or naturalistic monism inherent in Buckle's worldview. Moreover, while Buckle considered a paternalistic state an obstacle to progress and the free distribution of knowledge, Gedeonov portrayed the Russian monarchy as the most effective means of cultural progress. This combination of admiration for the centralized state and emphasis on intellectual development led Gedeonov to an unconventional picture of Russian history. He saw in the Russia of

Peter the Great a continuation of pre-Mongol Rus'. For him both epochs were characterized by the spread of education and, at the same time, by intensification of state power.

The nation-building project implied by this concept was the antithesis of Kostomarov's. A powerful centralized state was supposed to support and disseminate the culture of the "ruling people," thus consolidating the population into a homogeneous nation. This French-style institutional nationalism shaped not only Gedeonov's interpretation of the Varangian legend but also his bureaucratic career. As director of the Hermitage, he was the first to open the museum's doors to the general public. And as director of the imperial theaters, he worked to give the repertoire a more national character. Not only did he write plays himself on themes from Russian history and Slavic folklore; he also secured financing for the creation of such works and attracted notable playwrights to the project, above all A. N. Ostrovskii.[114]

Gedeonov's book enjoyed the enthusiastic approval of a wide public and earned a prestigious academic award, the Uvarov prize.[115] This was not because his vision of the nation was groundbreaking, but rather because it satisfied the mood and expectations of society. It tied up in one neat package three central themes of reform-era national discourse: assertion of the Russian people's position as "the ruling nationality," yearning for the dynasty to assume an explicitly national character, and glorification of Pan-Slavic unity. The final theme resonated particularly well at a time when sympathy for fellow Slavs, suffering under the Ottoman and Hapsburg empires, rose to a fever pitch in the days before the Russo-Turkish War. Even today Gedeonov's critique of the Normanist theory occupies a prominent place in Russian nationalist discourse, providing the conceptual framework for a group of historians who credit him with laying the foundations for the only scholarly solution to the Varangian question.[116]

Katkov's Inclusive Concept
of the Political Nation

While Kostomarov and Gedeonov emphatically excluded "the non-Slavic tribes" from the summoning, Katkov, surprisingly, enlarged the number of participants in this event, adding to the Varangian legend peoples mentioned neither in the chronicle nor by later scholars. To understand his version of the story and its implications, we must briefly establish the context in which it appeared.

In the 1860s the nationalist press whipped up a campaign against the "Germanization" imposed on the indigenous population of the Baltic provinces—Estonians and Latvians—by the local German elite. Katkov accused the German nobility of putting cultural pressure on these peoples in a far-ranging scheme to redirect their loyalties and ultimately annex the region to a then-consolidating Germany. He positioned himself not only as a champion of the Russian Empire's territorial integrity but also as a defender of the native Baltic population from greedy German masters, who were bent on erasing the national distinctiveness of the Estonians and the Latvians.[117] These "wretched tribes" with no "independent historical existence," writes Katkov, had longed for Russia's protection from time immemorial and naturally gravitated toward the Russian people long before Peter the Great's conquest of the region. To confirm his claim, Katkov turns to the foundation myth: "As the most ancient legend of our history relates," affirmed a lead article in *Moskovskie vedomosti*, the Finns, the Estonians, and the Latvians "together with our ancestors invited the founders of the Russian state and thus, at the very beginning of our history, linked their fate to that of the Russian people."[118] By inserting non-Slavic peoples into the sacred moment of Russia's birth Katkov seeks to prove that, from its inception, Rus' was a multiethnic state. He thus portrays Russia's imperial nature as a manifestation of its ethnohistorical distinctiveness.

Naturally, all the populations of the growing empire could not be shoehorned into the foundation myth, so Katkov put forward other collective memories to demonstrate Russians' centuries-long ties with regions far beyond Novgorod. Thus Katkov greeted the official announcement of the final subjugation of the Caucasus (1864) with a paean to the ancient longing that the Christian peoples of the Caucasus felt for the Russians. Here again, as with the Latvians and the Estonians, he places the first interethnic contacts in the most remote era: "In the period of Kievan Rus', when the Russian people and the Russian land first appeared on this earth, the Caucasus . . . was familiar . . . to our heroes (*bogatyri*), who traveled there at the very dawn of our historical life."[119] In his vision of Russia's expansion, each conquest, no matter what desperate local resistance it had to overcome, was preceded by a more distant epoch of sincere attachment to Russia: "If our contact with the Caucasus was concluded by force, it began with a plea for protection."[120] Pointing to the Georgian kings' appeals to their coreligionists, the Muscovite tsars, beginning in the sixteenth century, and to the request of the last Georgian monarch, George XII, that his kingdom be taken under the tsars' protection—which led to Georgia's incorporation into the Russian Empire (1800–1801)—Katkov depicts Russia's thrust into the Caucasus as initiated by the local people.[121] In the story of Riurik's summoning, he also emphasizes the agency of the non-Slavic groups: it was the Finns, Latvians, and Estonians who themselves "linked their fate to that of the Russian people."[122]

Katkov's vision of the Varangians' invitation encapsulated the new concept of national empire that he propounded on the pages of *Moskovskie vedomosti*. In Pogodin's version of the foundation myth, it was the Russian people who voluntarily submitted to Riurik and then gradually "infected" the empire's other ethnic groups with love for the ruler—a distinctly Russian trait. In Katkov's construct, it was the various nationalities of Russia who no less willingly subordinated themselves—not to the ruler alone but to the Russian nation, beginning with their participation in the collective act of founding the state. While Pogodin tended to downplay or even blur the lines between the ethnic core of the empire and its non-Slavic peoples (the entire population of the empire was equally subject to the monarch and equally distant from him), Katkov saw the relationship hierarchically: the Russians dominated the rest. He applied to the Russians the same concept of "ruling nationality" as did Kostomarov and Gedeonov, but he arrived at different conclusions. Though Katkov envisioned all groups of the empire as subject to the Russian nation, they were not necessarily doomed to be swallowed up by the dominant ethnic core—a fate Gedeonov and Kostomarov insisted on.[123] Katkov, an implacable foe of all separatist ambitions that threatened to undercut the integrity of the empire (above all, the Polish) or the unity of the single all-Russian nation (Ukrainian separatism), nevertheless tolerated cultural heterogeneity. His definition of a political nation explicitly permitted the Latvians, Estonians, Georgians, and even the "unreliable" Germans and the "rebellious" Poles to be accepted as Russians. Subject nationalities already in possession of a developed or developing high culture could keep their traditions, languages, and creeds and were to be considered Russians as long as they remained loyal to the state, accepted the dominant position of the Russian people, learned the Russian language, and (preferably) conducted their religious services in Russian.[124] Katkov's recipe for imperial integrity and longevity derived from observation of the separatist movements then shaking the Hapsburg and Ottoman empires.[125]

Like Gedeonov, Katkov was confident that the level of cultural develop-ment determined a nation's ability to dominate others. "Political might," he stated, remains "unstable" if it is not built upon "vibrant national civiliza-tion and intellectual productivity."[126] An ideologue of Russification, he constantly repeated that "the most lasting of all conquests is the conquest made by the language of a people."[127] At the same time—and in this he differed from Gedeonov—Katkov saw the sphere of culture as Russia's Achilles' heel. Today it is peculiar to read how this contemporary of such figures as Mendeleev, Tolstoy, and Dostoevsky despaired over Russia's lack of achievement: "We have no science of our own"; Russian literature does not bear comparison with its German and English counterparts; "the Ger-man language opens much broader mental horizons than does Russian."[128] These self-deprecating laments resemble P. Ia. Chaadaev's "Philosophical Letters." To complete the parallel, Katkov, like Chaadaev, saw Russia's back-wardness as reversible: "We came late to the feast," he wrote, contemplating how Russia lagged behind European countries in the sphere of high cul-ture, but "we can outpace the rest."[129] Attaining and exceeding European standards required a thorough study of classical languages. This was why over many years—and not without success—Katkov promoted a reform of education: intense study of Latin and Greek would, he claimed, develop the Russian language, transform it into a universal language, on par with En-glish, French, and German, and render it capable of uniting all the peoples of the empire.[130]

Scholars have long noted the derivative nature of nationalism in Eastern Europe, where historical conditions were less conducive to nation-building than in the West and where the nation appears largely a product of deliber-ate borrowing.[131] The formation of European nation-states, especially En-gland and France, drew Katkov's envious attention. Their imperial practices were equally intriguing, even though these maritime empires had little in common with the contiguous Russian Empire. As Seymour Becker has shown, the British and French empires differed from Russia in three re-spects: their colonies were separated from the metropolis by an ocean, colo-nial subjects were not expected to assimilate, and the overseas possessions were controlled not by supranational dynasties but by nation-states.[132] That final principle appealed to Katkov. Since he proposed the subordination of subject populations not only to the tsar but to the Russian people, it is pos-sible to view his construct of a ruling Russian nation as a transplantation of Western imperial practice to Russian soil.[133]

While rethinking Russia in terms of Western models, Katkov, like popular historians of his time, used collective memories to legitimize his project. Of many possible pasts, he chose Kievan Rus' to speak to Russia's future, even going so far as to suggest that the capital be restored to Kiev—a symbolic focus and actual site of Russian authentic culture in the eyes of the majority of nineteenth-century Russian intellectuals. Placing the court and government in Kiev, where "the most ancient memories of our people reside," would emphasize the dynasty's symbolic return to its national roots.[134] It would also fuel the hopes that the state should defend the interests of the Russian people, not those of the supranational elite associated with Petersburg. Above all, the transfer of the capital would address a number of problems that beset the empire. First, as Katkov often reiterated, the territories controlled by Kievan Rus' in the tenth and eleventh centuries were significantly wider than the European part of either the Muscovite state or the Russia of Peter I and could therefore provide Russians the most favorable measure of the "true" size of their ancestral land. Second, a capital in Kiev would underscore the unity of the Eastern Slavs as a single nation and thus undermine Ukrainian separatism. Third, an imperial center in Kiev would support Russia's geopolitical ambitions to the south and the east. Finally and most important for Katkov, Kievan Rus' represented in his eyes "a sacred symbol of the spontaneous unification" (*svobodnoe edinenie*) of various peoples who, beginning with the summoning, naturally gravitated toward Russians and acknowledged their dominant position.[135] In this way, historical memories made it possible to represent the construction of the political nation as a reconstruction, a return to the legacy of Kievan Rus'.[136]

As the last three versions of the Varangian legend show, its content and function changed dramatically in the reform era. For thinkers of the first half of the nineteenth century, the foundation myth had encapsulated the ideal relation of the people to the monarch. Despite fundamental disagreements over the nature of that relationship, all readings of the summoning articulated in the 1840s had depicted a humble people, voluntarily submitting to a Western ruler. In the 1860s the obedience to the leader remained voluntary, but the Russians came increasingly to see themselves as an energetic collective protagonist in history and the main agent of their own fate, capable of imposing their native values, customs, and institutions on the newly arrived ruler.[137] They were, in a word, capable of nationalizing the dynasty and building the state as an expression of the people's spirit. Even the official millennium celebration employed, however cautiously, memories of Novgorodian self-rule and *veche* symbolism, although it positioned this alternate historical narrative within what Wortman has called "the monologic universe of imperial ceremony," thereby foregrounding the conciliatory power of the monarchy, rather than the nation's distinctive qualities.[138]

Another fundamental shift in the 1860s interpretation of the legend also heightened the motif of popular agency, this time not at the expense of the ruler. In the reform era, the state-nation nexus was ever more clearly articulated as an empire-nation nexus. The new renditions of the foundation myth came to define the Russian nation not only in relation to the dynasty but also through its encounter with the empire's non-Slavic ethnic groups. In the first half of the century, the subject nationalities had figured in the legend, but they made only a cameo appearance: they stood as an attribute of Russia's grandeur (Karamzin), illustrated the unifying power of the emerging state (Solov'ev), or were portrayed as waiting passively for the Russian spirit to rub off on them—a process that led to blurring the boundary between non-Russians and the ethnic core of the empire (Pogodin). In the 1860s, new versions of the legend came to pay more attention to the non-Slavic tribes in order to dramatize their relations with the Russians. Now the myth emphatically justified the Russians' status as the ruling people, although, as we have seen, its varying versions construed the strategies and ultimate goals of their dominance in different ways. In the reform era, even Pogodin came to highlight the peoples' active role as builders of empire rather than bearers of all-embracing ideals. After his dispute with Kostomarov, he admitted that the Scandinavian Vikings had become subjects of Russian influence: "Our accommodating, feminine, Slavic soil has a particularly masculine power to remake those it welcomes and place its stamp on them: the grandsons of Tatars, Germans, and Cheremis become the most excellent of Russians, better than any native Russian could be."[139] Here Pogodin shifted his emphasis from domination by a Russian ruler to domination by the Russian people—and this change reflects the evolution in national discourse.

In the 1860s the Varangian legend assumed a developmental character, marking a new era of national mythmaking. Now intellectuals refashioned the foundation narrative to justify their nation-building projects. The three reform-era versions of the myth discussed here charted three competing visions of Russia's future, which corresponded to rival images of its heartland. Kostomarov distinguished between the Russian and the Ukrainian territories and transformed the myth that had previously buttressed the centralized state to bolster his federalist project. For Gedeonov, the Russian borders encompassed the entire area settled by the East Slavs and could even be expanded to include the West Slavs—his construct inclined toward Pan-Slavism and defined the nation in exclusive cultural and racial terms. Katkov identified the heartland with Kievan Rus' at its period of widest territorial extent and conceived the Russian nation in inclusive cultural and political terms. These three overlapping images of the homeland and the conflicting projects for national development that these images embodied all, however, addressed a single problem: how the empire was to evolve in an increasingly nationalistic era.

The growing vision of the nation as a political construct left less room for defining it through religion. For Pogodin and the Slavophiles, moral impulses and the people's "natural" predisposition to Christian values, anachronistically applied to the summoning, had played an overwhelming role in their understanding of Russianness. In the reform era, on the contrary, such mutually opposing thinkers as Katkov, Gedeonov, and Kostomarov all assigned Orthodoxy the least important role in their nation-building projects.

A highly adaptable, indeed protean legend, the Varangian myth still left many questions unanswered. How could the Russian people "rule" if they did not enjoy political rights that would grant them a higher status than nontitular nationalities of the empire? How could they control the subject populations if local ethnic elites often exercised social, economic, even political power over Russian peasants? How could one even speak about national will when the nation was deeply fragmented, culturally and socially, and mercilessly stifled by the regime?

Another myth offered a better framework for answering these questions. From the beginning of the Polish uprising, martial symbolism and the rhetoric of national self-liberation became central to the national discourse. Even though the most vocal nationalists seemed to agree that civic development, education reform, and the dissemination of Russian culture should be the primary instruments for forging the nation and for securing the Russians' dominant role in the empire, they nonetheless relied heavily on the cult of war to symbolically consolidate the Russian people and outline political changes that would enshrine their ruling status within the empire. As we shall see, it was the very contradictions inherent in Russian nationalism that prompted reform-era thinkers to articulate their nation-building projects by appealing to memories of war.

3

War as Peace

*The Symbol of Popular War
during the Polish Uprising
(1863–64)*

In his 1876 *Diary of a Writer*, Dostoevsky lays out a startling case for war. In the voice of a "paradoxicalist"—a "most peaceful person" who nonetheless advocates armed conflict—he articulates his own responses to the familiar moral dilemmas that accompany the use of force. According to Dostoevsky, war brings not misery, as people wrongly claim, but exultation and the "soul's delight." While prolonged peace breeds decadence and apathy, collective violence produces honor, beneficence, and magnanimity. Bloody conflicts nurture the imagination and inspire technological progress, so even the arts and sciences benefit. Moreover, he triumphantly concludes, Christianity often venerates warriors. With this justification of war—offered on the eve of the Russo-Turkish campaign (1877–78)—Dostoevsky marshals all the arguments that had been circulating among Russian nationalists over the two preceding decades. He crowns the entire edifice with his most telling point: war is a means of strengthening the national community. It brings "the equality of heroism" and a "strong bond among social strata." It gives the masses an opportunity to act and to "respect themselves."[1] How, one cannot help but ask, does Dostoevsky reconcile this advocacy of violence with his harsh denunciations of social evils and his belief in the Christlike nature and universal empathy of the Russian people?

The same paradox marks public speeches delivered by the Slavophile Ivan Aksakov before and during the Russo-Turkish War. In March 1877 he gave an address to the Moscow Slavic Committee, designed to provoke society's martial instincts and goad the government into declaring war on the Ottoman Empire.[2] A month later, when war finally did break out, he enthusiastically depicted the Russians as "the meekest, most peaceable people" who nonetheless take up arms and "go, rejoicing, to the feast of blood [*krovavyi pir*]" to liberate the Slavs suffering under the Turkish yoke. Like Dostoevsky, he also envisions mass sacrifice as a means of renewing the Russian nation and fostering brotherhood among social strata.[3] Dostoevsky's and Aksakov's saber rattling in the name of the nation was typical of the vocal group of nationalists (predominantly Pan-Slavists), who dragged Russia into the Russo-Turkish campaign.[4]

In the West, it was social Darwinism that justified nineteenth-century war propaganda. The "scientific laws" of evolution and the resulting "struggle for survival" legitimized, in the eyes of European liberals, conquest and imperial expansion by "progressive" nations.[5] Russian thinkers of a nationalist persuasion, however, utterly rejected social Darwinism.[6] How, then, did martial rhetoric come to occupy such a key place in their writings? Their advocacy of war is all the more striking, given that Russian cultural mythology, from the Slavophiles and Pogodin onward, advanced the thesis that love of peace, meekness, and humility were the nation's distinctive characteristics.[7]

This chapter approaches the war-peace paradox through exploration of the cult of popular war that developed during the reform era's opening decade. It argues that the fascination with military feats that defined the atmosphere of the late 1870s was rooted in the early 1860s—a period marking a threshold in the use of martial memories in Russian nationalist discourse. As we have seen, at the beginning of the Crimean campaign the Slavophiles had hoped that the war would lead to a relaxation of Nicholas I's despotism, "cleanse" Russia's morals, and make it possible to fulfill the nation's religious destiny. In the reform era, writers took this one step further, adopting the theme of the people in arms as the principal means of articulating their visions for building the nation.

As in other countries, in nineteenth-century Russia the remembrance of past conflicts crystallized a sense of national belonging and helped shape a national community distinct from its numerous Western and Eastern neighbors.[8] For Russian thinkers, however, commemoration of military victories played an even more important role: it allowed them to symbolically resolve central problems of nationhood that went unresolved in real life. The war topos opened up a unique mythic space in which irreconcilable contradictions could be reconciled—where the nation became a visible and independent agent of its own fate, and where, in many cases, it enthusiastically supported the very regime that suppressed it. Although the autocracy rejected the civic aspects of nationhood during peacetime, the people's active participation became indispensable in times of crisis. Only when the country found itself on the brink of disaster did the government manifest the ability to accept the nation as a meaningful entity separate from the state.

Hastening to take advantage of this modest loophole, 1860s writers turned the cult of war into the dominant form of national mythmaking. They utilized memories of the masses' taking up arms as a charter for changes aimed at consolidating the Russian people and making them the politically dominant ethnic group in Russia. What prompted the articulation of these new constructs was the January uprising in the Kingdom of Poland (1863–64), the most ominous sign of growing nationalism within the empire.

The Polish Question and
the War Topos

In the late eighteenth century, as a result of the three consecutive partitions of the Polish-Lithuanian Commonwealth, or Rzeczpospolita, undertaken jointly by Russia, Prussia, and Austria, Poland disappeared for more than hundred years from the political map of Europe. Russia annexed the lion's share of its lands and went on to enlarge this new domain in the early nineteenth century, at the conclusion of the Napoleonic wars. The ethnically Polish core of the newly acquired lands—in official parlance, the Kingdom of Poland (so constituted in 1815)—initially enjoyed administrative and legal autonomy within the Romanov empire; until the November uprising (1830–31) it even had a separate army, parliament, and constitution. The rest of the subject territories—historical Lithuania, a portion of Ukraine, and Byelorussia (absorbed into Russia in the late eighteenth century)— came to be known as the western borderlands (*Zapadnyi krai*) of the Romanov empire. This area was better integrated into Russia's administrative and judicial machinery, although this process of integration was a faltering one and Russian observers regularly lamented that Polish culture continued to hold sway there.

The *Zapadnyi krai*, Russians of all stations believed, was part of their "sacred" heartland: it had belonged to ancient Rus' but was wrested away by the Poles while Russia suffered under the Mongol yoke. Many thinkers justified the partitions of Poland with a belief in the Poles' "ineradicable thirst for expansion." Religious arguments often helped to bolster this claim, portraying Poland as the military vanguard of Catholicism, an allegiance that, some writers argued, guaranteed perpetual Polish hostility toward Orthodox Russia. Several generations of Russians thus legitimized the subjugation of Poland as a necessary—indeed, inevitable—resolution to the centuries-old "family feud" of the two Slavic peoples, as Pushkin had christened the conflict in his poem "To the Slanderers of Russia" (1831).[9]

But even though its fate seemed sealed, Poland remained a persistent source of unease for Russia. The Polish struggle for liberation culminated in two insurrections: the November rebellion of 1830–31 and the January 1863–64 uprising. Posing a challenge to government and public alike, both revolts demanded not merely a military but also an ideological response. The November rebellion, crushed by the imperial army, fueled the articulation of official ideology and provoked a burst of patriotic sentiment in Russian society. Attempts by some European powers, particularly France, to support Poland on the diplomatic front reinvigorated Russians' quest to define themselves vis-à-vis the West.[10] Yet the 1863 uprising elicited an even stronger reaction, occurring as it did in a period of increasing nationalism.

As the Russian and Polish projects of nation-building were taking shape, the question of who would culturally dominate the *Zapadnyi krai*— or *kresy wschodnie* (eastern borderlands of the Rzeczpospolita), as the Poles called this territory—not only remained on the agenda but took on new importance. The Poles envisioned the area as part of their fatherland and presented Byelorussians and Ukrainians, together with Lithuanians, as constituents of the Polish nation, stigmatizing Russians as an external threat to them all. The Russians, in turn, increasingly saw Byelorussians and Ukrainians as part of the Russian nation—in particular the peasants who, unlike the Polonized Russian nobility of the region, allegedly preserved their true Russian identity.[11] The preparations for the abolition of serfdom intensified the competition between Russians and Poles for cultural dominance in this area, giving new urgency to nationalistic arguments. Since the serfs—until then denied civil rights—were now supposed to become citizens and be fully incorporated into society, questions inevitably arose: Which society would they join? Where did the peasants' true loyalties lie and whom did they identify with—Russians or Poles?[12] With the introduction of emancipation, this dilemma became acute, determining both the character of the January uprising and its public perception in Russia.

The years preceding the uprising were a time of great hope for the Poles. The legislation of the peasant reform and the empire's foreign policy considerations—above all, the entente with France, the Poles' traditional protector—together informed Alexander II's attempts to reach compromise with various segments of Polish society, particularly the nobility (*szlachta*), the prime mover of the liberation movement.[13] In the immediate aftermath of the Crimean War, the tsar traveled to Warsaw and gave a speech to the marshals of the nobility that inaugurated a conciliatory policy toward Poland. He suggested that both sides "let bygones be bygones" but demanded that the Poles relinquish their "daydreams" of independence.[14] In the years that followed, as the government sought to come to grips with the Polish question, it employed a mixture of concession and suppression that served only to stoke the liberation movement.[15] Demonstrations for independence grew exponentially and at times led to armed conflict with Russian troops. The hope for a restoration of Poland within its pre-partition boundaries (including the western provinces of Russia) found articulate champions, and revolutionary activity spread from the Kingdom of Poland to the *Zapadnyi krai* (Lithuania and Byelorussia, in particular).[16]

In 1863, when the uprising—"mutiny" in the Russian official lexicon— erupted with a night massacre of Russian soldiers asleep in their Warsaw barracks, a groundswell of patriotic sentiment enveloped Russian society. It was not only the Polish insurgents who infuriated the Russians. Alexander II's previous conciliatory policy now provoked public indignation as well. His concessions to the Poles came to be seen as the continuation—indeed, the apotheosis—of the monarchy's traditional supranational policy, whereby the Romanovs cooperated with the empire's non-Russian elites. In reality, imperial policy on the eve of the uprising was not so straight-forward: it sometimes ran counter to the interests of the *szlachta*, seeking instead to foster loyalty to the Russian government among the peasantry in the Western borderlands and in Poland itself. Yet by appearing to favor the Polish nobility, the authorities opened themselves to charges of having betrayed the Russian cause. The stage was now set for journalists covering the uprising to press the government to alter the traditional imperial model and identify itself more closely with the Russian nationality.

The so-called patriotic, or Moscow, press—represented by Mikhail Katkov's *Moskovskie vedomosti* and Ivan Aksakov's *Den'*—exemplified the most articulate nationalistic response to the January uprising. These two publications espoused different and at times conflicting positions. Where Aksakov asserted that the world should be governed "according to moral principle" and, at the outset of the uprising, called on the Russian authorities to convene the Sejm—the Polish parliament—in order to decide Poland's future peacefully, Katkov upheld "the power of the sword" as the only means of resolving the crisis.[17] While Aksakov, in keeping with the Slavophile belief in the indivisibility of Russian national and religious identities, asserted that a Polish Catholic could never be considered Russian, Katkov advanced an in-clusive concept of a political nation that permitted non-Orthodox peoples to be accepted as Russians.[18] Most importantly, Aksakov saw the nation as centered on the people and called on the government to return to pre-Petrine institutions, while Katkov viewed the nation as being forged by the modern state and its bureaucracy.[19] Although these two journalists held sharply conflicting views, they ultimately converged on some points: as these areas of agreement gradually became clear, a common nationalist platform emerged that was to greatly influence Russian public opinion.[20]

Both *Moskovskie vedomosti* and *Den'* framed the January uprising as an interethnic conflict.[21] This vision of the revolt was dictated, as Dietrich Geyer notes, by the need "to channel anti-Polish emotions into a movement for Russian national solidarity."[22] In order to depict the Polish crisis in terms of the enmity of two peoples, it was necessary to contrast the insur-gents not with the state and its mechanisms of coercion but with the Rus-sian people. That in turn required "discovering" a Russian nation that was no longer stifled by the regime.

The January rebellion thus created a rare opportunity to turn the Russian nation into a decisive political player. As Aksakov sarcastically observed in 1863, the Polish crisis made it possible "to remind the clever politicians from Petersburg of the existence of an entire Russian nation, obscured for them by official Petersburg buildings."[23] Katkov also interpreted the Russian response to the Polish challenge as proof that "the Russian nation [was] alive and strong," "not a dead mass, but a living force."[24] The patriotic press argued so passionately for the viability of the Russian nation precisely because the Russians, as Katkov admitted with disarming frankness, were feeling "a lack of confidence in their own existence."[25] Indeed, the Russian intelligentsia was suffering a sense of national decline—if not nonexistence—in the face of Polish patriotism, whose mobilizing power stunned many Russians, even though the revolt itself was rather puny and the Polish peasants largely stayed out of it.

The word "envy" perfectly defined the attitude of many Moscow and Petersburg intellectuals toward the Polish national movement. The historian M. P. Pogodin confessed in the pages of *Moskovskie vedomosti*: "I give full credit to Polish patriotism. . . . The liveliness of Polish feeling . . . even inspires envy in me."[26] Elena Shtakenshneider, who was close to the Petersburg professorial and literary elite, admitted in her diary: "I would like to be a Pole now and fight with a clear conscience and with all my heart for my native land [*za rodnuiu zemliu*]."[27] The literary critic and philosopher Nikolai Strakhov surpassed them all in his article "The Fatal Question" (1863), in which he claims that the Polish question was "fatal" not for the Poles but for the Russians. With shocking candor, he juxtaposes the Polish nation—vibrant, active, possessed of a highly advanced culture—with a Russian nation that remained passive and insufficiently developed. Like so many Oriental civilizations, "we" could pride ourselves, he declares, only on the might of our state. The Poles, therefore, "can scarcely look upon us as anything but barbarians" and—even more frustrating—can readily vindicate their "moral right" to "civilize" the *Zapadnyi krai*, "our own ancestral land." But as soon as Russian government and educated society begin to cherish Russian native values, "then our stature will be no less than the Poles', and perhaps even greater." The entire world would then see, Strakhov concludes, that "the very same nation that built the great body of our state harbors its soul, as well."[28] The Polish rebellion thus made it imperative to allow the Russian people to express their unique nature and ultimately to turn the Romanov empire into a manifestation of the Russian nation.

Though *Moskovskie vedomosti* and *Den'* never fully agreed with Strakhov's harsh national self-criticism, both newspapers urged the government to respond to the Polish crisis with a radical shift away from supranational policies. In advocating this change, they drew extensive parallels
between the January uprising and the two periods of national calamity that
stood out in historical memories of Russia: the Time of Troubles (1605–13)
and the Patriotic War (1812–15). Nineteenth-century nationalistic discourse
often entwined these two campaigns as powerful outpourings of popular
patriotism, though in the first case it was the Poles who posed the threat to
Russia, and in the second the French. For Russians both enemies represented a similar type of aggression, given the traditional perception of
Poles as the military vanguard of Western civilization. In both wars Russia
faced a swift invasion followed by a sweeping advance into the country's
heartland; both times the crisis culminated in the occupation of Moscow,
and both wars concluded with triumphant expulsions of the intruders by
ordinary men who took up arms to defend their homes. This wide grassroots resistance made it possible for many writers to cherish the memories
of both periods of crisis as popular wars (*narodnye voiny*) and thereby to
portray the Russian people as the main historical actor, capable—to use
Strakhov's metaphor—of imbuing the state with their "soul."[29]

At first glance this rhetorical maneuver—the comparison of the January
rebellion with Russians' struggles against foreign enemies—seems ground-
less. The 1863 events lacked the principal—and, one would think, requisite—
condition for this analogy: Russia now faced no enemy incursion.[30] Yet the
patriotic press masterfully contrived to fill that void.

From early 1863, when the revolt broke out, Katkov and Aksakov presented Russians' reaction to the unfolding events as a spontaneous awakening of their martial instincts. They saw the unprecedented letter-writing
campaign that began in late March 1863 as the most tangible proof of a
nationwide enthusiasm for war. Representatives of the empire's various
regions and social strata sent Alexander II "statements of allegiance"
proclaiming their readiness to come immediately to the country's defense.
Katkov depicted this flood of letters, regularly published in the newspapers,
as "a phenomenon almost unparalleled in [Russian] history, or at least not
repeated since the memorable era of 1812."[31] These addresses to the tsar
themselves invoked analogies with wars of the past. "Command us, Sire,
and at a single word of Yours," proclaimed the Cossacks of Poltava province, "we will set aside the scythe and the plow, take up arms, and show the

enemies of Russia that . . . just like our grandfathers in 1812, we are ready to form a united militia at one word from our August Monarch."[32] Inspired by such declarations, Aksakov exclaimed: "Are we not still the men of 1812?"[33] A few days earlier he had referred to the Time of Troubles: "Are the people not preparing with such enthusiasm for war, because the old hatred has reawakened in them toward their old historical enemy, Poland, whose invasion in the seventeenth century is preserved in living memories to this day?"[34]

For both journalists, parallels between past wars and the Polish uprising became the foundation for a rhetorical strategy that rendered the Russian people visible and active. At the very height of the January rebellion, Katkov coined this optimistic formula: "A new 1812 would be a decisive triumph for us."[35] The very expression "triumph for us"—as opposed to "triumph over the enemy"—shows how he expected memories of the Patriotic War to assist in a national resurrection. "The war . . . shall awaken all our energy," affirmed Katkov. "It will bring out all the forces of our national spirit, cleanse us morally, and unify into a single whole our entire state organism."[36] Drawing analogies with 1812, Aksakov also ecstatically predicted: "The war, calling [Rus'] to life and vigor, will only give it new strength and solidity."[37] As the uprising progressed, Aksakov—following Katkov—relied increasingly on the Russian people's martial spirit, repudiating his initial hopes for the Poles' voluntary unification with Russia and taking every opportunity to remind his readers about the glories of the Patriotic War.[38]

The Moscow press profited from the symbolic power of war memories in several ways. First, it found in parallels with the struggle against enemies a ready tool for presenting the Russian people as a central political player, capable of defending its own national interest and ancestral land. Second, since the campaign against Napoleon combined defense of the fatherland with the mission of saving Europe, the events of 1812 allowed for a natural conflation of the war memories with the myth of the Russians' unique love of peace. The melding of these motifs muted the theme of violence and amplified the redemptive implications of Russia's sacrifice. Finally, the parallels with the expulsion of the Polish intruders in 1612 made it possible to mythologize the ongoing conflict with the Polish insurgents as a revival of the spirit of pre-Petrine Rus'. As we shall see, the patriotic press capitalized on all these motifs, making them serve as a justification for new nation-building projects.

The Polish Rebellion
as Enemy Invasion

The international response to the tsar's policy toward rebellious Poland reinvigorated the Russian tendency to view the January uprising through the prism of past wars. In 1863 the governments of the three great Western powers—France, England, and Austria—acting in concert, sent three sets of diplomatic notes to Petersburg (in April, June, and August) proposing concessions to Poland to resolve the conflict.[39] Such meddling by European states revived the long-standing opposition between Russia and the West. The Slavophile Iurii Samarin declared: "In response to the partition of Poland, Europe now calls for the partition of Russia."[40] Many contemporaries likewise perceived the Polish revolt as a harbinger of war, the prelude to inevitable armed intervention by England and France.[41] "We have every right to view the Polish mutiny," wrote Katkov, "as perhaps a final attempt by the Western powers to weaken and diminish the significance of Russia."[42] The January uprising came to be understood as a covert form of Western aggression against Russia, with Poland seen as an obedient weapon in the hands of the European powers, above all France.[43] Katkov even proposed that France's desire to avenge the defeat of 1812 was the chief cause of the Polish crisis and reminded his readers of Poland's "betrayal" in 1812: "The conqueror to whom all Europe had fallen then turned all its [Europe's] forces against us. Poland opened for him a path into our lands, fought with him under his eagles, and was present with him at the burning of Moscow."[44] The patriotic press developed the theme of Polish "treachery" into one of the key tenets of anti-Polish propaganda.[45]

While locating in the West the material and ideological resources of the Polish rebellion, the Moscow press nevertheless depicted the Poles as conquerors. It ascribed to the insurgents a desire to dominate the region, to subjugate the Russian population, and thus to reverse the outcome of the two countries' rivalry. Unlike the Russian people, who were supposedly "long-suffering and inclined to peace," "not vain or acquisitive," the Poles were portrayed as aggressive invaders who had been "consumed by political ambition" and "hunger . . . for military successes" throughout their history.[46] Katkov even interpreted the insurgents' demand for political independence as a pretext for territorial expansion: "Polish patriotism . . . seeks the restoration of Polish power over other nationalities; it seeks the restoration of the old Poland; it seeks the return of its conquests."[47] The irreconcilable conflict between two idealized fatherlands—the Rzeczpospolita and Rus'—made it possible to see in the January uprising not just a prelude to war but the beginning of an invasion of Russia's territory. "The Poles revolted," claimed Katkov, "in order . . . to drive Russia into the depths of the Asian steppe and occupy its place in the system of European states."[48] "Pole" thus simultaneously came to mean both "traitor" and "conqueror," reflecting the Kingdom of Poland's ambiguous status within the Russian Empire: Poland was so weakly integrated into Russia that it continued to be viewed as a foreign body.[49]

This construct implied a recasting of the empire-nation nexus. If the Polish uprising were regarded as a movement for national liberation, then it would pose a challenge only to the integrity of the multinational empire. State institutions would become the insurgents' immediate opponent; the Russian nation would be seen as less engaged in the struggle; and the monarchical empire would be viewed—as in fact, it was—as an instrument for suppressing the nationalities under its sway, Russians included.[50] Transform the Pole into an external foe, and the roles assigned to each player change completely. The Pole-as-conqueror became a threat not only to the empire but also to its constituent peoples, especially to the Russians, since the Zapadnyi krai—"holy Russian land"—was the territory being contested. An external threat united the Russian people and the Russian government against a common enemy. The state could thus appear not as an agent of coercion but as a bulwark of the nation's defense. To put it more succinctly, according to this mythologizing logic, exteriorizing the Pole inevitably turned the Russian people and the autocratic regime into allies, thereby permitting traditional forms of imperial loyalty to be rethought.

The patriotic press made it clear that loyalty to the dynasty alone did not guarantee the defense of Russian national interests. Aksakov asserted, "The Polish question is not a question for the government only, but for the entire Russian land," that is, for all of the Russian people (the metonymic substitution of land for people was a commonplace of Slavophile rhetoric).[51] Katkov even—theoretically, but boldly—dissociated dynastic and national interests, admitting only the latter as a basis for resolving the conflict: "If the Polish question concerned only the interests of the ruling Russian dynasty . . . then this question might be decided in a number of ways." Among possible resolutions, he contemplated the return of the western provinces to Poland, on condition that "subsequent Polish viceroys" be appointed "from among the members of the [Russian] imperial family," under the supreme authority of the tsar. "But the problem is," Katkov declared, "that . . . to the entire Russian people . . . all such plans would seem a fragmentation of the Russian Empire. . . . The entire Russian nation . . . would understand that its most vital interests were being sacrificed, that it was a matter of nothing less than its subsequent historical fate."[52] Arguing for the will of the Russian people as a decisive political force set current events in implicit contrast with the dynastic vision of the nation.

To minimize the supranational nature of the existing regime, the Moscow press persisted in replacing the official adjective normally applied to the empire, *rossiiskaia*, with an informal one, *russkaia*, usually used to describe the land and its people.[53] Such renaming reflected the journalists' drive to render visible the ethnic core of the state. "From behind official Russia," Aksakov observed at the height of the uprising, "there . . . is put forward Rus', with its ancient spirituality."[54] In the spirit of metaphysical musing expressed in the concluding pages of the first volume of Gogol's *Dead Souls*, Katkov wondered: "Where is it, our Rus'?" Then, quickly abandoning Gogol's tone, he answered concretely: "Even not so long ago, in reply to such a question, we would have glanced at a map with many-colored borders; but today each living human being feels our Rus' within himself, feels it as his own heart."[55] If prior to the January uprising Rus' had been drowning, as it were, in the limitless expanse of empire, it was now rising up from the depths of history, like the invisible city of Kitezh from the bottom of the legendary lake. The Russians were now acquiring the "native land" (*rodnaia zemlia*) for which Shtakenshneider, who dreamt of becoming a Pole, had longed to fight.

Having "discovered" Rus', the patriotic press had no intention of eroding the symbolic boundary between the Russian core and imperial space. Using the declarations of allegiance sent to Alexander II by non-Russian and non-Orthodox groups during the letter-writing campaign of 1863, Katkov and Aksakov affirmed that the "diverse regions that [lay] along the marches of the Great Russian world" were ready to defend Rus'.[56] According to both journalists, almost the entire population of the multiethnic state (except for the less reliable upper-class inhabitants of certain border regions, such as the German elite of the Baltic provinces) was rising in defense of Rus'.

The myth of the entire empire fighting for Rus' became the basis for a renewed conception of imperial loyalty, one that the Moscow press formulated during its discussion of the letter-writing campaign. Aksakov scorned those "German missives from the cities and nobles of Estland, Livonia, and Kurland" that expressed only regional patriotism: "We are sure that the borders of that side of the empire will find in the Germans the most brave, honorable, and steadfast defenders, but we, the Russians, need patriotism of another type and character: mere attachment and devotion to the integrity of the empire means little to us; we need devotion to the Russian nationality as well!"[57] Responding to a letter from the Catholic nobles of Kiev (traditionally equated with Poles because of their religion), Katkov declared: "There is no doubt that if the Kievan . . . nobles of the Roman Catholic faith . . . have good sense, they should . . . join the great Russian family, pin all their hopes on it."[58] Thus, without overshadowing or displacing the category of "dynasty," the patriotic press proposed the Russian people as an object of political allegiance. This renewed conception of imperial loyalty highlighted what Ronald Suny describes as a distinguishing feature of empire: "inequitable rule," the superiority of one group over others.[59] Now it was not the ruling house or the social elite but the Russian core of the empire that was "imagined" as prevailing.

The Memory of 1812 and the Triumphal Consolidation of the Russian Nation

At least two closely connected circumstances posed obvious impediments to the new principles of imperial loyalty. First of all, in several regions Russians constituted the most numerous ethnic group but, as the patriotic press emphasized, in these areas local non-Russian elites dominated and even "oppressed" the "state-forming" nationality. Second, the journalists had to contend with the fragmented nature of the Russian nation. They were concerned not only with its disunity across social strata but also with the limited integration of the Ukrainians and the Byelorussians into the "Russian" nation. The symbolism of the years 1812 and 1612 addressed both concerns. It provided a capacious framework for interpreting the 1863 patriotic upsurge as resistance to a foreign oppressor and a triumph of the nation's centripetal forces.

Paradoxically, the Moscow press transformed the Polish rebellion into a Russian one. By representing the January uprising as yet another chapter in the struggle between Russians and Poles over the western borderlands, the nationalists imagined the Polish crisis as the Russian people's revolt against the Poles. Inasmuch as the *Zapadnyi krai* was held to be sacred Russian land, the "Poles" who had settled there were labeled "newcomers." These "newcomers," the patriotic press insisted, had "seized" the dominant position in the region and set about mercilessly exploiting the "Russian" peasants. By describing the struggle between the "Russian *muzhik*" and the "Polish *pan*" as continuing from "time immemorial," the journalists portrayed current events as a welcome opportunity to cast off the "Polish yoke."[60]

Although only the local peasants' clashes with the Polish insurgents in the western provinces could be described as an "uprising of the Russian people," the patriotic press sought to represent the battle with the "Polish oppressors" as a broad national movement to "liberate" the downtrodden "Russians" and "return" the region to Russia—not merely to absorb it into the empire, as had been the case with the partition of Poland, but to integrate it more fully into the Russian whole. *Moskovskie vedomosti* and *Den'* launched a large-scale campaign aimed at creating the impression that the entire Russian nation had risen as a single body against the "Polish yoke."[61] Parallels with 1812 made this task possible. "Step forward, Russian Land," appealed Aksakov, "call forth from the depths of your bosom . . . as you did in 1812, not just outward and material forces, but the forces of the Russian spirit."[62] An anonymous writer for *Moskovskie vedomosti* compared 1863 with 1812 precisely because in both cases the suffering of one part of the "Russian land" called its other parts to arms: "One quite wise and observant old man, who recently traveled through several internal, ethnically Russian provinces, told me that as far as he could remember, the current patriotic movement among the peasantry closely resembled the national movement of 1812 *in the second half of the campaign*. Only after the occupation of Moscow by the French and rumors about the sacrileges committed there . . . did *the people* manifest the ire and grim determination to grapple with the adversary, without which many feats and many horrors of 1812 would have remained unknown. At present, the simple people are every bit as irate and just as determined in their wrath."[63] The author emphasized the belligerent feelings that had swept core Russian areas in response to the Polish oppression of the "native population" in the western provinces.

In developing the theme of national integration through warfare, the patriotic press also appealed, naturally enough, to the Time of Troubles. A contributor to *Den'* drew a parallel between the letter-writing campaign of 1863 and the "declarations from the cities that in 1612 gathered together to save Moscow." In the wave of enthusiasm of 1863, he found the same "firm links of unity" (*prochnye sviazi edinstva*) that had saved Rus' in the seventeenth century.[64] *Moskovskie vedomosti* published a notice from Khar'kov about an episode prompted by the transfer of an uhlan regiment to a region where there had been clashes with the insurgents: "During a banquet given for the regiment by the local inhabitants . . . one peasant . . . addressed these words to the soldiers: ' . . . if you perish, we will all go as warriors.' . . . The peasant who said this was born in Riazan' province and was 'a scion [*otkolyshek*] of Minin and Pozharskii,' as he himself put it."[65] The paper makes this Riazan' peasant's response, with his mention of the voluntary mobilization of 1612 and its heroes, an emblematic voice of the Russian core, determined to liberate the suffering *Zapadnyi krai*.

"A Terrible Dilemma"

For Katkov and Aksakov, the heroic memories of 1812 and 1612 played one more critically important role: more vividly than anything else, they embodied the "harmonious" and "triumphant" accord between ruler and people. Exploiting these connotations of the Time of Troubles and the Patriotic War, the Moscow press urged the government to abandon traditional imperial practices of cooperation with non-Russian regional elites and to join the "downtrodden Russians" in their struggle with the Poles. Clashes between the "Russian *muzhik*" and the "Polish *pan*" in the northwestern region prompted the journalists to articulate this program.

Since all the nobles of the western borderlands were considered Poles (or hopelessly Polonized Russians) who participated in or sympathized with the "mutiny," and since all peasants were considered Russians with unswerving loyalty to the authorities, ethnopolitical tensions (treacherous Poles vs. loyal Russians) tended to align with social tensions (Polish landowners vs. Russian peasants).[66] In the course of the uprising, incidents of "Russian" peasants refusing to obey their "Polish" masters multiplied rapidly. The government realized that resolving this conflict in the usual manner—that is, by applying force to the peasants—would be counterproductive.[67] Yet the need to choose sides in this conflict posed a conundrum for the regime. If, on the one hand, the authorities followed the traditional dynastic practice of showing solidarity with the regional nobility, they would be acting against Russian peasants to defend the interests of Polish landowners. Given the official interpretation of the "mutiny," such a stance would mean siding with the regime's own enemies. On the other hand, if the government supported the Russian peasants against their Polish masters, it would directly or indirectly undermine the foundations of the autocracy.

The imperial authorities sought to avoid this dangerous choice. On March 1, 1863, they promulgated a decree that expedited the process of emancipation in the northwestern provinces: it ended the peasants' direct dependence on their former masters sooner and on more favorable financial terms than in Russia's other regions.[68] This measure, however, did not achieve the expected pacification of the region. The press began to report more and more frequently spontaneous resistance to "mutinous Polish landowners" by "Russian peasants" in that area. In April 1863 the newspapers published a telegram announcing that in the Dinaburg region of Vitebsk province, "a gang of mutineers . . . attacked a Russian weapons transport." But, the report triumphantly continued, "the attack had scarcely taken place when peasants from all the neighboring villages, armed with whatever came to hand . . . set off against the mutineers and succeeded in retaking part of the transport and then, not letting the gang out of their sight, held them until troops arrived."[69] To emphasize the combined efforts of the "villagers" and the regular army, local authorities published a series of caricatures depicting the clash at Dinaburg and the Poles' comeuppance. The first picture portrays a gang of well-armed and obviously well-fed rebels energetically marching to meet other mutinous forces waiting for them in a forest (fig. 5). The second depicts the capture of the mutineers by Russian peasants, male and female, armed only with staves (fig. 6). The concluding caricature shows the gang, now looking famished, being led off by a joint convoy of Russian *muzhiks* and imperial cavalry (fig. 7).[70]

The peasants, however, were far from law abiding.[71] A few days after the first report from Dinaburg, there came disheartening news that those same brave villagers—Old Believers, as it soon was discovered—were now carrying out pogroms against their Polish masters.[72] Thirst for vengeance had turned into peasant revolt. Katkov, who clearly understood the need to control popular anger, nevertheless concluded rapturously: "The people's

Figure 5. "The 1863 Rebels: The *Pany* March into the Forest." Censorship permission granted on March 25, 1864, Vilnius. (Lithuanian State Historical Archive [LVIA], F. 439, ap. 1, b.227)

Figure 6. "Russian Male and Female Peasants Seize and Bind Insurgents in the Dinaburg region, the spring of 1863." Censorship permission granted on March 25, 1864, Vilnius. (Lithuanian State Historical Archive [LVIA], F. 439, ap. 1, b.227)

Figure 7. "The 1863 Rebels: The *Pany* March out of the Forest." Censorship permission granted on April 10, 1864, Vilnius. (Lithuanian State Historical Archive [LVIA], F. 439, ap. 1, b.227)

passion has been unleashed [*Narodnaia strast' zagovorila*]."[73] Once again—and now even more acutely—the authorities found themselves confronting the problem they had tried to evade with the March 1 decree.

The journalist and historian Mikhail Koialovich described the difficult challenge facing the regime in his article "The Popular Movement in Western Russia." Focusing on the Dinaburg pogroms, which he called "the prologue to a great national drama," Koialovich urged the government to work out a new approach to the nationality problem: "What a terrible dilemma—to strike our own people in Western Russia or the Poles! . . . Can it be that . . . Great Russia even now, enriched by the fruits of Western European civilization, will prove powerless to contend with this dilemma? . . . This is the dilemma that must be pondered before all the rest!"[74] Koialovich so emphatically propounded the necessity of correcting traditional imperial policy that his article, originally published in *Russkii invalid*, was reprinted and widely discussed elsewhere. In *Den'*, Aksakov placed the article alongside his own editorial comments, unhesitatingly proclaiming: "It seems to us that there can be no question of *striking* our own people—those Russian people who arise in justifiable indignation to defend *their own*, Russian land."[75] Katkov expressed his opinion just as forcefully: "We will contend with the terrible dilemma. . . . We will not strike the Russian forces."[76] The

Moscow press called on the government to strengthen the position of the Russian population of the western provinces: "Can the government not acknowledge itself as the organ of the ruling nationality," asked Katkov, "and hold its banner high over all the foreign elements living under its rule?"[77] Emphasizing that the Dinaburg Old Believers "now—to the salvation of the region—strike fear in the hearts of the mutineers," he expressed the hope that the government would empower the Russian people in the area and better defend their interests: "There is reason to believe that in the recently announced local elections in the Lithuanian and Byelorussian provinces, the civic rights of Old Believers will no longer be restricted."[78]

Although hope for a rapprochement between the regime and the nation had occupied intellectuals since the beginning of the reform era, Katkov now envisioned it as a revival of the "deep-seated trust" between the ruler and the people.[79] Their fundamental unity had always revealed itself in times of national calamity, he claimed, and so it was revealed now, as the people rushed to form volunteer units to resist the Poles.[80] Discussing this grassroots mobilization, Katkov evoked associations with the Patriotic War as the finest hour of Russian history, when Alexander I, "always favorably disposed" to the Poles, temporarily withheld support for their political aspirations and came to the defense of his own people.[81] Aksakov also understood the victory over Napoleon as a result of cooperation between the government and the people. In the aftermath of the uprising he wrote, "The power of the Russian Empire has always depended, and continues to depend . . . on how close the government is to the people . . . as we saw in 1812 and in part in 1863."[82] The tendency to make concessions to Poland that Alexander II had shown in the first years of his reign came in for unprecedented criticism. The Moscow press declared imperial policies in the western borderlands to be against the interests of the Russian population and called for an immediate return to the legacy of 1812, which implied the empowerment of the empire's ethnic core.[83] In this way, the momentous year served to legitimate transformations being proposed to the government.

For the Moscow journalists, the memory of the Patriotic War symbolized the "nationalization" of the emperor, a necessary condition for bridging the gap between the state and the people. Many nineteenth-century intellectuals were inspired by a brief moment in 1812 when Alexander I adopted the role of national leader and declared that, in the event of a French victory, he was ready to assume the appearance of a *muzhik*, grow a beard, and share the fate of his people to the very end.[84] Reflecting on this episode, Aksakov cited Napoleon's phrase: "The Russian emperor need only grow a beard, and he's invincible." Aksakov applauded Napoleon's words because they linked Russia's victorious future with the prospect of reviving the dynasty's national character and consolidating the government and the people, as had happened in 1812. "It is hardly necessary to explain," continued Aksakov, "that the beard symbolizes here the spiritual and moral character of the Russian people."[85] The nationalists used the memory of the Patriotic War to stress that their vision of uniting ruler and people was not a Western innovation but a restoration of deeply ingrained, native patterns, manifested during popular wars. As we shall see, official ideology's symbolic response to the proposed changes also drew on the victory over Napoleon.

Count Borodinskii, or Russians in Paris

Back in 1856, Alexander II's coronation had been set to coincide with the anniversary of the battle of Borodino (on August 26) and thus symbolically efface the painful defeat in the Crimean War. After the coronation, however, external political factors—above all, the entente with the France of Napoleon III—prevented the government from extensively invoking the memory of 1812. Even two consecutive jubilees of the Patriotic War—the fiftieth anniversaries of the Battle of Borodino and the expulsion of Napoleon's army from Russia—were not widely commemorated in 1862.[86]

At the end of the January uprising, however, the tsar sensed a propitious moment to reappropriate the memory of the campaign against Napoleon. In 1864, when the "diplomatic attack" of the Western powers had been repulsed and the Polish revolt largely put down, Alexander undertook a voyage abroad. En route to Germany, he stopped in Dinaburg and received a deputation of those same Old Believer peasants who had disarmed the band of Polish insurgents. The eloquent counterpart to the emperor's meeting with the Russian peasants was his refusal to receive a deputation of Polish nobility and Catholic clergy in Vilna on the way back to Russia. After a brief return to Petersburg and Moscow, Alexander set off again at summer's end for Germany, where he took part in Prussian military maneuvers. In October the imperial family arrived in Nice, where the tsar met with Napoleon III.[87]

Throughout the entire voyage, the Russian emperor traveled incognito under a symbolic pseudonym, which was greeted enthusiastically by the Moscow press. "We are delighted to note," wrote a contributor to the Sunday supplement of Katkov's *Russkii vestnik*, "that our sovereign traveled abroad under the modest—but memorable for Europe—name of Count Borodin-skii."[88] Alexander II's route followed the path of the Russian advance from Germany into France in 1813–14. The emperor's participation in the Prussian military maneuvers served as a reminder of the two countries' joint action in the campaign of 1813. By evoking memories of the Borodino battle and of the Russian army's triumphal progress through Europe after Napoleon's expulsion from Russia, the tsar's foreign journey symbolically established a parallel between that victory and the conclusion of the Polish crisis.

Though this symbolism seemed to buttress the war rhetoric of the patriotic press, unlike Katkov and Aksakov, Alexander II downplayed the events of 1812, in which Alexander I had not taken part, and highlighted the Russian army's foreign campaign of 1813–14, led by the emperor himself. The ruling tsar thus portrayed Alexander I as the chief architect of Russia's victory over Napoleon—remaining faithful to the interpretation of the Patriotic War employed by official ideology throughout the nineteenth century.[89]

Another gesture by the emperor also vividly demonstrated his fidelity to the vision of the Patriotic War as the monarch's achievement. On March 19, 1864, Alexander II staged a parade of all the guards units in Petersburg to honor the fiftieth anniversary of the Russian takeover of Paris. The ceremony was a grand performance: it lasted more than two hours, occupied all three of the city's central squares (Palace Square, Admiralty Square, and St. Isaac's Square), and drew a huge throng of spectators. "The parade was a grand and poetic spectacle that brought forth, unbidden, feelings of patriotic pride," A. V. Nikitenko excitedly noted in his diary.[90] The drama centered on the Alexander column, the monument to Alexander I unveiled by Nicholas I in 1834. First, Alexander II placed himself at the head of the troops and, as newspapers reported, "led them in a ceremonial march past the monument to Alexander the Blessed, at whose feet were gathered the veterans of 1814."[91] Then the emperor "saluted the monument" and stood beside it, thus allowing the troops to parade past two Alexanders, one living and one bronze. By saluting the monument, Alexander II paid tribute to Alexander I, his uncle, as the embodiment of victory; by accepting the parade on his namesake's behalf, the ruling emperor symbolically identified himself with his uncle. Alexander I was also the focus of a ceremonial dinner given by Alexander II at the Winter Palace on the eve of the parade. In welcoming his guests, who included all living veterans of the 1814 campaign, Alexander II acted as the inheritor of his forebear's accomplishments.[92]

Contemporaries diverged in their perceptions of the 1864 jubilee. Some of Alexander's advisors opposed it, arguing that "such a demonstration [would] be offensive to France." Alexander, however, would not yield. On learning of the emperor's intractability, P. A. Valuev, the minister of internal affairs, wrote in his diary—not without sarcasm—"*Ce sera la parade 'du bon ami'*" (This will be the parade of a "good friend").[93] The "good friend" was a direct reference to a dispute that had broken out on the eve of the Crimean War concerning the title of Napoleon III, who had declared himself emperor in 1852. At the time, Nicholas I was the only European monarch who refused to call the new emperor "*mon frère*," but instead called him "*mon ami*."[94] Valuev's phrase located the jubilee ceremony squarely in the context of conflict between royal families, accentuating the Russian monarchy's continual role as unbending defender of legitimacy.

While Alexander II's attitudes toward the Patriotic War foregrounded the ruler's role in times of national crisis, Katkov's and Aksakov's coverage of the jubilee tended to present the people as the main political player. How did these constructs interact? This question raises an even wider problem. How could the nationalist leaders of public opinion collaborate with the government, if the former held up the people as an object of allegiance and the latter demanded loyalty to the emperor? The patriotic press's reaction to the 1864 jubilee sheds some light on the issue.

In their coverage of the celebration, the Moscow journalists built on the traditional representation of Alexander I as noble savior of nations and merciful deliverer of Europe. At the same time, they elaborated in a new way the theme of great Christian feats persistently associated with this emperor. If official ideology depicted his magnanimity, nobility, and mercy as virtues inaccessible to mere mortals,[95] *Moskovskie vedomosti* attributed them to the Russian people as a whole, while claiming that these distinctive national qualities found their perfect embodiment in the Russian tsar. The patriotic press thus transformed the clement monarch into the nation's ideal incarnation. "We rose up first against the common enemy of the enlightened world," claimed Katkov. "We were at the head of those who deposed him; we held in our hands the fates of France and Europe—and did not abuse either our glory or our strength."[96] By using the pronoun "we," Katkov spoke for the nation, not the emperor alone. Seeing the Russian people's benign nature in Alexander I's humane conduct of war, the patriotic press turned the founder of the Holy Alliance, the recognized champion of dynastic universalism, into the personification of the Russian nation's true self.

The journalists thus achieved two goals. First, by ascribing the Christian mercy and redemptive potential associated with Alexander I to the entire nation, they managed to reconcile the theme of a people at war with the long-cherished myth of Russians' meekness and exceptional love of peace. Still more important, the press combined the rhetoric of national distinctiveness with the Romanovs' imperial glory in a fundamentally new way. Prior to the reform era, the two visions of the Patriotic War—as a popular victory and as the triumph of autocracy—had appeared compatible only within the framework of official nationality, where the former was strictly subordinated to the latter: memory of mass struggle against the invaders served to confirm the people's utter devotion to the throne. Reform-era journalists dramatically recast this pattern. They proved willing to attribute victory over the Grande Armée to the emperor, but only if he embodied native Russian virtues and assumed the role of national leader. The jubilee publications therefore enshrined Russia's resistance to Napoleon as a moment of truth when the ruler expressed the nation's moral values, thus demonstrating loyalty to his own people.[97]

The 1612 Militia Redivivus

If the Patriotic War offered a rich trove of motifs to be used in enlisting the ruler in the national cause, then the Time of Troubles—the period of political breakdown precipitated by dynastic crisis and followed by the enthronement of the Romanovs—provided the press an epic stage on which to display the autocracy's true Russian identity. The formation of the popular militia by Koz'ma Minin and Prince Dmitrii Pozharskii, the triumphant expulsion of the Polish intruders from Moscow, the election of Mikhail Romanov to the throne, and the peasant Ivan Susanin's self-sacrifice for the young tsar—all these stirring narratives of the seventeenth-century struggle with the Poles gave journalists an ideal stock of motifs to draw upon as they worked to restore the monarchy to its native roots. Moreover, as we shall see, reform-era writers invoked these events to virtually transform the Romanov empire into a national one and to affirm the Russian people's commitment to building and sustaining their empire.

Moskovskie vedomosti made eloquent use of the Time of Troubles in its coverage of an extended journey undertaken in the summer of 1863 by Grand Duke Nicholas Aleksandrovich, heir to the throne, along the Volga River, from the north of the empire (the Olonetskii region and Petrozavodsk) to its southern frontiers (the Caspian Sea and the Crimea). The heir's two tutors, the jurist K. P. Pobedonostsev and the economist I. K. Babst, accompanied him and chronicled the entire tour. Their *Letters on the Grand Duke's Travels from Petersburg to the Crimea* turned the journey into a showcase for the nationwide repercussions of the Polish uprising.[98] The coauthors gloried in the "exultant masses" who rose up "in dense waves" to surround Nicholas at many stops along the way.[99] In some areas, inhabitants handed him missives to be passed on to the emperor, expressing their eagerness to go off at once and crush the Polish insurgents. In other places, the crowds simply shouted to the grand duke: "Tell your father . . . that we will all go to meet the enemy, every last one of us!"[100] Pobedonostsev and Babst ecstatically commented that at such moments "thousands were animated by a single ardent feeling."[101] When Nicholas traveled through Russia's heartland, the report portrayed these bellicose throngs as a reenactment of the 1612 militia. In Iaroslavl', streams of peasants, "not only from neighboring villages but from afar," converged on the city to greet the heir. Observing the "sea of faces" and listening to their "deafening" shouts, "we could not help but recall," wrote Pobedonostsev and Babst, that "in 1612 Iaroslavl' had served as an assembly point for the popular forces that took up arms to defend the fatherland."[102] Reporting the jubilant reception of the heir in Kostroma, they stated that in this region, home to Ivan Susanin, "his memory is alive to this day among the people."[103] The coauthors saw that everywhere the people displayed the same fundamental virtues that had saved Russia in the seventeenth century.

Chief among these national virtues was religious devotion. When Pobedonostsev and Babst described the enthusiastic crowds in Rybinsk, they approvingly quoted the sermon of the local priest Rodion Putiatin, who assured the grand duke: "Russia will never lack for Minins and Pozharskiis so long as its sons remain sons of the Orthodox church."[104] The *Letters* depicted the dynasty's bonds with the people in religious terms. Recounting Nicholas's visit to the Ipat'evskii monastery in the Kostroma region, from whence the young Mikhail Romanov had departed to assume the throne 250 years earlier, the coauthors claimed that the monks had not only nurtured Mikhail's decision but endorsed his election, "by crowning him in a solemn national ceremony [*vsenarodnyi obriad*] in the ancient Troitskii Cathedral."[105] The word *vsenarodnyi* is used to give an aura of popular approval to the consecration of the new dynasty. The Orthodox church figures here as a manifestation of the people's will and a guarantee of the Romanovs' union with the nation. The *Letters* interwove all these motifs—ecstatic popular reception of the heir, grassroots enthusiasm for war, and deeply entrenched religious bonds between the people and the imperial family—to turn the trip into a symbolic return to the monarchy's native heritage.

At the beginning of the nineteenth century—on the eve of the French invasion and still more intensively after it—a group of conservative poets, playwrights, and journalists construed the memories of the 1612–13 war as the people's struggle for their very existence and for the restoration of autocracy. As Andrei Zorin has demonstrated, these writers promoted the Time of Troubles as the foundational period of national history.[106] While preserving all the traditional connotations of the 1612 memories, Pobedonostsev and Babst imbued them with the imperial theme, thus rendering the imperial an intrinsic part of the national. The *Letters* recast the ultimate purpose of Minin and Pozharskii's militia as a struggle "to restore the unity of the state."[107] It was the common people's determination to build the empire and sustain its integrity that, according to the report, saved Russia in that period of national calamities. As they observed the bellicose crowds greeting the heir in Rybinsk, the coauthors harked back to the Time of Troubles and portrayed the assembled throng as "the Great Russian born and bred, who gathered up our Mother Russia and made it whole."[108] The Polish uprising revitalized the people's commitment to safeguarding the state and moved them to resume their innate role as builders of empire: "The people hear from everywhere about the enemies of Russia, about threats to its unity and integrity—and awareness of the state's integrity is awakened in them with an intensity that the present generation has not felt for a long time."[109] Thus the parallel with the Time of Troubles made it possible for the coauthors not only to bring the dynasty back to its national roots but also to restore the entire Russian nation to its natural-born vocation of empire building.

The national and imperial themes dramatically merged at the climactic moment of the grand duke's voyage: his investiture as Ataman of the Don Cossacks. When Nicholas arrived in the lower Don to take part in the ceremony, half the Cossacks were off fighting the Polish insurgents. The remainder of the Don troops came out to greet the heir and assured him, as the report stated, of their readiness to join the battle.[110] To demonstrate that he shared their martial fervor, the grand duke sailed up to each Cossack settlement "to the strains of the old Cossack march of 1812."[111] In Novocherkassk, after the investiture ceremony, he offered the Cossacks a toast: "To our common brothers in arms [*za nashikh obshchikh tovarishchei*], the Don Cossacks, as they shed their blood for tsar and fatherland against the Polish mutineers."[112] Nicholas thus positioned himself as a member of the Cossack community, a group regarded in the nineteenth century as the very embodiment of Russianness.[113]

At the same time, the report drew on another traditional representation of the Cossacks: as prime movers in the empire's expansion and as bearers of the Russian national spirit. And here the coauthors elaborated on the imperial theme with particular intensity. Stating that true Cossack culture originated from the lower Don, the report gave a vivid account of the ethnic diversity of the region. From time immemorial, "people of different tribes and tongues converged here from various places in search of freedom." In the typical Don Cossack visage, one discerns, the coauthors observed, Kalmyk, Tatar, Greek, and Turkish features—to say nothing of the diverse cultures that one can still trace in their attitudes, tastes, and habits.[114] But the dominating Russian presence had ultimately engulfed and transformed all non-Russian elements: "In this region throbs the same life force that is to be seen and heard everywhere in the Russian lands."[115] As the grand duke traveled from the Don River down to the southern frontiers, the variety of the subject nationalities increased along the way. Pointing to the Cossacks as the main assimilative force, Pobedonostsev and Babst described how the clearly foreign was transmuted into the truly Russian. As they drew closer to Astrakhan, in the welcoming crowds the Greeks, Armenians, Persians, Kalmyks, and Tatars began to outnumber the Russians. But even confronted with this motley array, "we felt," the coauthors stated, "that the mixture of dress and faces and tongues was given its essential tone by that consolidating element, the Russian people."[116] The Russians gathered, absorbed, and cemented all the diverse ethnic groups into a new whole. The *Letters* portrayed the empire as a broadly based Russian community that embraced all the constituent ethnicities, while tolerating a limited cultural heterogeneity—a concept fully in accord with Katkov's inclusive project of the empire as nation.[117]

The coauthors understood the empire as a work in progress, an attitude made abundantly clear by such declarations as, "It will not be long before the Caspian Sea becomes our lake."[118] They envisioned the future absorption of Central Asia and further eastward enlargement as part of a natural growth process: Russia, they observed, borders on tribes that "chafe at its domination" and on open steppe "where little by little the Russian people with their all-encompassing civilization intrude."[119] By joining the Cossacks, the grand duke symbolically stood with them in both of their missions: in the fight with the Polish enemy and in the task of expanding and Russifying the country's borderlands. Thus, by enlisting the heir in the national cause, Pobedonostsev and Babst drew him into what they understood as the principal vocation of the Russian people: the building of empire. While official ideology presented emperors as heroic conquerors who dominated all their subjects, including the Russians, the *Letters* portrayed the ruler as a national leader who joined the Russian people in their commitment to create and dominate the multiethnic state. In short, Pobedonostsev and Babst depicted two forces—the imperial family and the Russian nation—as leading and prevailing over the rest of the population.

Nicholas Aleksandrovich died unexpectedly less than two years after the trip.[120] This loss—a personal trauma for Pobedonostsev—left him, and the wider group of nationalist thinkers, with no choice but to place Nicholas's younger and less intelligent brother, Grand Duke Alexander Aleksandrovich (the future Alexander III, 1881–94) at the center of their nationalist schemes. Pobedonostsev instilled the ideal of a national monarchy in him by presenting memories of the Time of Troubles as historical justification for rethinking the empire in nationalistic terms and promoting coercive policies of Russification.[121] It was, however, the Polish crisis with its mythical overtones that set the terms for a new vision of Russia's development. In 1863 the patriotic press definitely, emphatically, and systematically formulated the principle of "nationalization" of the dynasty and the empire and thus laid the foundations for the model of autocracy implemented in future decades.[122] To recognize and celebrate these efforts, in 1865 the Moscow gentry presented Katkov with an inkwell adorned with an idealized figure of an ancient Russian prince: dressed in chain mail and with sword in hand, he carries a banner with the words "Unity of Russia" (fig. 8).

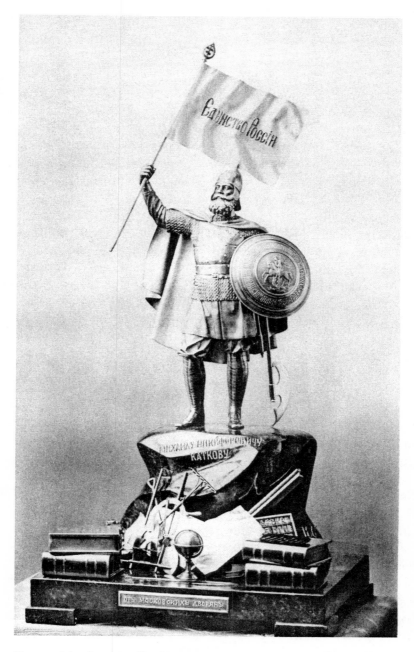

Figure 8. Inkwell presented by the Moscow gentry on December 25, 1865 to Mikhail Katkov in recognition of his role as leader of the "patriotic press." (From *Katkov, Sobranie peredovykh statei "Moskovskikh vedomostei": 1866 god*, title page)

A Second Susanin

How did the constructs articulated in 1863 function later, after the rebellion was crushed? Did war memories and the concept of public involvement in political life remain interwoven in the patriotic press? The way *Moskovskie vedomosti* perceived and construed the first attempt on Alexander II's life reveals much about how the cult of war developed as the reform era unfolded.

In April 1866 in Petersburg, the young revolutionary Dmitrii Karakozov fired a shot at Alexander II as the tsar was leaving the Summer Garden. News of the attack quickly spread—and with it, rumors of a Polish conspiracy as the force behind the attempted regicide. In fact, it may have been Alexander II himself who gave rise to this perception of the event. Numerous sources reported his first words to the criminal, moments after the assault: "Are you a Pole?"[123] Before the would-be assassin's identity had been determined, the press unanimously declared him Polish.[124] When it emerged, however, that the shooter called himself by a Russian name (initially a false one) and spoke perfect Russian, Katkov hastened to denounce what he believed to be a fabrication: "The malefactor rushed to proclaim himself a Russian in order to injure Russian national feeling."[125] In its report on a public prayer service held in the Kremlin in gratitude for the tsar's deliverance, *Moskovskie vedomosti* approvingly quoted the exclamations of the assembled crowds: "*He* is not Russian; *he* cannot be Russian!"[126] This interpretation of the assassination attempt transformed an internal conflict into a struggle with an external enemy—a rhetorical maneuver that made it possible to perpetuate national self-definition through war.

Memories of the Time of Troubles once again offered a powerful lens through which to view the crisis. Before the immediate anxiety produced by the assassination attempt could subside, *Moskovskie vedomosti* played out the 1612–13 narratives against the backdrop of Alexander II's "miraculous salvation": the newspaper hastened to draw a parallel between his escape and that of Mikhail Romanov, who, legend has it, was pursued by the Poles only to be rescued by Susanin. "Next to the murderer," Katkov commented on the shocking story from Petersburg, "there appeared a peasant, originally . . . from the very same place where Ivan Susanin was born and gave his life for the founder of the dynasty—a peasant drawn here by the desire to pray to God on his name day, and by whose hand Russia was saved along with the life of its Tsar."[127] The peasant Osip Komissarov, who happened to be standing next to the would-be assassin and allegedly shoved his arm aside just as he raised the weapon, was made into a new Susanin. This parallel gained currency and proved so resilient that it withstood the final disclosure of Karakozov's Russian identity.[128] Though rumors circulated that Komissarov merely witnessed the event and had nothing to do with Alexander's narrow escape, celebration of the "new Susanin" grew into an astonishingly productive legend. Newspapers and popular booklets re-fashioned Ivan Osipovich (Susanin) and Osip Ivanovich (Komissarov) into mirror images; as doubles they proved the unchanging nature of the Russian people across the generations. These two saviors, as one writer de-clared, "are neighbors and brothers united by their great deeds and shared feeling."[129] Although Komissarov had left his native village near Kostroma while still a child, lived ever since in Petersburg, and completely lost his traditional peasant appearance, the press and visual representations none-theless played on his legal status as a peasant in order to evoke mythical as-sociations. The front of one of the medals cast to commemorate the event depicts Komissarov, as the description says, in a "peasant's winter coat," while the obverse features an Orthodox cross (fig. 9).[130]

In Moscow and Petersburg, public spaces—squares, monuments, and theaters—served as settings for mass reaction to the assassination attempt. *Moskovskie vedomosti* presented the outraged crowds that every day filled Red Square and the Kremlin as a replay of popular war: "On the Minin and Pozharskii monument, right among their bronze figures, a portrait of the emperor was placed. Below them, on the monument's pedestal, a printed portrait of Osip Ivanovich Komissarov was affixed. . . . In the evening the monument was illuminated and musicians . . . played the national anthem" (that is, "God Save the Tsar" ["Bozhe, tsaria khrani"]).[131] In his articles, Katkov made the crowds that gathered around the Minin and Pozharskii monument into an emblem of national unity across social divides. When Moscow University students came to the monument to sing "God Save the Tsar" under the direction of Anton Rubinstein, as Katkov excitedly reported, the common people "raised the shout, *Hurrah, students!*" This greeting met with an apt response: "*Hurrah, Komissarovs!* shouted the stu-dents."[132] These demonstrations symbolized for Katkov a national mobil-ization akin to war: "As if Russia in all its immensity were gathered now in Moscow . . . the thousand-headed throng and the individual—all came to-gether in empathy and became one."[133] And just as it had during the Polish

Figure 9. Osip Ivanovich Komissarov-Kostromskoi. Medal cast "in memory of the miraculous salvation of Emperor Alexander II from Karakozov's attempt on his life, April 4, 1866." (From Ivers, *Medali v chest' russkikh gosudarstvennykh deiatelei i chastnykh lits*, table 24)

uprising, *Moskovskie vedomosti* capitalized on the events of the day to turn Alexander II into a true national leader (*narodnyi vozhd'*), Katkov asserted that at this turning point in Russian history, "there [was] no Russian force that would not flock to his glorious banner."[134]

Glinka's opera *A Life for the Tsar* figured in the daily press as the ideal outlet for expressions of devotion to the throne, patriotic fervor, and bellicosity.[135] It was performed in both the Mariinskii and Bol'shoi theaters, but, at the request of the public, without the second act, which is set in the Polish camp.[136] *Moskovskie vedomosti* reported with fascination that the public could not tolerate seeing the "Poles" on stage, but demanded "God Save the Tsar" instead and joined with the actors to sing it. The actor playing Susanin "sang out his thunderous answer to the Poles":

> Strakha ne strashus',
> Smerti ne boius',
> Liagu za tsaria, za Rus'
>
> [No terror do I feel,
> No death do I fear,
> I will die for the tsar and for Rus']

and "the public made him repeat it three times, so apt was it to the present situation."[137] In Petersburg, Komissarov was present in person at a performance of *A Life for the Tsar* at the Mariinskii Theater. Disrupting the performance, the public called him to the stage, and during the third act, after Susanin sang the words "and my tsar is saved," Komissarov again appeared onstage at the audience's request "and again was met with shouts and protestations of general delight."[138] Reporting similar eruptions of mass enthusiasm and indignation from all over the country, Katkov's newspaper offered them as proof that Russia's enemies could never hope "to fragment this nation—so firmly united in spirit—into a rabble of tribes."[139] Thus, much as in 1863, *Moskovskie vedomosti* used anti-Polish sentiments to reassert the empire's integrity.

In its coverage of the assassination attempt, *Moskovskie vedomosti* revived all the connotations of popular war employed during the Polish uprising. Once again, war appeared as a way to argue for the national character of the empire, consolidate the people, and imagine them as a decisive political actor. But there was also a fundamental difference between the rhetoric of 1863 and that of 1866. During the Polish uprising, Katkov had used the symbol of popular war as a way to propose expanding the civic rights of the Russian people. Now there was no discussion of political reforms, no hint at involving the nation in political life, apart from fighting the foe. As a result, the cult of war was transformed from a historical justification for reform to a substitute for it. The regime blocked all institutional avenues for building civil society, and war became the only arena for mass participation in political life.

This conflation of war memories with projects for popular empowerment encouraged violent forms of national self-expression in the decades to come, preordaining the aggressive orientation of Russian public nationalism. In the 1870s, nationalists harried the government until they succeeded in dragging Russia into the Russo-Turkish War. What made them advocate war with the Ottoman Empire was not merely sympathy with the growing liberation movements on the Balkan peninsula (particularly the outbreak of uprisings in Bulgaria and Serbia), nor even the expansionist project aimed at increasing Russia's political power, but rather the hope of consolidating the nation. With the onset of hostilities, Dostoevsky mustered all his arguments for war (which we examined at the beginning of this chapter) to declare that it would "strengthen the spirit of the entire nation," engender "mutual solidarity," and bring the Russians closer to fulfilling their collective destiny.[140]

Yet the depression that enveloped Russian society after the Russo-Turkish War clearly exposed the cult of war as a self-defeating substitute for popular sovereignty. As Vasilii Vereshchagin's paintings and Vsevolod Garshin's stories—both produced in the aftermath and under the impact of this war—make clear, the campaign stripped Russian society of its sense of collective identity.[141] In the late 1870s, journalists across the political spectrum began to write that military assistance to the Slavs was a noble sacrifice, but one that would only impede Russia's development and distract society from the resolution of internal problems. Indeed, the war contributed to growing discord among social strata and intensified the revolutionary movement—that is to say, instead of the promised results, it yielded the exact opposite.

In response to the Polish uprising, the patriotic press adopted memories of popular wars as the dominant form of national myth-making. War-bound self-definition helped to cast the people as a decisive political player and

propose the ethnic core of the empire as the main object of political allegiance. It symbolically enlisted the tsar in the "Russian cause" and served to
chart Russia's future as a national empire ruled by an emperor who identified himself with the "state-forming nationality." The journalists thus pre-
pared the ground for a turn to a new model of autocracy and to more aggressive policies of Russification, which would be implemented during the
next reign, when Alexander III assumed the throne. Since militant nationalism seemed able to resolve problems that the government could not, for
Russian thinkers war remained the only arena for mass participation. As a
result, iconic images of the nation encapsulated in war memories dominated the national imagination. As we will see in the next chapter, the war
theme resonated powerfully with reform-era poetry and prose. Together
with the patriotic press, literature contributed to an enduring link between
war memories and demands for popular empowerment, a coupling that
was to become characteristic of Russian culture.

4

Literary Representations of a Nation at War

From Apocalyptic Battle to Beehive

During the reform era, war memories proliferated in poetry and prose. This is not to say that authors turned to battle scenes and plots more frequently during the 1860s and 1870s than they had in the past. Rather, the literary works produced during this period tend to conceive of the ongoing reforms in terms of struggle, expressing even peaceful themes through martial analogies and metaphors. The work of Nikolai Leskov, author of antinihilist novels and numerous stories about the clergy, the Old Believers, and peasants (characters who at first glance would seem to have little to do with war), provides a striking example of this tendency. His novel-chronicle *Cathedral Folk* (1867–72) portrays the 1860s as a battle for the revival of the nation by depicting the "Polish conspiracy" and homegrown revolutionaries as intruders on Russian soil. The chronicle's underlying comparison of the reform era with warfare culminates in a legend about an ancient Russian *vitiaz'*, a nameless hero in the struggle against the Tatar yoke. Beset by enemies, the legendary warrior prays to God for a quick death and is immediately struck by lightning. On the spot where he perishes, a spring of "life-giving water" begins to flow and the chronicle's protagonist, the priest Tuberozov, drinks from it, thereby drawing strength for his own struggle with destructive forces.[1] In keeping with recurrent cultural idioms, the first published version of *Cathedral Folk* projects this battle onto the events of 1812,[2] while the drafts of the novel evoke the leaders of the popular war of 1612, who once again are called upon to save Russia: "Arise, our Russian prince [Pozharskii], take up your sword and sever . . . the knot tied by foreigners! Stand forth, Minin of Nizhnii Novgorod, and teach your grandsons to count themselves as nothing before the grandeur that is Rus'!"[3] Not only does Leskov deploy the rhetoric found in the patriotic press of 1863, but he also sees the struggle in mystic terms, as an impending apocalyptic battle to be followed by the establishment of the kingdom of Christ.[4]

After the defeat in the Crimean War, the cult of military victories took on compensatory functions in Russian national discourse. The recollection of military triumphs offered one of the few opportunities to assert Russia's status as a European power of the first rank, if only in an earlier period. The Polish uprising of 1863 and its treatment in the patriotic press gave new currency to war memories. As we have seen, Katkov and Aksakov employed them to transform the Russian people into the empire's politically dominant group, to epitomize the national community's consolidation along social and regional lines, and to unite ruler and people. Many memoirists confirm that Katkov's coverage of the Polish crisis profoundly affected the Russian intellectual landscape. Though Aksakov enjoyed considerably less popularity, the cultural elite read his newspaper very attentively. Quotations from articles by both Katkov and Aksakov filled drafts of *Cathedral Folk*. Leskov's work demonstrates the pervasiveness of the war theme (as popularized by the patriotic press) but also exemplifies the problems it created for national discourse.

Although in the first half of his career Leskov subscribed to many nationalistic idioms, he repudiated most of them at the beginning of the 1880s, as he moved gradually to the left. Even a decade earlier, while working on the final version of *Cathedral Folk*, he had muted parallels with the 1812 and 1612 campaigns and eliminated the apocalyptic theme. This shift in attitude reflects Leskov's reaction to the dilemmas confronting many intellectuals who sought to define the nation by combining memories of popular war with religious motifs.

This chapter explores how reform-era literature contributed to war-bound national self-definition and how, depicting the people at war, writers treated the relationship between the ethnic, imperial, and religious aspects of Russian national identity. It focuses on two strikingly different works—Fyodor Tiutchev's five-stanza poem, "A horrid dream has been burdening us" (1863), and Lev Tolstoy's four-volume novel, *War and Peace* (1863–69)—to elucidate two opposing tendencies in the approach to these problems. Although these works differ in their underlying visions of history, as well as in genre, style, and poetic devices, they both utilize war as a means of national self-definition, and tackle the problem of the relationship between nation and empire. Tiutchev and Tolstoy both show how war awakens and energizes the national community, evokes a powerful sense of belonging, and provides an avenue to the fulfillment of its historical destiny as ordained by Providence. Their texts seek to fuse God and the Russian people into a single agent of national salvation. Finally, both Tiutchev's poem and Tolstoy's novel exemplify how tensions between ethnic and religious aspects of national identity intensified in the reform era, undermining attempts to build a coherent expression of the nation on both principles at once.

Battling with Corpses:
The Russian Empire against the Vampire Pole

"A horrid dream has been burdening us," written in August 1863, appeared in Ivan Aksakov's newspaper *Den'* within days of its composition. Tiutchev sent it to the printers on the eve of his departure from Moscow, where he had spent nearly two months in the summer of 1863, living, as he told his wife, "in the very center of the Moscow press, between Katkov and Aksakov."[5] Although all three writers held firmly to their own beliefs, there was some commonality in their views, and they undoubtedly discussed the very problems—the prospect of war between Russia and the West over Poland, the fateful nature of the impending battle—that constitute the poem's central theme. Personal friendship and shared Pan-Slavist views account for Tiutchev's intensive contacts with Aksakov, the poet's future son-in-law.[6] As to Katkov, the poet followed his editorials with great interest and considered

him the most articulate spokesman for "the Russian cause."[7] Tiutchev had
made the trip from Petersburg to Moscow at the behest of the minister of
foreign affairs, A. M. Gorchakov, who hoped the poet would restrain Katkov from agitating for war with Western Europe.[8] The rhetoric of the patriotic press, possibly developed with Tiutchev's participation, may thus serve
as the point of departure in interpreting the poem.

The text of the poem, together with a translation in English, follows:

> Uzhasnyi son otiagotel nad nami,
> Uzhasnyi, bezobraznyi son:
> V krovi do piat my b'emsia s mertvetsami,
> Voskresshimi dlia novykh pokhoron.
>
> Os'moi uzh mesiats dliatsia eti bitvy,
> Geroiskii pyl, predatel'stvo i lozh',
> Priton razboinichii v domu molitvy,
> V odnoi ruke raspiatie i nozh.
>
> I tselyi mir, kak op'ianennyi lozh'iu,
> Vse vidy zla, vse ukhishchren'ia zla! . . .
> Net, nikogda tak derzko pravdu Bozh'iu
> Liudskaia krivda k boiu ne zvala! . . .
>
> I etot klich sochuvstviia slepogo,
> Vsemirnyi klich k neistovoi bor'be,
> Razvrat umov i iskazhen'ie slova—
> Vse podnialos' i vse grozit tebe,
>
> O krai rodnoi! takogo opolchen'ia
> Mir ne vidal s pervonachal'nykh dnei . . .
> Veliko, znat', o Rus', tvoe znachen'ie!
> Muzhaisia, stoi, krepis', i odolei!
>
> [A horrid dream has been burdening us,
> A horrid, monstrous dream:
> Drenched in blood, we grapple with dead men
> Arisen in order to be buried again.
>
> For eight months now these battles have dragged on;
> Heroic passion, treason, lies,

A den of thieves in a house of prayer,
Crucifix and knife held in the same hand.

The whole world, as if drunk with lying,
Every form of evil, every wicked artifice! . . .
No, never has human falseness
Challenged God's truth to battle so brazenly! . . .

And this cry of blind compassion,
This worldwide call to desperate battle,
Debauched minds and distorted words—
All this has risen, and all of it threatens you,

O native land! Such marshaled hordes
Have not been seen since the world was new . . .
Great must be your significance, O Rus'!
Take heart, stand firm, and overcome!][9]

Although Tiutchev masterfully avoids mentioning the words "Pole" or "Poland" even once in five stanzas, the poem clearly deals with the January rebellion. The line "For eight months now these battles have dragged on" dovetails with the insurgents' activities, begun nearly eight months before the poem's composition. The line "A den of thieves in a house of prayer" refers to the widespread representation of Catholic clergy as instigators and leaders of the "mutiny."[10] Nor could Tiutchev's readers doubt that the joint diplomatic initiatives of the three European powers—France, England, and Austria—which demanded that Russia make concessions to Poland and proposed a system of measures to regulate the conflict, underlie the central theme of "universal" hatred toward Russia. At least two lines—"The whole world, as if drunk with lying" and "This worldwide call to desperate battle"—clearly depict Western European reaction to the Polish uprising, or more precisely, the Russian reception of that reaction.

Viewing "A horrid dream" as a direct response to the European powers' diplomatic campaign does not, however, account for the poem's hyperbole, especially in its final stanza: "Such marshaled hordes / Have not been seen since the world was new."[11] Why do diplomatic notes cause such alarm? Also it is not entirely clear which diplomatic campaign the poem is intended to reflect. Between the start of the uprising and the time of the poem's composition, Russia received three sets of notes from the Western countries, in April, June, and August 1863. The August démarche, in which the Western powers appeared to back down and were out of step with one another, aroused no great alarm in Petersburg and could hardly have inspired such a response.[12] But the first two diplomatic campaigns provoked lively discussions concerning the prospect of war; these discussions had been going on for over half a year before Tiutchev wrote his poem.[13] In May the poet himself was firmly predicting war.[14] If we are to read "A horrid dream" as a response to the April and June notes, then we must see it as a delayed response, indeed emphatically delayed, given that the poem points to the date of its own composition by referring to the eighth months that have passed since the beginning of the uprising. Why, if the poem refers to the April and June diplomatic actions, does Tiutchev emphasize the temporal distance between the publication of the text and the European countries' anti-Russian campaign? Was he covertly pointing to some significant event that fell within this interval, so clearly demarcated in the text? Nor is it clear that the poem was inspired exclusively by the three powers' official protest against the suppression of the uprising, rather than by the massive anti-Russian campaign already under way in the parliaments and press of England, France, and Austria during the winter of 1863.

The poem's thematic structure is also perplexing. The "horrid dream" of the first stanza, its nightmarish battle promising "us" no hope of victory, is transformed in the last stanza to a vision of triumph: "Great must be your significance, O Rus'! / Take heart, stand firm, and overcome!" What motivates this thematic transformation? The poem's use of metaphor begs for interpretation as well. Why is the uprising called a "horrid, monstrous dream?" It is, of course, tempting to read the whole first stanza simply as a comparison of the Polish crisis with a nightmare. But such a trite metaphor cannot explain the key image, the "dead men arisen in order to be buried again."[15] What political associations lie behind this image?

In Russian literature of the second half of the nineteenth century, dead bodies, apparitions, and shades signify otherness.[16] In his analysis of the official rhetoric of the "Russian cause" from the early 1860s, Mikhail Dolbilov identifies "the theme of death as an attribute in the propagandistic depiction of the Polonized Russian nobility."[17] Yet the necrological metaphor found an even wider application: it stigmatized not only a certain stratum of the nobility in the western borderlands but also Polish patriotism and Polish statehood as a whole. In 1863, corpses moved to the very center of political rhetoric, becoming one of the main tools for mythologizing the Polish uprising.

Already in 1844 Tiutchev had accused the West of seeking to manipulate Poland like "a dead body." At that point, he saw Poland as the victim of attempts by Catholic countries—especially France—to erase its Slavic identity.[18] In 1854 Pogodin linked the theme of death with another aspect of the Russian-Polish dispute. He proclaimed the Rzeczpospolita dead and presented the Poles' territorial claims as an effort to resuscitate a corpse: "Let the past rest in its grave. We will leave the dead to bury their dead."[19] When the January uprising broke out, the Gospel adage cited by Pogodin (Matt. 8: 22) took on new meaning, and the necrological metaphor enjoyed an ever-increasing popularity. The Moscow press described Poland as an apparition, a corpse, a shade desperately and vainly asserting its right to life. Katkov never tired of proclaiming its death: "Poland died, the world attended its funeral, and grass has grown over its grave."[20] No efforts on the part of Europe, claimed the editor of *Moskovskie vedomosti*, could ever "resurrect the outworn and truly dead Polish state."[21] During the very days when Tiutchev was writing "A horrid dream," the lead article in *Moskovskie vedomosti* put forward what may be the most striking necrological image of Poland: "Polish patriotism is a revenant from the tomb [*mogil'nyi vykhodets*]; it has not a single thing in common with real life."[22] In the same issue of *Den'* where Tiutchev's poem first appeared, Aksakov also called Polish statehood "a rotten corpse" that exudes "a constant, secret poison."[23]

The necrological rhetoric that gripped the patriotic press in 1863 served two purposes. First, Poland as "a revenant from the tomb" symbolized the hopelessness of the unrest and stood as a final confirmation of Russia's victory in its age-old dispute with Poland. Second, it proved a potent weapon against pro-Polish propaganda, arising as it did in direct opposition to both Polish and Russian revolutionary discourse. Herzen responded to the January uprising with an article eloquently titled "Resurrexit!" He made the triumph of life over death the central theme in his coverage of the crisis. "These Poles are really tireless. For almost a hundred years they haven't been able to die," Herzen sarcastically observed. "It seems as if everything is over; generations pass, all is quiet, *finis Poloniæ*, Europe's sterile feelings of pity subside—What can you do? You can't resurrect the dead! Who could possibly survive so many wounds and blows? The proud warrior is forgotten under the earth—when suddenly from one end of the earth to the other a groan resounds, shaking everyone's conscience, disturbing everyone's sleep: the groan of a people buried alive, standing up with their bloody wounds and rusty chains to announce that they *are not dead!*"[24] Gospel parallels mingle here with historical allusion: following the defeat of his army at the Battle of Maciejowice during the anti-Russian insurrection of 1794, the Polish general Tadeusz Kościuszko allegedly exclaimed, "Finis Poloniæ." In another article, describing the emigrant Poles eagerly returning en masse to their homeland to take part in the uprising, Herzen noted: "One does not visit the dead thus; even those who went to the tomb in Jerusalem were visiting not the dead but the resurrected."[25] Herzen's wording draws an explicit parallel between the 1863 uprising and Christ's resurrection: in Russian the verbs *voskresnut'* (to rise, be resurrected) and *vosstat'* (to rise up, rebel), derivatives of different roots, often function as synonyms, particularly in liturgical texts. The Gospel references allude to the rhetoric of Polish messianism, the discursive backdrop to the representation of Poland as a "revenant from the tomb."[26]

Tiutchev radically reconfigured this treatment of biblical motifs. In calling the Polish insurgents "dead men arisen in order to be buried again," he substitutes for the image of Messiah-Poland that of a living corpse, thereby equating Poland with the "false Messiah," that is, the Antichrist. Tiutchev depicts the Polish uprising not so much as a struggle between nations as an unprecedented clash between the forces of good and evil: "No, never has human falseness / Challenged God's truth to battle so brazenly!" The poet reinforces these apocalyptic associations by introducing a reference to the Creation: "Such marshaled hordes / Have not been seen since the world was new." The Creation motif testifies eloquently to the poem's eschatological subtext, since, in accordance with Christian theology, the Creation can be compared only to the Apocalypse. The two endpoints of history—Creation and Apocalypse—form two discontinuities in the flow of time. Seen in this context, the corpses, resurrected but doomed to perish anew, are servants of the Antichrist, forever excluded from "the book of life" (Rev. 13:8).[27]

This biblical subtext sheds light on the thematic structure of Tiutchev's poem. The first four stanzas, devoted to "desperate battle" and the dominion of evil, can be read as a depiction of the Antichrist's temporary triumph, which will be followed by Christ's reign. If one identifies the false Messiah with Poland, then the authentic Messiah is Russia. The triumphal notes that sound in the poem's finale are prompted by the poet's faith in Russia's future as the coming kingdom of the true Christ. While the patriotic press viewed the events of 1863 as a clash between two peoples, Tiutchev relocates the conflict outside the temporal plane and translates the national question into a providential one.

The mythological juxtaposition of the two forces by no means implies the poet's indifference to the concrete political issues discussed by Katkov and Aksakov. The governing dichotomy of the poem's first stanza—risen corpse/living sleeper—resonates with similar images in the patriotic press. If Katkov saw the Pole as the "revenant from the tomb," then he depicted the Russian—whether soldier, administrator, or bureaucrat—as somnolent. Katkov, who openly criticized the Russian government, exploited the metaphor of drowsy impotence and portrayed the Russian authorities in Poland as sunken in lethargy. He declared that Russians must throw off "the nightmare that robs [them] of [their] determination and energy"; they must free themselves from "the grip of an incomprehensible nightmare."[28] Aksakov extended the sleep metaphor to all of Russian society, "so long asleep, listless, and apathetic," only now awakening, thanks to the Polish threat.[29] Behind the contrast "living sleeper/risen corpse" stood two mirror images, full of associations that simultaneously reinforced a conception of Russia as a force for renewal, revival, and awakening, and a vision of Poland as a dead body.[30]

Through the use of such images, the Polish crisis was recast as the attack of a "dead" people on a living one. Not surprisingly, the attack of "revenants from the tomb" took on vampiric form. "Our enemies are nameless," wrote Pogodin, "their places of residence unknown. They don't even have a body. They are shades, sent out at night from some infernal region and vanishing with the sunrise."[31] Katkov further elaborated the comparison: "Poland has died, but its specter comes as a vampire to suck the blood of the living."[32] In his poem "To Prince Drutskii-Liubetskii," A. N. Maikov also forcefully articulates the link between Poland and vampires. In the aftermath of the uprising, Prince A. I. Drutskii-Liubetskii, a Polish aristocrat of Russian origins from the northwestern province, converted—or, as the press put it, "reverted"—to Orthodoxy. The poem celebrates the event as a restoration of his true Russian identity. The prince proudly declares that he is shaking off the demonic temptation of Catholicism and the Poles' "vampiric" enchantment:

O net, begi kto khochet za vampirom!
Kak korennoi, prirodnyi russkii kniaz',
Ia s predkami teper' pred tselym mirom
Vozobnovliaiu prervannuiu sviaz';
Vse s Pol'sheiu i Rimom uzy rushu.

[No, let who will run after vampires!
As a natural-born Russian prince,
Now before the entire world I restore
The broken bond with my ancestors;
I sever all ties to Poland and to Rome.][33]

By transforming Russia from executioner to victim, the "vampire Pole" metaphor conflated war symbolism with the theme of national suffering, a recurrent cliché in the representation of Russianness. Better still, the "vampire Pole" undermined Polish territorial claims. As we saw in the previous chapter, the Western provinces of the Russian Empire served as the apple of discord in the clash of the two idealized fatherlands—Rus' and the Rzeczpospolita. Typically, the rhetoric of blood and bones allows nationalists to symbolically appropriate a contested land.[34] The right to a particular territory is often confirmed by the burial of ancestors in that land. The patriotic press asserted Russia's claim to the disputed territories through frequent references to the "Russian blood" spilled and the "Russian bones" buried in the Western provinces. Many writers also proclaimed that while the Western provinces had been sown with "Russian bones," Poles could find no rest in "our" earth. The Russian soil rejected them, because it did not belong to them. To put it another way, the Pole as wandering vampire and Poland as unburied "rotting corpse" proved the Russian right to the western borderlands. A more elaborate logic may also have been at work. According to the popular belief of many peoples, including Russians, a vampire can only be eliminated when his heart is pierced with an aspen stake, which pins him to the ground. The image of the vampire foreigner drinking the blood of another people, made famous in *Dracula* (but alive in literature before and since), can, as Katherine Verdery has astutely observed, be taken as "a creative inversion of the idea that proper burial . . . must occur in one's own soil."[35] Wandering Polish vampires thus symbolically disproved Polish territorial claims to the "Russian heartland." In this context, Tiutchev's appeal to Rus' (not to Russia) at the very end of his poem can be interpreted not merely as poetic convention but also as part of a political discourse that designated the Western provinces as "sacred Russian land" and labeled the uprising an attempt to tear Rus' asunder.

At those points where it resonated with key episodes of the 1863 struggle, the "vampire Pole" metaphor assumed greater importance and merged the political and the religious. The January uprising began with coordinated night assaults on sleeping soldiers of the tsar's army.[36] Horrified by what they saw as an atrocity, Russian commentators often emphasized that the insurgents' activities peaked at night. "The Poles," wrote Pogodin, "burn people alive at night, stab sleeping soldiers . . . for the sole crime of being Russian."[37] Reports of such nocturnal sorties inspired panic even in the capital. In the spring of 1863, "during Holy Week a rumor spread that Poles living in Petersburg would slaughter the city's inhabitants on Easter night. Consequently regiments of guards were ordered to patrol the streets of Petersburg with loaded weapons."[38] This rumor of nocturnal attacks timed to coincide with Easter, Orthodoxy's most holy season, resonated with Tiutchev's vision of the Polish crisis as a struggle between servants of the Antichrist and those of the risen Messiah.

If one interprets the image of servants of the Antichrist—Tiutchev's "dead men arisen"—as vampires, then the line "Drenched in blood, we grapple with dead men," suggests not only blood spilt in battle but also the blood sucked from "us." This reading of the poem highlights the Russians' Christlike meekness and humility and suggests how the Polish events affected Russians simultaneously on a personal and a national scale. When the "dead men" took on vampiric form, the confrontation with Poland became an intimate struggle, in which everyone was left to face the enemy alone. When the "dead men" took the shape of the Antichrist's servants, the whole Russian nation had to unite to fulfill its high mission. By mythologizing the suppression of the uprising as a battle with the Antichrist, Tiutchev depicts the events as an awakening and unification of the Russian nation.

This mythical subtext suggests why the poem avoids ethnonyms for Poland. For Tiutchev the Poles are not so much a people as a weapon of worldwide evil. In vanquishing this evil, Russia becomes identified with the kingdom of Christ. Rus' thus becomes not merely an ethnonym but also the locus of Christianity's earthly triumph. The struggle for the unity of Rus' (including the Western provinces) is thus conflated with the enactment of the divine plan of salvation and the establishment of God's rule on earth.

One more reason why Tiutchev avoids using ethnonyms for Poland is that his "dead men arisen in order to be buried again" refer not only to the "mutinous" Poles of 1863 but also to Napoleon's defeated troops. Tiutchev's poetic lexicon itself reveals these associations. Poets who lived through the War of 1812 identified Napoleon with a "night shade" (*nochnaia ten'*), a "specter" (*prividenie*), or a "nightmare" (*durnoi son*), and saw his downfall as the coming of the dawn. In his ode "The Liberation of Europe and the Glory of Alexander I" (1814), Nikolai Karamzin compares the Napoleonic invasion with a "monstrous dream" (*bezobraznyi son*):

> Zlodei torzhestvoval, gde on?
> Ischez, kak bezobraznyi son.
>
> [The evildoer triumphed—and where is he?
> He has vanished like a monstrous dream.][39]

By adopting the symbolic vocabulary of 1812—even reviving the metaphor of the "monstrous dream"—Tiutchev poetically links the Patriotic War and the January uprising.

The representation of the new enemy as an incarnation of the French army has a particular genealogy in Russian poetry—a genealogy connected with the Polish question. In his poem "To the Slanderers of Russia" (1831), discussed in chapter 1, Pushkin projects the Polish insurgents and their Western supporters onto Napoleon's army and prophesies a humiliating defeat for the Western countries, should they enter into open conflict with Russia in solidarity with "mutinous" Poland. On the eve of the Crimean War, Tiutchev himself compares the combined forces of Turkey, England, and France with the Grande Armée in his poem "Nieman" (1853). Earlier still, in Tiutchev's triptych "Napoleon" (1850), the French emperor appears in the form of a restless "corpse." In the final poem of this triptych, which commemorates the removal of the emperor's remains from St. Helena to Paris (1840), Napoleon's "uneasy spirit" is said finally to "sleep," though memories of Russia still trouble him. "The corpse brought home to his motherland" (*na rodinu vernuvshiisia mertvets*) rises from his tomb to gaze toward Russia. While the metaphor of "enemy as risen corpse" is only hinted at in "Napoleon" and "Nieman," it finds its full expression in the poem "A horrid dream has been burdening us."

If the "dead men arisen in order to be buried again" represent not only the Polish insurgents but also the French troops, doomed once again to destruction, then the long-established tradition of rhetorically equating Napoleon with the Antichrist further enhances the poem's apocalyptic implications. Using the symbolic repertoire and vocabulary of Russian poetry to enrich the associations with apocalyptic battle, Tiutchev portrays the Russian nation awakening once again to decide the world's fate, as it did in 1812. It thus becomes possible to see the poem "A horrid dream" not merely as a response to the European powers' diplomatic notes, nor even as a direct reaction to the Polish rebellion. The poem instead alludes to the Russian people's "awakening" by the Polish "mutiny." Tiutchev so clearly marks the chronological distance separating his poem both from the beginning of the uprising and from the Western powers' diplomatic campaigns because the repercussions of the "mutiny"—the awakening of the peace-loving Russian people and the impending fulfillment of their unique historical mission—constitute the poem's dominant theme.

"A horrid dream" signals Tiutchev's shift from seeing the Russo-Polish conflict within the Pan-Slavist paradigm to understanding it within the Christian mystical tradition. This evolution emerges clearly if one juxtaposes "A horrid dream" with his earlier poem "As Agamemnon sacrificed his daughter" ("Kak doch' rodnuiu na zaklan'e") (1831), dedicated to the previous Polish rebellion. Though in 1831, as in 1863, the poet supported the suppression of the Polish uprising, at that time he regarded Poland's future somewhat optimistically. As A. L. Ospovat has demonstrated, in 1831, the poet viewed Poland's role as that of redemptive sacrifice, offered up in the name of future Pan-Slavic unity. He depicts Poland as poised for rebirth through the struggle for "our common," that is, Pan-Slavic, freedom.[40] The brutal suppression of the November uprising is thus justified by the poet's belief in Russia as the only country capable of fighting for the Slavs and their unity:

> Slavian rodnye pokolen'ia
> Pod znamia russkoe sobrat'
> I vest' na podvig prosveshchen'ia
> Edinomyslennykh, kak rat'.
>
> Sie to vysshee soznan'ie
> Velo nash doblestnyi narod.
>
> [To gather kindred Slavic tribes
> Beneath the Russian banner

And lead to the task of Enlightenment,
United in purpose, like an army.

This supreme consciousness
Led forward our valiant people.]

In Tiutchev's eyes, this "supreme consciousness" of the Russian people
earns Poland a future rebirth and place within a united Slavdom:

Ty pal, orel odnoplemennyi,
Na ochistitel'nyi koster!
Ver' slovu russkogo naroda:
Tvoi pepl my sviato sberezhem,
I nasha obshchaia svoboda,
Kak feniks, zaroditsia v nem.

[You fell, O eagle of our fraternal people,
On the purifying pyre!
Believe the word of the Russian people:
Your ashes will be treasured, like a holy object;
Our common freedom, like the phoenix,
Will be born within them.][41]

In his 1863 poem "A horrid dream," by contrast, Tiutchev not only terms
Poland a "dead man"; he also excludes it from the long-sought union of the
Slavs by associating it with the Antichrist.

This new attitude toward Poland brought Tiutchev closer to Pushkin's
vision of the conflict, as expressed in "To the Slanderers of Russia" and
"The Anniversary of Borodino." In the 1830s Tiutchev had voiced some reservations about these poems; in the 1860s, however, he would certainly
endorse the famous line of Pushkin's "Anniversary of Borodino" that emphasized Poland's hopeless condition: "Poland's fate is decided" (*Pol'shi
uchast' reshena*). Following Pushkin's lead, Tiutchev links the West's intention to interfere in the Russo-Polish conflict with the defeat of Napoleon's
army in 1812. Tiutchev's representation of enemies attacking Russia—"dead
men arisen in order to be buried again"—resonates with Pushkin's image of
"embittered sons" of the West, whom fresh destruction awaits "in Russian
fields, / Among the graves of their kinsmen" ("To the Slanderers of Russia"). Now Tiutchev, too, sees the readiness of Russians to rise in defense of
their country as the only way out of the conflict, but with one significant

reservation. While Pushkin presents an imperial space seized by patriotic fervor, Tiutchev refers only to Rus'. The glaring absence of empire from "A horrid dream" does not signify, however, Tiutchev's indifference to the problem; rather, it reflects his understanding of the empire-nation nexus.

The Rus' of Tiutchev's imagination is characterized by a profound duality: it belongs to both the earthly and transcendental worlds. The fleshly embodiment of Rus'—that is, the Russian core of the empire—seeks to establish the kingdom of Christ on earth and thus to merge with its metaphysical prototype. Transient by nature, Rus' therefore is not bound to any time or territory: it is a constantly expanding space, with fluid borders, whose growth is conditioned by mystical forces. In the poem "Russian Geography" (1848–49), defining the "limits" of this "kingdom" is left to Providence; the reader sees only its grandeur:

> Ot Nila do Nevy, ot El'by do Kitaia,
> Ot Volgi po Evfrat, ot Ganga do Dunaia . . .
> Vot tsarstvo russkoe.
>
> [From the Nile to the Neva, from the Elbe to China,
> From the Volga to the Euphrates, the Ganges to the Danube . . .
> Here is Russia's kingdom.][42]

In "A horrid dream," Rus' "awakens" to fight with the "whole world" and thus establish its universal power. This construct arose out of Tiutchev's belief in an eternal Christian empire. For him Russia, the true inheritor of the Byzantine Empire, was predestined to rule the world. He mythologized all of Russian history, including 1812 and the conflict with Poland, as a sequence of transformations that was leading Rus' into this all-embracing power.[43] While Pushkin equated Rus' with Russia, and the patriotic press imagined the entire empire, in all its ethnic diversity, rising to the defense of Rus', Tiutchev's ever-expanding Rus' was an atemporal, providentially defined entity meant to eclipse the existing state. As noted in chapter 1, the rhetoric of the Crimean War period presented Russia's lack of natural barriers to enemy incursion as its most reliable defense. Tiutchev recast this cliché as a symbol of Russia's natural inclination toward military expansion. The country's very boundlessness came to symbolically justify its "limitless" growth.

Rooted in national mythology, this construct represents one of the reform era's paths to self-understanding—a path that also beckoned

Dostoevsky and Leont'ev. "A horrid dream," a poetic incarnation of the aggressive type of nationalism, replaces the flow of time with eschatology and removes Rus' from historical time. It subordinates Russian distinctive features to universal religious values and, as a result, dilutes and obscures the nation's ethnic uniqueness. Even more important, Tiutchev's poem elides the contours of the real Russian Empire in the name of an imaginary universal one.

Biological Metaphor
in *War and Peace*

The symbolism of the nation in *War and Peace* contrasts sharply with that in Tiutchev's poem. While the poet defines Rus' in terms of its religious mission and merges it with the transcendental, Tolstoy elaborates his vision of the Russian people through comparison with the mundane activities of insects. Tiutchev's Rus' eludes human temporality; Tolstoy's nation, on the contrary, submerges itself in a biological time punctuated by birth, growth, death, and continuation of the species. In Tolstoy's novel, "swarm life," captured in images of the beehive and the anthill, forms one of the central metaphors of national community. Bees and ants, "biological and poetic relatives," exhibit highly social behavior and thus represent in literature an orderly society.[44] *War and Peace* places particular emphasis on the swarm's organic wholeness and its tenacious life force, two underlying themes in the novel's representation of the Russian people.

Despite the profound differences in their understanding of the nation, Tiutchev and Tolstoy do converge on one important point. Like Tiutchev, Tolstoy conceives of the nation within the framework of divine law. According to his fatalistic conception, each person unconsciously contributes to historical events that, taken together, enact the will of Providence—though individuals are usually moved by deeply selfish, even "wild and bestial" impulses.[45] One key segment of *War and Peace* dramatically connects the metaphor of "swarm life"—and, by implication, the Russian nation—with divine will. Comparing the abandoned Moscow of 1812 to an empty and "queenless hive," Tolstoy counterposes the hive and the beekeeper, endowing the latter with Godlike functions. In this juxtaposition, it is the beekeeper who "peers into" the hive, "examining" it from on high, who comprehends both the complex collective life of the swarm and the actions of each individual bee. And most of all, it is the beekeeper who decides when to burn the hive.[46]

The metaphor of Moscow as doomed hive foreshadows not only the burning of the city but also its subsequent rebirth. Tolstoy depicts the dysfunctional swarm on the eve of its collapse and contrasts it to its former thriving state. The detailed description of disarray alongside an equally detailed vision of bustling activity invites readers to imagine Moscow in its future restored wholeness. At novel's end, Tolstoy indeed revisits the metaphor of swarm life in order to describe the ancient capital's restoration. Like ants around an "overturned anthill," Russians crowd the liberated city, full of "tenacity," "energy," and a devotion to "something immaterial that constitutes the strength of the anthill Moscow."[47] By inscribing Moscow's fate within the plan of Providence, Tolstoy locates the nation's history within a teleological narrative and, quite paradoxically, infuses that narrative with biological associations that help the author graphically convey his philosophical reflections and strengthen them with quasiscientific observations.

It is easy to imagine how shocking this insect metaphor must have sounded in a novel about a war that belongs to the pantheon of national triumphs. Even Nikolai Strakhov, the literary critic whom Tolstoy held in the highest regard, could not—for all his delight with the novel—reconcile himself to its prosaic explanation of the victory: "If the author had concluded his book with some thoughts of a philosophical or other nature, which might have clarified for us . . . the ideal that saved us then and animates us still to this day—we would have been satisfied."[48] Aksakov, to whom Tolstoy read the first section of *War and Peace* in 1864 and who seemed at the time to approve of it, rejected the completed novel precisely because it desacralized the memory of the Patriotic War and denied "the moral virtue exhibited by the Russian people during the burning of Moscow."[49] Indeed, Tolstoy, with his metaphor of swarm life, rebelled against the conventional representation of 1812.

Since Tolstoy assumes the primacy of impulse and intuition in human life, biological metaphors underlie many crucial scenes of *War and Peace*.[50] More than once, he expresses in the novel—and still more explicitly in the diaries that accompanied its composition—the belief that "everything, everything that people do, they do at the behest of nature. And the mind merely counterfeits for each act its transient pretext, which for one person is called conviction or faith, and for an entire nation, *ideas*."[51] This denial of the role of "ideas" in the life of a nation stemmed from Tolstoy's distrust of governments, politicians, and intellectuals who foisted their theoretical constructs on the people. In applying these views to the Russia of his day, Tolstoy turned an especially skeptical eye on the cultural elite, which advocated social and political transformations, and the patriotic press, which articulated a new vision of the nation that relied on the memory of the triumph over Napoleon.[52]

The beginning of the author's work on the novel coincided with the Polish uprising, which patriotic journalists mythologized as a "new 1812." Since Tolstoy had long planned to write a work about the early nineteenth century, the anti-Polish campaign cannot be seen as the prime impetus for his embarking on the novel. Nonetheless, Katkov's and Aksakov's articles constitute an important context for understanding *War and Peace*.

Scholars have long drawn attention to the novel's dual perspective on war. On the one hand, the writer condemns military action as mindless cruelty. On the other, he tends to aestheticize battle, to find hidden meanings in war, and even at times to justify it.[53] As it had for many Russian thinkers, war helps Tolstoy find the nation. Significantly, the metaphor of the hive nation appears only in the second half of the novel, which chronicles the Patriotic War. Absent from the recounting of the events of 1805–11, "swarm life" emerges in the author's reflections on the incursion of Napoleon's army into Russia, culminates in his depiction of abandoned Moscow, and from this point on never leaves the novel (not even the epilogues). Tolstoy depicts the events of 1812 as a debacle so great as to render the nation not only visible but also recognizable for its distinctive qualities. Thanks to the war, Pierre discovers "a potent life force, a power capable in this snow, in this landscape, of sustaining the life of a whole, distinct, and cohesive nation."[54] Moreover, according to Tolstoy, war gives ordinary people occasion for self-reliance and scope for independent action. Crisis frees them from the laws, rules, and administrative demands that normally regiment and limit their lives. On the field of battle, Tolstoy claims, the power of military commanders becomes useless: "Nowhere is a man more free than at the time of battle, when it's a matter of life or death."[55] Once Napoleon's army advances into Russia, the Russian land becomes a battleground, and the actions of the entire population — not just of the army — assume a spontaneous character. While the "sea of history" is calm, it appears to the "ruler" (*pravitel'-administrator*) that he controls the nation's progress, "but as soon as a storm arises" it immediately becomes clear that "the ship of nation is moving at its own majestic pace, not governed by anyone."[56] If in *The Cossacks* Tolstoy found the nation's true expressions on the margins of the empire, now he finds it in time of national calamity.

As we have seen, the patriotic press of 1863 also used the memory of 1812 as a tool to discover the nation. Yet whereas Katkov and Aksakov sought in the victory over Napoleon an effective blueprint for consolidating regime and people, Tolstoy, on the contrary, emphatically separates the two in his depiction of war: for him, the nation reveals itself in those grassroots and instinctive acts that defied official orders—acts that either ran counter to the generals' plans (the abandonment of Moscow) or preceded them (the guerilla war). Tolstoy the anarchist is equally critical of Katkov's and Aksakov's claims that in the face of the enemy in 1812, the monarch joined the nation. To emphasize the Court's alienation from the people, Tolstoy repeatedly notes the tsar's hostility toward Kutuzov, whom the novel upholds as the embodiment of the national will. This tension becomes especially evident when Tolstoy writes of "the general acclaim that accompanied the choice—both popular and contrary to the court's wishes—of Kutuzov as commander in chief."[57] While Tolstoy attributes to Alexander I the same intention to assume the role of national leader that so fascinated the patriotic press (in *War and Peace* the tsar declares his readiness to lead "his good *muzhiks*" in their struggle with the enemies), Tolstoy treats this rhetoric as an object of derision.[58]

Tolstoy also challenges the recurrent cliché about the Napoleonic invasion's having instantly inspired a patriotic groundswell among all Russians—a cliché central to official historiography of the War of 1812 and to Katkov and Aksakov's writings in 1863. *War and Peace*, on the contrary, recounts soldiers' carefree mood in the first weeks of the war, the merry days they spent near Vilna, the "drunken camp" at Sventsiani, and the lively social scene in Moscow in the summer of 1812.[59] Most characters don't experience the slightest bit of patriotism until they become personally involved in the calamity.[60] Princess Mary reaches her turning point when her father dies, after which she suddenly begins "to think the thoughts of her father and brother," adopts their sense of national pride, and realizes the impossibility of remaining under French authority. Natasha begins to feel herself a part of something wider than her family when she helps the wounded and comes upon Prince Andrei among them. The questions thus arise: If the sense of involvement comes to each character individually, does this liminal moment also come for the entire national community? And if so, when and how?

War and Peace gives a very definite answer to these questions. The author portrays the Russian army's retreat at the beginning of the campaign with no particular drama, for he considers the entire space from the Nieman to Smolensk—that is, the Western borderlands of the empire—to be "the Polish provinces." One might think that Tolstoy is simply repeating the name often applied to these regions during the early nineteenth century (although the novel's authorial voice generally remains untouched by the stock images of the period).[61] Yet the author himself draws a sharp distinction between the western parts of the empire and Russian lands proper by portraying the indifference among the people and within the army before the war reaches, in Tolstoy's own words, the "Russian borders" (though by that time military action had been taking place on the territory of the Russian Empire for several weeks) and Smolensk—the gateway to what Tolstoy views as Russian ancestral territory. The "patriotic fervor" emerges after the city's surrender and intensifies as military action moves closer to Moscow.[62] After Smolensk, the *muzhiks* "slaughtered the French as instinctively as dogs instinctively attack a stray mad dog."[63] *War and Peace* thus undermines the fundamental axiom of the patriotic press, which held that the Western provinces were part of Russia's ancestral lands. Tolstoy asserts that the decisive battle was fought at Borodino not because it was strategically more convenient "than any other place in the Russian Empire," but because earlier, before the army's retreat toward Moscow, "the people's thirst for a decisive battle had not expressed itself sufficiently strongly."[64] Tolstoy thus constructs an ethnocentric story about 1812, circumscribing the boundaries of the Russian land and sharply distinguishing it from imperial space.[65]

Like many others, Tolstoy sees popular war as a time when the nation consolidates itself naturally, gathering individuals into an organic whole.[66] Although the novel describes the centripetal forces of the nation through the familiar idiom of kinship, *War and Peace* contradicts the vision of unity across social divides as a matter of brotherly self-sacrifice, as expressed in the official propaganda of 1812 and reiterated in the patriotic press in 1863. For Tolstoy, on the contrary, his characters' sense of the nation as a family arises at the time of the French invasion from the same instincts, mundane concerns, and emotional patterns that motivate their behavior elsewhere in the novel. Since their actions during the war are spontaneous and instinctual, in any given moment they might or might not overcome social barriers, might or might not contribute to the nation's cohesion—although, taken together, they lead in the direction of national consolidation. The epicenter of the kinship idiom is Moscow, whose "maternal significance" is on display throughout the novel. It is in Moscow that the peasant Platon Karataev watches over Count Pierre Bezukhov like a mother (fulfilling the role of the peasant mother whom Pierre cannot remember), that the Rostovs' housekeeper Mavra Kuzminichna shows maternal affection to a nameless young nobleman with "the Rostov features," and Pierre, moved by an emotion he cannot quite fathom, declares the girl he saves to be his daughter. Yet in time of war people can also exhibit class hatred, like the rioting Bogucharovo peasants, or senseless mutual aggression, like the crowd that beats Vereshchagin to death, a scene that mirrors the killing of bees in a destroyed hive. Such examples of disintegration and disarray within the community resemble the image of the dysfunctional swarm in the hive: they constitute a backdrop to the predominant tendency toward national consolidation in wartime and help the author depict this consolidation as a complex (on the surface, even chaotic) process, driven by natural impulses that have nothing to do with the exalted notion of brotherly self-sacrifice.

War and Peace also distinguishes itself from the patriotic press of 1863 by completely ignoring the commonplace parallels between the expulsion of Napoleon's army in 1812 and the victory over the Polish invaders in 1612. This historical rhyme sacralized both popular wars, elevating them to the pantheon of national triumphs. Just as the novel refuses to show the Patriotic War in an exclusively heroic light, so it emphatically makes no distinction between profane and sacred epochs. Tolstoy attaches major importance to the people's unchanging nature and the constants of human behavior, operative in all periods. The novel claims that during the military campaign of 1805—a time of defeats for the Russian army—the soldiers exhibited the same emotional and behavioral patterns that would bring victory in 1812. For instance, describing both campaigns, Tolstoy insists that on the eve of battle everyone feels a growing sense of being part of a whole. Before the Battle of Austerlitz, the soldiers seek to "set aside the interests of their regiment" and speak of the entire Russian army—"in a word, Moscow!"— despite the fact that the engagement is taking place on foreign soil.[67] On the

eve of Borodino, a passing soldier expresses to Pierre the same overwhelming feeling in exactly the same phrase: "in a word, Moscow!"[68] Using situa-
tional rhymes, fixed patterns of behavior, and other forms of repetition,
Tolstoy fosters a sense of the nation's sameness over time.[69] He extends this
panchronic vision of the true Russian self not only to epochs that inspire the
worship of posterity but also to epochs that posterity would prefer to forget.

This technique helps Tolstoy not only to link the chronologically remote
episodes of *War and Peace* with one another but also to collapse the distance
between text and reader. Tolstoy regularly, and most often in battle scenes,
shifts from past to present tense and speaks in the first-person plural, assum-
ing a Russian community outside time, one that also encompasses his contemporary readers: "The armies are divided at the start of the campaign. . . .
We try to unite them. . . . We lead the French to Smolensk. . . . We depart at a
sharp angle."[70] In such passages the narrative makes the past immediately
present and lumps the reader together with the novel's characters. The battle
scenes provide the best opportunity for including Tolstoy's audience in the
collective "we," since the author sees in all wars the same universal patterns:
"No battle ever goes as planned," and "nowhere is a man more free than at the
time of battle."[71] Yet alongside this "we" that distinguishes the Russian
people from the enemy, there is another "we" at work in the novel—the generation of the 1860s, rather than that of 1812: "Naturally . . . an endless variety
of causes [of war] presented themselves to contemporary observers, but *for
us—their descendants* . . . these causes seem insufficient."[72] Thus, alongside
the panchronic "we," Tolstoy develops its time-bound version, accentuating
the historical changes and the differences between the generations.[73]

Significantly, however, the second "we" does not undo the sense of
national unity conveyed by the first "we." Despite temporal fluctuations,
Tolstoy positions the novel's heroes as the reader's ancestors, thus once again
evoking a sense of biological time. On the very first page, he observes that
Prince Vasilii speaks "that refined French in which our grandfathers
thought." At the novel's end, he invites readers to look on the victory over
Napoleon as an event that "unfolded before the eyes of our fathers."[74] The
idiom of kinship, which, as we have seen, is used in *War and Peace* to convey
the centripetal forces of 1812, now unites readers and characters. Moreover,
references to "our fathers" unite "us," their descendents, not only with the
previous generation but with one another. The integrity of the "ancestors"
assumes a corresponding integrity of the descendents, who share something

in common—if only the ways in which all descendents differ from their forebears: "we" have all lost the refined French of our "grandfathers"; "we" can only imagine what our "fathers" saw with their own eyes. In this way, Tolstoy opens out the novel's internal time and connects his readers with their ancestors and contemporaries, making them feel part of the national community.[75]

Tolstoy employs one more technique to bind his readers and characters together: he locates them on a single temporal axis. *War and Peace* dates not only battles, truces, and other historical events but also events in the lives of the fictional characters. Having mentioned in the novel's first scene that Anna Pavlovna Scherer's soirée took place in late July 1805, the author becomes ever more pedantic about dates. As the story unfolds, we learn that the "little princess" Bolkonskaia's labor began on March 19, 1806; that the Rostovs went hunting at Otradnoe on September 15, 1811; that Pierre stood at the threshold of the prisoners' barracks playing with a dog on October 6, 1812; and that French soldiers shot Platon Karataev on October 20, 1812. In a fictional text, it is always important to know what happens *before* or *after* a particular event. Tolstoy provides not only the contingent *befores* and *afters* but also the absolute *whens*, making it possible for the readers to synchronize their *when* with that of the characters.

Perhaps the most striking example of this technique involves the date Tolstoy chooses for one of the key scenes at the beginning of the novel—the name-day party at the Rostovs', where many of the central characters, and even chance visitors, are welcomed into the warm family atmosphere of the household. Although Tolstoy does not give the date of the party outright, the information he provides—that the Rostovs are celebrating the name day of two Natalias, mother and daughter, at the end of the summer of 1805—clearly situates the scene on August 26. Seven years later, on precisely the same day, comes the battle of Borodino—a turning point in the lives of many of the characters, the basis of a shared memory not only for them but also for the entire nation. The inclusive power of the Rostovs' party, with Natasha—a girl endowed with quintessentially Russian traits—playing a pivotal role in the scene, foreshadows the all-embracing power of the battle that serves as a defining moment for national self-perception in both the fictional and the real world. The symbolic potential of this temporal marker allows Tolstoy to establish a link between an event important for one family and a battle that affects the entire Russian people. Thus Tolstoy

inculcates in his audience an emotional connection with the Rostovs, inviting readers to see the characters' story as the history of their own ancestors.

In describing the repercussions of the Battle of Borodino, Tolstoy juxtaposes two dates—the date of the battle (August 26) and Alexander I's birth-
day (August 30; actually Tolstoy made a mistake: it was the tsar's name
day). All the courtiers are expecting good news of the war on August 30.
For them the date of the Battle of Borodino means nothing, whereas for
Tolstoy's readers August 26, 1812, is a defining component of Russian identity. Here the narrative reaches into the future, since in subsequent decades
August 26 will be celebrated not only as the anniversary of Borodino but
also as the day of Alexander II's coronation in 1856, which was deliberately
set to coincide with the date of the battle. August 26 was also the day of the
Decembrists' amnesty in 1856. This last detail is particularly important for
the novel, since one spur to its creation was the history of Decembrism.
Thus not only does *War and Peace* locate its characters and first readers, the
people of the 1860s, in a calendar punctuated by dates significant for them
all, but it also shows how the temporal frame in which they live was formed.

An emotional attachment to certain dates and places unites the Russian
people across generations and serves to distinguish them from the "other."
Although Tolstoy depicts an unrecognizable French-occupied Moscow, he
emphasizes certain unchanging features of the landscape, thereby evoking a
sense of belonging on the part of the reader. For the French, Tolstoy writes,
Moscow is "the new locus of a new field of battle," a phrase that flattens
the city into a featureless expanse. "This place was not Vzdvizhenka, Mo-
khovaia, Kutaf'ia, and the Troitskii Gates" for the invaders.[76] But for Tolstoy's readers these streets, towers, and gates were home. By emphatically
naming them throughout the chapters that describe the French occupation
of the city, Tolstoy restores to Moscow its familiar and (supposedly) unchanging topography and creates a bond of complicity among characters,
readers, and author. Temporal markers function similarly. Since the Julian
calendar, in effect in nineteenth-century Russia, differed by twelve days
from Western Europe's Gregorian calendar, for the Russians the Battle of
Borodino took place on August 26, while for Napoleon's soldiers it occured
on September 8. When Pierre converses with Captain Ramballe, they give
different dates for the battle, and Tolstoy preserves the confusion to show
that Napoleon's soldiers and the Russian people literally reckon time differently. Tolstoy dramatizes this temporal disconnect when the captive Pierre,

having lost track of days, is led through burning Moscow: hearing the ringing of church bells, he realizes that it is the Feast of the Birth of the Mother
of God. For the conquerors, the date is unmarked (the Catholic Church
would have celebrated the Birth of the Virgin Mary twelve days earlier), so
in deserted Moscow "it seemed there was no one left to observe the holi-
day."[77] In this way, Tolstoy employs spatial and temporal markers to present
the Russian nation as a single entity, coherent across temporal divides.

In cultivating a sense of the nation's commonality and continuity, the
novel draws together what for Tolstoy's contemporaries seemed disparate
and discontinuous: the defeat at Austerlitz and the victory at Borodino,
Russian life of the early nineteenth century, and the reform era of the
1860s.[78] War thus allows Tolstoy not only to find the Russian people and
their historical homeland unobscured by the imperial space, not only to
create an emphatically ethnocentric, as opposed to imperial, narrative of
1812, but also to present the nation's past and present as elements of an
organic whole. Just as the picture of the dysfunctional swarm invites the
reader to imagine Moscow as a future healthy hive, so the depiction of the
catastrophe of 1812 points to Russia's restored state and thus highlights
the nation's continuity.

Though celebration of Russian national distinctiveness plays a prominent role in the novel, it is counterbalanced by universal Christian values.
And it is Tolstoy's depiction of the people at war that gives voice to both
viewpoints. Pierre is the character through whom the two views are most
often expressed. During the war he overcomes his own ego and joins the
Russian people, discovering their kindness, simplicity, and cooperative nature on the Borodino battlefield, in captivity, and, most important, through
his encounter with Platon Karataev. But Pierre also joins humanity and
indeed the whole universe, as symbolized by his dream of the liquid globe
with God inside it and by the sky and stars—constant images in the story
of his captivity.[79] The authorial voice oscillates between these two notions
as well. On the one hand, Tolstoy proudly claims that the Russian people
have demonstrated in battle the strength to decide the fate of peoples and
proved their national greatness.[80] On the other, Tolstoy claims that the
only criterion for greatness is "the measure of good and evil given us by
Christ."[81] How does the novel reconcile these contradictory ideas?

In keeping with national mythology, Tolstoy portrays the Russian
people of 1812 primarily as defenders of their homeland, not so much

the perpetrators of violence but rather its sufferers. Kutuzov—the novel's incarnation of the national spirit—would like to replace cannons and rifles with "patience and time," which at campaign's end he calls his main weapons. The prisoner Pierre amazes those around him with his combination of humility and strength. Significantly, he finds inner freedom not on the battlefield but in captivity. The soldier Karataev, who has spent most of his life on active duty in the army, is also shown not in battle but in captivity. The novel's embodiment of Russianness, Karataev meekly accepts his death at French hands. At Borodino, Prince Andrei and his regiment neither attack nor kill but rather passively "stand" under fire.[82] These constructs—victory without violence, freedom in captivity, passive standing in place rather than active fighting—allow Tolstoy to discover the nation through war, while minimizing the depiction of violence. Tolstoy thus reconciles the novel's conflicting ideas by portraying 1812 more as calamity and suffering than as collective violence, but this balance cannot last. Later in life, he will preach the primacy of moral and universal values.

War and Peace—the high-water mark of Russian literature's attempt to define the nation through war—demonstrates the limitations of war-bound national self-definition. Like the patriotic press of 1863, Tolstoy employs martial memories to define the Russian nation. Tolstoy even outdoes his contemporaries: using images of war, he restores the ethnic community to wholeness, overcoming temporal and spatial divides. Yet unlike Katkov and Aksakov, he emphasizes war's immorality, seeing not in victory but in suffering the power to unite the nation, for suffering elicits the people's natural tenacity and makes clear their divine calling.

Tiutchev's poem and Tolstoy's novel define the Russian people quite differently with respect to their conceptions of time, their visions of the community's future, and their understandings of the nation-empire nexus. If for Tiutchev imperial mission prevails over Russian ethnic culture, Tolstoy tells an ethnocentric story of the nation at war, ignoring the imperial dimension of Russianness. While Tiutchev endows the Russian people with a universal mission and thus justifies violent and expansionist nationalism, Tolstoy proclaims the superiority of the universal over the Russian, ultimately denying nationalism (a tendency, discernible already in *War and Peace*, that will find still more direct and uncompromising expression in his later works). As representatives of the main lines of thinking about national self-definition, Tiutchev and Tolstoy demonstrate the contradictory and ambiguous forms taken by Russian national discourse under an absolutist regime that made war the only arena for mass participation in political life. Both writers also reveal that in the reform era it became increasingly difficult to combine the ethnic and religious aspects of national identity into a coherent expression of the national self.

5

The Myth
of Spiritual Descent

Remapping the Empire

t is well known—indeed, almost a cliché—that Russia's national self-image is pervaded by religious motifs. Many nineteenth-century thinkers, above all the Slavophiles, found in Orthodox culture the key to Russian uniqueness.[1] What real impact, however, did religion have on reform-era constructs of the nation? Did the sacred help to shape emerging nation-building projects, with their ultimate focus on the profane? The previous chapter discussed how Tolstoy's and Tiutchev's writings reveal the increasing difficulty of combining the ethnic and religious aspects of national identity into a coherent expression of the nation. Did more politically oriented intellectuals seek to harmonize the two? And if so, did their efforts strengthen or challenge imperial consciousness?

To address the issue we will focus here on the myth of the nation's spiritual birth and on the symbolic representations that arose from it. Though the Varangian tale—Russia's canonical founding myth—was remarkably resilient (as we have seen in chapter 2), by the end of the nineteenth century historians were searching for an alternative version of the starting point of Russian history, one that would enable them to trace the origins of the nation, rather than those of the state. This proved a challenge, however, since previous epochs did not provide thinkers of the 1860s with a coherent story that could command the same respect as the Varangian tale. Scholars experimented with several episodes from the past that, with careful pruning, could be shaped into alternate accounts of the nation's origins. N. I. Kostomarov identified one potential starting point for national life in the migration of the most strong-minded Slavs from the Danube River to regain freedoms curtailed by their Roman conquerors.[2] V. O. Kliuchevskii located another in a development he depicted as even more heroic: the rise of a powerful military alliance among Eastern Slavs in the Carpathians, following their departure from the Danube area.[3] Although these two constructs never achieved wide popularity, they signaled an increasing need to complement the story of the foundation of the state with a narrative of the people's pedigree.

It was the myth of spiritual descent that allowed reform-era writers to virtually remove the nation from the shadow of empire by contrasting the origins of the people with those of the state. The story identified the nation's birth with the mission of two brothers, the saints Cyril and Methodius, Greek monks, who in the ninth century came to the Slavs to translate the scriptures into old Church Slavonic, a written language they devised for the purpose of evangelizing these peoples. By presenting them as the "saintly teachers" of all Slavdom, this narrative blurred the distinctions among the various Slavic nationalities, thereby appealing particularly to those who envisioned Russia's future in a Pan-Slavic framework. Building on the Slavophile legacy, the Pan-Slavists viewed Orthodoxy as the core of Russianness and traced the nation's beginning back to the first seeds of Christianity among the Slavs. Yet, unlike their predecessors, the Pan-Slavists embroidered the religious account to justify Russia's expansionist project and endow its imperial mission with an aura of moral imperative. The acquisition of Slavic territories figured in their constructs as both the Russian people's recovery of their spiritual cradle and the liberation of their "suffering brothers" from the "foreign" yoke. In this way, the Pan-Slavists sought to reconcile the imperial, ethnic, and religious aspects of national identity.

The Spiritual Birth of the Nation

In spring of 1862, when preparations for the celebration of the Millennium of Russia were well under way, Pogodin published a missive, *To the Slavs*, in which he juxtaposed Russia's upcoming jubilee with another one, equal in age, that marked the threshold of civilization for all Slavs: "By an amazing confluence of circumstances, the Russian millennium coincides," he declared, with "the millennium of the Slavic liturgy and literacy."[4] Pogodin proposed to commemorate Cyril and Methodius's mission immediately, in 1862—the same year the government was to celebrate Riurik's arrival, but with a separate ceremony. In his missive, he invited scholars, priests, poets, and political activists from all the Slavic lands to come to Russia and observe this formative date together. He even went so far as to claim the "emergence of the Slavic liturgy" as the spiritual genesis of all the Slavic peoples: "At the beginning of Slavic history, by some mysterious predestination, it fell to the same hands to scatter the same seeds across all the Slavic lands."[5] Back in the 1830s and 1840s, Pogodin had construed the Russian people's voluntary submission to an invited ruler as their most distinctive feature and contrasted it with the violent foundations of Western states whose populations were conquered by their kings.[6] Now he recast this construct in ethnoreligious terms: it was the spiritual birth, distinct from that of the Russian state, that he set alongside the bloody foundations of those European polities: "The Western European nations," he maintained, "consider their states to have been founded at sword point. We in the East must begin our history precisely with the apostolic activities of the immortal brothers."[7] Like the Varangian legend, this narrative of descent drew on the *Primary Chronicle* (which contains an account of Cyril and Methodius's mission) and thus enjoyed an aura of antiquity.[8] Yet, unlike the Varangian tale, it tracked the origins of the people only to find them in a place that had never belonged to Russia: Cyril and Methodius performed their apostolic work far from the territory of Kievan Rus' and more than a hundred years before its conversion to Christianity. Pogodin thus not only contrasted the people and the state but also implicitly justified Russians' right to absorb the land of their spiritual origin and thus expand their empire.

Since Russians could boast neither of a genealogical link with the saintly preceptors nor of their having preached on Russian soil, Pogodin resorted to religious ties and cultural affinity (as opposed to blood kinship) to connect Cyril and Methodius with the Russian people.[9] In this construct, Orthodoxy came to represent the main force that not only linked Russians with their putative "founding fathers" but also bound Slavs together across time and space. Though Pogodin seemed to be neglecting the Catholic, Protestant, and Muslim Slavs, in fact, he was adhering to the rather common view of Russian Pan-Slavists that the non-Orthodox groups among the Slavs—owing to either external pressure or internal squabbles—had only temporarily betrayed the legacy of their "immortal mentors" but would return to Orthodoxy, their timeless heritage, at some point in the future.[10]

Of course, it is not only Orthodoxy that binds the Slavs together. They also speak kindred tongues, a fact Pogodin by no means overlooked. But rather than treating their linguistic and confessional bonds as separate, he chose to tie them up in a single, neat package: as the common liturgical language of all Orthodox Slavs, Old Church Slavonic had influenced their vernaculars and inculcated shared religious assumptions, thus reinforcing the primordial linguistic unity of the Slavs.

This focus on the church-language issue allowed Pogodin, once again, to sharply distinguish the Slavs from other European nations. In the West, he asserted, indigenous culture and Christianity constitute two separate and potentially conflicting objects of allegiance, as reflected in the linguistic duality (i.e., the coexistence of vernacular languages and Latin). This duality alienates the common people from the church: "Catholics were long condemned, hearing, not to hear, and seeing, not to understand." In the Slavic lands, on the contrary, Cyril and Methodius "conveyed the Word of God to us in our own tongue" and therefore "we" have been hearing it all these thousand years.[11] In this construct, Pogodin blurred the line not only between the Slavic vernaculars but also between the vernaculars and Old Church Slavonic, presenting the latter—quite surprisingly—as a "native" language for all Slavs.

With linguistic truth thus conveniently stretched, Pogodin addressed—though not explicitly—reform-era developments that complicated the status of Church Slavonic. In 1858, after many years of disagreements within the Russian ecclesiastical hierarchy and between the government and the church, the Holy Synod set about translating the Bible into modern Russian.[12] The speedy completion of a New Testament in Russian (1862) triggered an increase in requests for a Ukrainian Bible. Such a project would, however, have been tantamount to a recognition of Ukrainian as a language separate from and equal to Russian—a direct assault on the notion of a single Russian nation that included Ukrainians, Russians, and Byelorussians.[13] But now, recast by Pogodin as both native and secular, Church Slavonic seemed immune to these challenging national realities: it could still represent "the basis of our [common Slavic] nationality, the anchor of our salvation, the token of our success."[14] Moreover, it could help to subsume under "our nationality" not only the East but the South and the West Slavs, thus eliminating the threat posed to Pan-Slavic unity by their rapidly developing literary languages. With this interpretation of Church Slavonic, one could render Orthodoxy the focus for a national identity that was deeply embedded in all Slavic cultures.

The missive *To the Slavs* partakes of a broader reform-era tendency to fuse the Slavophiles' people-centered vision of the nation with a glorification of Russians as empire builders.[15] Pogodin, who almost thirty years earlier had established the canonical form of the Varangian legend, now juxtaposed the two jubilees, not to repudiate the myth of the state's founding but to reconcile it with the story of the nation's spiritual birth and rethink the imperialist overtones of his earlier concept. Then he had rhetorically transformed Russia into a national empire, folding the nontitular nationalities into the myth of voluntary—and uniquely Russian—submission to a ruler. He thus erased the boundaries between various ethnic groups within the state, making them all equally submissive, all moving toward eventual convergence. Now he emphasized Russians' supremacy within the empire. He envisioned them as the "state-forming" people who would embrace other Slavs, restoring their primordial unity, and thus make Russia into a Slavic empire. Moreover, Pogodin managed to cast this project in the typical nineteenth-century language of irredentism (that is, gathering up ancestral territories seized by greedy neighbors), then widely used to justify the formation of nation-states. He longed for Russians to play the same role in the Slavic world that Piedmont had played in the recent unification of Italy or Prussia in the ongoing unification of Germany. "The face of Europe is being renewed," he observed. "Nations are coming to understand their needs. . . . Italy has almost achieved independence and is freeing itself from foreign influence. Divided Germany is seeking the means to unite." Only the Slavs, he lamented, remain scattered across many lands, as these centripetal processes passed them by.[16]

Although Pogodin constantly asserted that Pan-Slavism had no political agenda, he nonetheless interpreted the coincidence of the all-Slavic religious and Russian state millennia as a providential sign and a justification of the potential expansion of the Russian Empire into Slavic lands. In this way, Pogodin outlined the principal components of Russian Pan-Slavism: a conflation of national and religious identities and glorification of the Russian people's imperial vocation as the primary means of bringing salvation to all Slavs.

Pogodin's missive was part of an unfolding Pan-Slavic campaign. In May 1862 I. S. Aksakov published a report on the resumption—"after many centuries of neglect"—of "the religious observance commemorating the first saintly teachers of the Slavs." Initiated by a group of activists, the service reflected, for Aksakov, the awakening of "the Slavic idea" in the Russian public and a growing movement to restore the unity of the "scattered Slavic brothers." Aksakov approvingly quoted from the sermon preached on that occasion, reiterating Pogodin's view of Old Church Slavonic as the native language of all Slavs.[17] A few days after Pogodin's missive appeared, the linguist and folklorist A. F. Gil'ferding began to publish a series of "letters" in the newspaper *Den'* on the millennium of Slavic literacy. The commemoration of "our saintly teachers" will make clear, he declared, that "the brotherly unity of the Slavs, which had appeared faintly at the time of Cyril and Methodius, now after a thousand years is being renewed."[18] But in reemerging, Gil'ferding maintained, this unity was to assume a new shape. Since, with the fall of Constantinople to the Turks in the fifteenth century, Moscow had become the center of Orthodoxy, the Slavs should redirect their allegiances toward Russia: "For a Slav, wherever lies the center of his spiritual world, there, too, is his fatherland."[19] If the myth of spiritual descent sought to instill in Russians the belief that their origins lay beyond the borders of their state—in common Slavic historical and geographic space—then all the remaining Slavs were invited to see their futures beyond the limits of their lands. The gathering of representatives of all Slavic peoples in Moscow—the idea Pogodin proposed in his missive—now placed Russia at the center of the Pan-Slavic project.

The thought of celebrating the millennium of "Slavic enlightenment" won some attention in official Petersburg. The empress herself, influenced at the time by the Pan-Slavists, took an interest in it.[20] The ober-procurator of the Holy Synod, A. P. Akhmatov, submitted a request to Filaret (V. M.

Drozdov), the metropolitan of Moscow, "to inform her Highness of his opinion concerning the idea expressed by several people about holding in Russia a religious celebration for the prayerful remembrance of the preceptors of the Slavs."[21] Filaret's political acumen prompted him to block the project: "To have the celebration of a religious millennium and the celebration of a state millennium in one year, but in different months and days," he wrote, "would give the appearance of a certain awkwardness and disarray."[22] For Filaret, counterposing the two ceremonies implied a symbolic disjuncture of Orthodoxy and autocracy, two pillars of the doctrine of official nationality. He also opposed blurring the line between Russian history and that of the other Slavs and suggested that for Russians it would be more appropriate to commemorate events "belonging to the Russian church and the Russian people," like the baptism of Princess Ol'ga or of Prince Vladimir.[23] A clever prelate, Filaret discerned the danger concealed in the proposed commemoration: it represented a symbolic expansion of the boundaries of the Russian state and had the potential to subvert the ideological heritage of Nicholas I.

In Pan-Slavist circles, the project of the all-Slavic gathering in 1862 evoked doubts of another sort: controversy emerged over the dating of the saintly brothers' mission. While Pogodin and Gil'ferding accepted the year 862 as the date when work began on translating the liturgy into the newly created Slavic written language, other scholars pushed it back to 855.[24] Aksakov disappointed Pogodin: "It turns out," he averred, "that it is impossible to celebrate the millennium [of Slavic Orthodoxy], because it has already happened."[25] Aksakov went on searching for another date to commemorate and came up with the millennium of the arrival of the Slavic apostles in Moravia, which the Czechs planned to celebrate in 1863.[26] Yet it could not serve the purposes that animated Pogodin's missive: "They are perfectly within their rights to celebrate the occasion in Brno or Prague. This will be a purely *local* commemoration," Aksakov observed sadly, "not for us to direct."[27] In 1862 in Russia, the date Pogodin had planned to commemorate with other Slavs was marked only by a service in honor of Cyril and Methodius conducted in the chapel of Moscow University. As a correspondent for *Pravoslavnoe Obozrenie* (The Orthodox Review) reported, in the course of the service a canon taken from the ancient Mineia manuscript was read to the two saints and after the liturgy a prayer was said. "And so we remembered our enlighteners," reported the journal. "One wants to think that we [in Moscow] were not alone in remembering them, but others did as well, in various corners of Orthodox Russia."[28] The all-Slavic celebration was still waiting for a reason to happen.

The Ethnographic Exhibition:
Extending the Reach of Empire

A springboard for the revival of this project presented itself during preparations for the 1867 ethnographic exposition organized by the Society of Friends of Natural Science at Moscow University. With the aim of educating the public about Russia's variegated population, the organizers of the exhibition first focused only on the exotic peoples of the empire. As the project took shape, however, it came to include a Russian section, intended to show, as Nathaniel Knight has observed, the dominance of Russians over the state's multifarious inhabitants.[29] Ironically, an exhibition designed to showcase the dizzying ethnic diversity of the empire paved the way for a campaign that envisioned Russia's future in predominantly Slavic terms.

In 1865, while the plans for the exhibition were still being developed, the organizing committee endorsed a proposal by the historian N. A. Popov to add a section that would acquaint visitors with the West and South Slavs. These Slavic peoples, ran Popov's argument, provide a comparative perspective necessary for understanding Russians, and in any case some of them belong to the settled populations of the empire (he pointed to the Kingdom of Poland and the Bulgarian and Serbian communities within Russia).[30] All at once, as the Slavophile newspaper *Moskva* (Moscow) later recounted, huge numbers of private individuals began to donate Slavic exhibits, demonstrating "the unanimous sympathy with which Russian society greeted this fortuitous idea."[31] Then materials started arriving from Slavs abroad, thanks to the enthusiastic assistance of a wide group of Pan-Slavists.[32] "In this way," concluded *Moskva*, "our Russian exhibition becomes Russo-Slavic, the more so since the subject nationalities [*inorodtsy*] will be presented in it as secondary and subordinate tribes."[33] It was precisely this aggressive Slavic ethnocentrism that inspired Popov to suggest making the Slavic section the second in importance after the Russian one.[34]

Though the ethnic diversity of the empire remained the exposition's guiding theme, the Slavic section took up a disproportionate share of the exhibit space. The West and South Slavs were represented by 63 mannequins in authentic dress and surrounded by household objects, while all the non-Slavic peoples of Russia taken together claimed 114 mannequins.[35] Thus, the "all-Russian exposition" not only reached out to the West and South Slavs; it granted them a prominent place in the visual representation of Russia, thereby expanding the empire's imagined geographical contours.

To dramatize Russia's symbolic remapping, the exhibition's organizers enacted Pogodin's 1862 project, inviting scholars, journalists, poets, and political activists from various Slavic lands to attend the Moscow exposition.[36] In early May 1867, eighty-one guests—Czechs, Serbs, Croats, Slovaks, Slovenes, Montenegrins, Bulgarians, and Kashubians (in view of the bloody suppression of the January uprising, the Poles declined the invitation)—came to Russia to set in motion what soon became known as the Slavic Congress. Despite this resounding name, the event took the form of what Sergei Nikitin has called "a rather disorderly exchange of speeches and greetings," held initially in the provinces along the delegates' route and later culminating in a series of gatherings in Petersburg and Moscow.[37] With their arrival, discussions about the Slavs' collective future and Russia's historical mission eclipsed the exposition's educational goals. The congress posed the questions: In what direction should Russia develop? With whom should it ally itself? An unequivocal answer emerged from the contrast between the dead exhibits—the mute and immobile mannequins representing the multiethnic inhabitants of the empire—and the flesh-and-blood Slavic guests, who turned the congress into a living, breathing spectacle that occupied the front pages of the major newspapers for several weeks.

The daily press devoured the array of sumptuous receptions, festive assemblies, mass meetings, and excursions (to libraries, cathedrals, and convocations of learned societies) held for the guests in both Petersburg and Moscow. Even newspapers that were not partisans of Pan-Slavism—*Golos* (The Voice) and *Russkii invalid*—amiably and in many cases ecstatically reported the entire campaign. Moreover, rival groups of intellectuals participated in the congress and in some respects found themselves in agreement, albeit temporarily. Apart from Pogodin, Tiutchev, Aksakov, Popov, and many other Pan-Slavists, the delegates were addressed by the historian S. M. Solov'ev, the journalist M. N. Katkov, the minister for education D. A. Tolstoi (none of whom fully subscribed to Pan-Slavism), and by many others, including scientists and poets.

Several factors contributed to this wide support for the congress. As a project conceived and implemented by leaders of educated society, it embodied the spirit of public activism awakened at the dawn of the reform era. The congress, however, took place at a moment when that spirit seemed to be faltering. After Karakozov's attempt to assassinate Alexander II (1866), the authorities took a reactionary turn. In the new political climate, the Slavic campaign drew overwhelming attention from a public that seemed to sense its last opportunities for exprsssion draining away. Another reason for the congress's enthusiastic reception stemmed from the desire to regain a sense of Russia's historical mission. The familiar image of Russia as the sole protector of oppressed Slavs and Orthodox Christians ideally satisfied this longing, felt ever more keenly after the disastrous defeat in the Crimean War.[38] The hosts of the festivities desperately wanted to hear their guests acknowledge Russia's unique role—and ascribed deep political meaning to pronouncements like the one made by an Austrian Serb, the jurist and politician Mihajlo Polit-Desančić: "Russia does not belong to Russians alone."[39] In other words, Pan-Slavist expansionism arose not simply out of a hunger to control foreign lands but also from a desire to restore Russia's sense of national destiny and the country's prestige vis-à-vis the West.[40] Finally, the congress seemed to resolve problems that the exhibition could not. As Nathaniel Knight has shown, the representation of Russians at the exhibition provoked profound critiques from the press: contrary to its own design, the exposition did not succeed in presenting the Russians as superior to other nationalities within the empire.[41] Press coverage of the congress compensated for this failure. As we shall see, the Russians' imperial mission and the role of Moscow as the spiritual center of the Slavic world became the congress's main themes.

The Slavic Congress:
Reenacting the Past and Projecting the Future

Although newspaper accounts acknowledged the spontaneous nature of the congress, the symbolism of many of the meetings and receptions was thoroughly thought out in advance. On the very eve of the gathering, Pogodin called upon its organizers—or rather drew public attention to a preexisting plan—to arrange each event "so that every detail [had] its significance, so that meaning, feeling, and history [were] to be seen in everything."[42] The newspaper accounts not only highlighted the "meaning and history" inscribed in the events, but also smoothed rough edges, excised undesirable statements, and put forward those speeches and slogans that resonated best with the journalists' own views. For this reason, the daily press accounts discussed here present not the ambiguous character of the real Slavic Congress, where the interests of different groups diverged and sometimes clashed, but rather the way it was conceived, perceived, and presented by the intellectual elite.[43] Although various periodicals supported different political programs and thus did not follow a single discursive strategy in reporting the gathering, they nonetheless concurred on some points.

The myth of the Slavs' common descent served as an overarching theme in coverage of the congress. Many newspaper accounts presented the convergence of delegates as a metonym for the past unity of all Slavic peoples. "For the first time since the very beginning of our history . . . ," declared *Moskovskie vedomosti*, "the brothers, so many long years scattered by ill fortune, have finally come together."[44] In his newspaper *Russkii* (The Russian), Pogodin published an anonymous poem, purportedly sent from the Trinity Monastery, which portrayed the congress as a family reunion following a thousand years of separation:

> Na zemliakh slavian zaria gorit,
> Se Zhenikh griadet vo polunoshchi.
> "Edem, brat'ia, na Sviatuiu Rus',
> Povidaem bogatyr'-brat'ev . . ."
> Pozdno vecherom ne spit Moskva,
> Brat'ia krovnye beseduiut . . .
> Tysiachu let my ne vidalis'.

> [Dawn burns in the Slav lands,
> Lo, the bridegroom at midnight approaches.
> "Let us ride, brothers, to Holy Rus',
> "To visit our heroic brothers . . ."
> Late at night Moscow does not sleep,
> Blood brothers converse . . .
> A thousand years we've not seen one another.][45]

The key line of the poem—"The Bridegroom at midnight approaches"— is a direct quotation from the New Testament (*Matt.* 25:1–13) sung in

Orthodox liturgical services during Holy Week. Given that the Bridegroom is a metaphor for Christ who comes to reward the righteous with eternal life, the religious subtext of the poem makes it possible to transform the anticipated all-Slavic reunion into a fulfillment of the divine plan of salvation.

Newspapers capitalized on religious bonds between the Slavs and downplayed their confessional differences in order to highlight their common spiritual descent—a relatively easy task, given that, with the Poles' absence from the congress, Orthodox delegates far outnumbered the Protestant and Catholic ones. Before the guests had even reached Moscow, in a sermon given in the chapel of Moscow University on May 11, the Orthodox day of devotion for Cyril and Methodius, the priest N. A. Sergievskii cast the Slavic gathering as the fulfillment of a covenant with their saintly preceptors. Recalling the relic of the "incorruptible hand" of St. Cyril brought by Pogodin from Prague to Moscow in 1855, the priest asserted: "[The saint's finger] shows our brothers the way to us and guides both them and us to a single, true and life-giving union."[46] He thus rehearsed the references to Cyril's prophetic hand that were already circulating in the press in 1862, when Pogodin first proposed the gathering.[47]

On this same Cyril and Methodius Day, with the majority of guests assembled in Petersburg, the congress's organizers arranged its first full-scale ceremony celebrating the Slavs' spiritual and linguistic bonds. In the morning, the delegates attended liturgy in St. Isaac's Cathedral and then took part in a festive dinner at the Noble Assembly. They exchanged speeches beneath a "marvelous white and gold banner [khorugv']" that bore the images of Cyril and Methodius and "the Savior, blessing them in their apostolic deeds."[48] A second banner emblazoned with the words "The Slavic and Russian languages are one" hung above the khorugv'. "The truth of this motto," Moskovskie vedomosti observed, "was made evident at the feast itself," where guests and hosts conversed easily with one another.[49] Russkii invalid also claimed that orators from the various lands need only speak clearly and slowly in their own tongues and no interpreters would be necessary.[50]

For the organizers of the congress, Russian was to be the lingua franca of the Slavic world. "Our brothers," proclaimed Pogodin, "who say the Lord's Prayer [Otche nash] almost as we do," will realize of their own accord that "the Slavs need a common language."[51] Of course, the hosts of the gathering asserted that this role should fall to the Russian language. As the first step toward this goal, they suggested that the Cyrillic alphabet be used by all Slavs without exception.[52] Russian nationalists saw in this project a potential counterweight to the Austrian government's attempts to introduce the Latin alphabet in Galicia among the Ruthenians.[53] "The idea of a common Slavic alphabet and orthography is not at all an empty utopia, as it might at first glance seem," wrote N. A. Popov in 1865, claiming that the Croats were inclined to mark "the millennial celebration of Cyril and Methodius . . . by adopting Cyrillic."[54] One month prior to the guests' arrival in Moscow, Pogodin published a letter from the Czech scholar František Jezbera, who called on the Slavs to embrace the Cyrillic alphabet.[55] The campaign for Cyrillization of the Slavs unfolded rapidly and assumed very articulate form on the eve of the congress.

The program of linguistic unification implied political union. The menu for the Noble Assembly's festive dinner—"a work of art rather than a bill of fare" (as one of the reporters observed)—made these aspirations visible.[56] Executed by the artist M. O. Mikeshin (according to the design of the historian S. N. Palauzov, a Pan-Slavist of Bulgarian descent), it depicts joyfully converging Slavs. From one side a Russian peasant advances to offer bread and salt to his Slavic brethren. Behind him three other hosts, one of them recognizably Ukrainian, wave their hats in the air. The guests in their various national costumes come forward to meet them. It is symbolic that the Slavs converge in front of a church circled by the inscription "Christ is risen." The image suggests a parallel between the Savior's resurrection and the Slavic resurgence. Cyril and Methodius appear on the church's dome, which is made to look like a gate and thus symbolizes the threshold of the sacred the Slavs have collectively entered. The saintly preceptors tower over a rudimentary map of Russia and Europe affixed to the front of the church. The map outlines all the Slavic lands in a way that suggests their continuity with Russia. To the right and the left of the map, as though inscribed on the walls of the church, appear the names of prominent Slavic writers, scholars, and political activists. And as if to give voice to their common desire, the slogan "May the same sun warm us" crowns the tableau. Famous landmarks from important historical centers—Moscow, Kiev, Vyšehrad, and Constantinople (the latter, in accordance with Russian tradition, called Tsar'grad)—and the coats of arms of various Slavic cities surround the church and the Slavs who converge in front of it (fig. 10).[57] During the dinner, newspapers reported, at the hall of the Noble Assembly, the flags and

Figure 10. Menu for the festive dinner to honor Slavic Congress participants, held in the hall of the Petersburg Noble Assembly, May 11, 1867. Executed by the artist M. O. Mikeshin according to a design by the historian S. N. Palauzov. (Fedor Tiutchev State Museum, Muranovo, inv. no. KP-3924)

mottos of the Slavic lands were hung along both sides of the main banner. Pennants representing "significant years" in Russian history were interspersed with shields depicting the heroes and historical figures of the various Slavic peoples.[58] The design of the dinner thus wove the pasts of the Russian and other Slavic peoples into a single historical narrative, at whose beginning stood Cyril and Methodius.

The *khorugv'* portraying the saintly preceptors traveled with the guests from Petersburg to Moscow, serving as the fixed center of the congress's symbolic space. At the banquet at Sokol'niki, the main Moscow feast, it was placed in the pavilion where the delegates gathered and became a point of reference for many addresses.[59] After the dinner, it was ceremoniously taken outside and paraded before a huge crowd of Muscovites who had gathered to greet the Slavic guests. For journalists, this moment was emblematic of the Slavs' religious ties: "That sea of humanity covering the entire slope from the pavilion to Sokol'nich'ia Grove fell silent for a moment before the holy symbol of Slavic unity. Everyone bared his head in the presence of the *khorugv'* carried by one of the Slavic delegates, an Orthodox priest."[60] Katkov also depicted this scene as the emotional culmination of the entire congress, but in his account it was all the guests together who carried the *khorugv'* out of the pavilion "to give salutations to Moscow and to the Russian people . . . on behalf of their distant homelands." This spontaneous exchange of greetings produced, he claimed, "an astonishing effect," expressing the meaning of the Slavs' gathering "better than any speech. . . . Here, in this place, first stirred the breath of a new, broader life, wafting over Moscow, which up to then had been stagnating in its estrangement from the rest of the world."[61] For Katkov, the congress marked Russia's joining in the march of nationalism then progressing across Europe. Nor was Katkov alone in this understanding of the proceedings. A few months before the congress, Aksakov stated, employing the term *tribes* for *nationalities* (a conventional usage at that time): "A kind of centripetal movement has taken hold of Europe. All the scattered fragments of tribes are gathering around a single tribal focus, like sheep in a single herd, and are seeking to express their shared tribal individuality in the form of political unity."[62] At the banquet at Sokol'niki, he proclaimed that the Slavs, too, were now crossing this threshold: "Here begins a new period, a new epoch in the history of Slavdom."[63] Thus, the main message of Pogodin's 1862 missive grew into a program of Russian nationalism.

Some newspaper accounts of the congress explicitly presented the convergence of the Slavic delegates in Petersburg and Moscow as a sign of an impending change in the political map of Europe, one that would remake Russia as a Slavic state in direct competition with the imperial ambitions of its neighbors. *Russkii invalid* reported that the Czech and Serbian delegates from Austro-Hungary had valiantly overcome all obstacles placed in their paths by their government. The article concluded by predicting similar success for the entire centripetal movement of the Slavs: "Barricades on the road to Moscow will be of no avail. . . . Historical truth is sacred and inviolable!"[64] Pogodin expressed this idea in a still more metaphoric way: "Distance must bow to the power of kinship."[65] The scientist G. E. Shchurovskii, president of the Society of Friends of Natural Science, also reiterated this formula greeting the guests.[66]

The organizers of the congress used the location of the main festivities to display their political project in the most dramatic possible light. Prior to the guests' arrival, Pogodin announced that he had grown disillusioned with the long-cherished dream of Constantinople as capital of Slavdom and would from now on assign that role to Moscow.[67] Some weeks later he described the delegates' trip as a spiritual pilgrimage: "Moscow has become the pantheon of the Slavic world. The Slavs are coming here to venerate [the ancient city]."[68] As Aksakov claimed, Russia's old capital would become both the political center and "the focus of moral energy for all of Slavdom."[69] The Russians' thirst for political domination became so obvious at the congress that the Czech delegation felt the need to assert its right to an independent future and demand that the Russians repent their brutal suppression of the Polish uprising.[70]

In their cultural Russocentrism, territorial expansionism, and pretensions to political hegemony, the hosts of the gathering were neither more creative nor more aggressive than other European nationalists of their day. The Pan-Slavist program was in perfect accord with Western liberals' understanding of nationalism in the middle of the nineteenth century. In the words of Eric Hobsbawm, "national movements were expected to be movements for national *unification* or expansion," undertaken only by "state nationalities" capable of absorbing smaller communities, which otherwise were seen as doomed to extinction.[71] This ideology justified the unification of Germany and of Italy and inspired the Russian thinkers. Rather than merely serving as a pretext for imperial conquest, the Pan-Slavic project thus testified to Russians' membership in the club of "chosen" nations and their ability to secure a place in the future world for themselves and for other Slavs, on condition that they unite under the aegis of Russia.

Moreover, since only "state nationalities" could claim a place in the circle of nations, this project legitimized the existing Russian Empire on nationalist terms and justified the violence that had accompanied its growth. During the congress, Katkov glorified the use of force quite bluntly: "The history of Moscow is a harsh history. . . . The policies of the Muscovite state were pitiless and cruel. . . . But were it not for that harsh past, where would the Slavic world be now and what would have become of the Slavic cause?"[72] As the leader of the Petersburg Pan-Slavists, Professor V. I. Lamanskii proclaimed in his speech at the congress, it was "the military triumphs of the Russian *bogatyr'*, who has built himself the largest state in the world," that guaranteed the safety of the Slavs.[73]

The congress played out against the backdrop of two unfolding developments that, Russian thinkers believed, posed new challenges for the Slavs. Prussia's stunning victory in the Seven Week War with Austria (1866) demonstrated the Germans' growing power and expansionist ambitions and seemed to place the very existence of their Slavic neighbors in jeopardy. The war led to radical administrative reforms in Austria that further weakened the position of the country's Slavic subjects. In February 1867 Emperor Franz Josef came to terms with the Magyars' aspirations and agreed to grant Hungary internal autonomy within the Hapsburg Empire, henceforth to be known as Austro-Hungary. This change excluded the Austrian Slavs from the national compromise and was perceived as detrimental to them.[74] The congress's participants referred indignantly to the notorious dictum of Friedrich Ferdinand von Beust, Prime Minister of the Hapsburg Empire, who, seriously concerned about Pan-Slavism, proclaimed: "The Slavs must be cornered."[75] The necessity of defending the entire Slavic world against a perceived external threat made a powerful, centralized Russian state indispensable and provided a moral justification for Russian hegemony.

Just as they had during the Polish uprising, newspaper accounts of the congress emphasized the solidarity of the Russian people across classes as they expressed their empathy with the Slavic guests. In Moscow, Pogodin reported, despite the inclement weather, "crowds from all social strata" gathered at the train station to greet the deputies. "All the Russian people transmit their feelings to one another as though they were joined by an electrical wire."[76] A correspondent for *Russkii invalid* took as the center-piece of one of his reports the admiring words of a guest who observed that "from the general to the villager, everyone in Russia greeted the delegates cordially."[77] Once again, like memories of popular war in 1863, the myth of Slavic unity transformed the tsar into the national leader. Report-ers repeated the words of František Rieger, one of the leading Czech politi-cians, who dared to call Alexander II "not only a great ruler, but also a noble Slav."[78] Although the guests' fulsome praises were clearly aimed at winning the tsar's support in the international arena, the Russian press exploited this rhetoric to present him as the natural defender of the Slavic cause. For Pogodin, the congress revealed that Alexander II shared "the thoughts and feelings" of the entire Russian people, "down to the very humblest."[79]

Alexander II himself, though very cautiously, encouraged such inter-pretations. The tsar and members of the imperial family granted audiences to some of the delegates, while Prince A. M. Gorchakov, the minister of foreign affairs, received others. Nationalist writers took this encouragement from above as a sign of the tsar's willingness to explicitly identify the government with the Russian nationality. The belletrist and chamberlain B. M. Markevich, Katkov's informant on the atmosphere inside the Winter Palace, hastened to report to the editor of *Moskovskie vedomosti* how gra-ciously and enthusiastically Alexander had greeted his guests. For Marke-vich, it was a confirmation of the tsar's "true and truly Russian instincts," not yet corrupted by "various German and Polish influences." Markevich was thrilled to inform Katkov (relying on Tiutchev's account of the event) how Alexander had expressed his wishes concerning the public reception of the Slavs: "The more boisterous it is, the happier I will be."[80] The words the tsar spoke on parting with his guests (not "farewell" but "until we meet again") were interpreted as a promise that Russia would protect the Slavs.[81] The Slavophile writer General A. A. Kireev in his diary excitedly called the congress "a manifestation of national life," which evoked "the same feelings as reading an epic poem." For him the expected turn in national policy was signaled both by the tsar's audience with the Slavs and by the fact that on the day of the meeting Gorchakov allegedly rebuked high-ranking officials from the ministry of foreign affairs who criticized Katkov's advocacy of turning Russia into a national empire.[82] It was in this circle of influential Pan-Slavists and leading journalists that the idea of founding a Western Slavic empire under Russia's aegis developed during the congress.[83]

To project Russia's future with regard to the Slavs, the organizers and observers of the congress employed two different—and at first glance mutually incompatible—strategies. On the one hand, they sought to fit Russia into the paradigm of national unification exemplified by Germany and Italy. They thus declared Russia fundamentally different from other empires and therefore immune to the processes of disintegration already well under way in its two neighboring rivals, the Hapsburg and Ottoman empires. On the other hand, coverage of the congress maintained an imperial tone: the journalists envisioned a future Russia as a Slavic empire peopled by a variety of ethnic groups, predominantly Slavs, and led by Russians. Throughout the festivities, the press emphasized the multiplicity of cultures to be found within the Slavic world. The ethnographic exhibition that gave rise to the congress offered journalists a rich trove of material to draw on in portraying the Slavs' vibrant range of experiences and traditions. The colorful menu for the Petersburg dinner discussed earlier depicted the Slavs in authentic national dress. Newspapers reported the "picturesque national costumes" of the Montenegrins.[84] Though the other guests disappointed the organizers by attending the celebration in European dress, the idea of cultural diversity figured prominently at the congress as both Russia's defining quality and a token of its viability.

These two visions of Russia reflect the double-edged nature of empire as it appears in the Pan-Slavists' project: for them, the empire is at once an instrument and a goal. It serves as a precondition to and a tool for the Slavs' survival and for Russia's advancement in a world of expanding nations. At the same time, it is an unfolding project geared toward reasserting Russians' imperial impulse and confirming their right to dominate other nationalities. By broadening the Slavic core of the Romanov empire, Russians would alter its ethnic composition in order to give it a more national character, but this transformation by no means implies that the ethnic differences are fated to fade away or that Russians would ultimately cease to rule over the other groups. The imperial mission of the Russian people is once again inscribed into the national mythology. Russia's recovery of its spiritual birthplace offers the nation what Anthony Smith has called "conditional salvation": revival of the saintly preceptors' legacy promises all Slavs "collective sanctification" and long-term survival, while guaranteeing Russians the leading role in the empire.[85]

Pan-Slavism versus Pan-Orthodoxy:
The Impact of the Greek–Bulgarian Church Schism
on Russian Self-Perception

It was precisely the fusion of the imperial, national, and religious aspects of Russian national identity that allowed the Pan-Slavists to distinguish the Slavic future from that of other European nations, which were understood to be profoundly alienated from the sacred. Tiutchev made this disparity into the main theme and structural principle of his poem "The Two Unions" (1870) ("Dva edinstva"). While calling Bismarck's Germany "a union bonded by iron and blood" (a reference to Bismarck's own words), the poet contrasts it with the emerging Slavic union, governed by the Christian imperative:

> No my poprobuem spaiat' ego [edinstvo] liubov'iu—
> A tam uvidim, chto prochnei.
>
> [But we will attempt to bond ours with love—
> And we shall see which is the more lasting.][86]

Though, from the inception of their project, the Pan-Slavists had conflated secular and religious visions of the nation, towards the 1870s, when national movements began to develop in the Balkans, Russian thinkers found themselves confronted with the necessity of decoupling these two aspects of national identity. The Greek–Bulgarian church schism (1872) posed a particular challenge in this regard. As we shall see, this seemingly arcane issue prompted Russian thinkers to question their own national self-perception, that is, the synthesis of the imperial, the national, and the religious, which had looked so plausible at the Slavic Congress.[87]

To understand the nature of the Greek–Bulgarian conflict, we need a glimpse at its origins. In the fourteenth century, with the decline of the Byzantine Empire, the Bulgarians emerged from ecclesiastical subordination to their religious mentors—the "Greeks," or, to be more precise, the patriarchate of Constantinople—and established an independent, or autocephalous, national church. This was part of a broader process typical of the period: around the same time, the Serbs freed themselves from the control of Constantinople, and the Russians followed suit later. In the fifteenth century, however, as a result of the Turkish conquest of the Balkans and the fall of Constantinople, the Bulgarians lost not only their political but also their ecclesiastical independence.[88] The Turks compelled them to return to the jurisdiction of the patriarch of Constantinople, since the Ottoman Empire regulated the civil and religious life of its subject nationalities through a single—centralized and relatively autonomous—administrative body established for each confession.[89] This centuries-old pattern of administration proved increasingly untenable with the rise of national movements across the Balkans in the nineteenth century. The division of the population along religious lines came into conflict with the various peoples' growing ethnic aspirations—and autocephalous churches began to reemerge in Southern and Eastern Europe (first in the Greek Kingdom, then in the Principality of Serbia and Romania).[90]

Throughout the nineteenth century, the Bulgarians, like their neighbors, struggled to achieve ecclesiastical autonomy, at least in part. The Constantinople patriarchate, as the Bulgarians constantly complained, was stifling its Slavic flock and filling the church administration with Greek hierarchs. The "Greeks" levied discriminatory taxes against the Slavs, appointed priests of Greek origin, and conducted liturgical services in Greek in dioceses with largely Bulgarian populations. In their attempts to promote their native culture through education and publishing, the Bulgarians were also dependent on Constantinople, since the Porte authorized the patriarchate to regulate the secular affairs of all Orthodox subjects of the Ottoman Empire. The Bulgarians accused the patriarchs—all of them ethnic Greeks—of using their power to Hellenize the Slavic population. The head of the Orthodox church was seen by the Bulgarians to be as much an obstacle to the development of their nation as was the Porte.[91]

Almost everywhere in Southern and Eastern Europe, the church question boiled down to a question of nationhood, but the Bulgarian case was peculiar. While establishment of a national church generally followed the attainment of either internal political autonomy or outright independence, in Bulgaria it worked the other way around: the Bulgarians declared their church autocephalous *before* being recognized as a separate political entity.[92] They quite openly turned their crusade for ecclesiastical freedom into a weapon in their struggle for political freedom—a maneuver clearly understood by all parties involved. In 1867, when Patriarch Gregorios VI proposed a compromise that he hoped would satisfy the Bulgarians' demands, he told Count N. P. Ignatiev, Russian ambassador to the Ottoman

Empire: "I have built with my own hands a bridge to the political independence of the Bulgarians."[93] The compromise, however, did not accommodate the Bulgarians' aspirations and did not work out.

Although the Turks harbored no illusions about the political nature of the Bulgarian church question, in 1870 the Porte, resorting to the perennial tactic of "divide and rule," authorized the establishment of a Bulgarian exarchate over the patriarchate's objections. On May 11, 1872, the feast of Cyril and Methodius, the first Bulgarian exarch celebrated the liturgy in the Bulgarian church in Istanbul and afterward read an act that proclaimed the independence of the exarchate. This step brought the Bulgarians to an open break with the patriarchal throne. In response to these events, Patriarch Anthemos (the successor of Gregorios VI) summoned a local church council, attended by the heads of the churches of Antioch, Alexandria, and Jerusalem. They declared the hierarchy and laity of the autocephalous Bulgarian church "schismatic."[94]

The Russian press followed the Greek–Bulgarian church controversy with rapt attention. While the Holy Synod—and the Russian government as a whole—refrained from interfering in the conflict and did not openly choose sides, the majority of the Russian public praised the Bulgarians and celebrated their ecclesiastical autonomy.[95] In 1862, in Pogodin's missive to the Slavs, the Bulgarians had figured as defenseless victims, deprived of the right to pray in their native tongue and therefore doomed to near-certain extinction.[96] In 1873, thrilled by the establishment of the exarchate, Pogodin welcomed it as a sign of Bulgarian—and, by extension, Slavic—national resurrection.[97] Many Russian intellectuals delighted in pointing out how a populous Slavic nation was rising to prominence.[98] As Katkov enthusiastically stated in 1871, "after centuries of darkness," when the Bulgarians were mistakenly lumped in with the Greeks, "the government of the Ottoman Empire finally recognized the Bulgarians as a distinct people."[99] Slavic nationality now became a visible reality in a place where it had previously been obscured.

For the Russian public, however, this conflict was not merely a thrilling spectacle. The break between the Greeks and the Bulgarians became a testing ground for Russian attitudes towards the religion-nation nexus. Accustomed to playing the role of protector of all the Orthodox peoples under the Ottoman "yoke," without regard to ethnicity, now, with the independent Bulgarian church declared schismatic, Russians were faced with the need to take sides among their quarreling coreligionists. The decision proved so momentous that the philosopher, diplomat, and novelist Konstantin Leont'ev proclaimed: "Because of the Bulgarians, we [Russians] come to a Rubicon."[100] In this forced choice between the Greeks and the Bulgarians, the Russians confronted a dilemma that had the potential to undermine the basic precept of their national self-understanding: the conflation of Orthodoxy and nationality.

At the time of the Crimean War, in an article arguing that Russia must come to the aid of Christians suffering under Ottoman rule, Aleksei Khomiakov presented Orthodoxy and nationality in terms of the Russians' twofold links with the Orthodox inhabitants of the Balkans: "The Russian people are bound by ties of blood to the Slavic peoples and by ties of faith to the Greeks. These are such ties as we can never forget or reject."[101] Khomiakov declared the two types of connection crucial and inseparable in determining Russia's future, and established a firm hierarchy among them. "From now on, two great principles are on the rise: the first, the Russian or rather Slavic principle of true fraternity of blood and spirit; the second, incomparably higher, the principle of the church—under whose sheltering wings that brotherhood is preserved in the midst of a world of strife and discord."[102] In the reform era, however, contrary to Khomiakov's predictions, the intellectual elite found itself obligated to choose between the two aspects of Russian national identity, a decision encapsulated in the need to side either with the Bulgarians or with the Greeks.

As clashes between the adversaries intensified, it was Khomiakov himself who openly condemned the "Greeks." In his missive to the Serbs (1860), he stated: "The starkest example of spiritual pride is to be found not in Rome . . . but among the present-day Greeks." By praising themselves as "God's only chosen people," the Greeks—he meant the Constantinople patriarchate, rather than the nation—depart from the true Orthodox legacy of universalism, proclaimed Khomiakov.[103] Though in this missive he did not contrast "the principle of the church" with that of nationality, he did discuss the bitter political reality in which the former proved incompatible with the latter. The dilemma assumed such a sharp form that in 1864 Pogodin began a campaign to detach Cyril and Methodius from their Greek identity: "What were Saints Cyril and Methodius—Slavs or Greeks? . . . These days, in this epoch of rising national consciousness, the question assumes a new importance. We would very much like to place the icons of these two great figures in the temple of Slavic history."[104] Though this campaign elicited no wide support from either the public or academics, it is a salient example of how ethnic sentiments came to outweigh religious ties.[105]

The Greek–Bulgarian problem would bedevil—and divide—the Russians for years. In 1873, when Dostoevsky, then editor of the newspaper *Grazhdanin* (The Citizen), received Pogodin's article in support of the Bulgarians, he flatly refused to publish it. Explaining the rationale for his rejection, Dostoevsky firmly asserted the preeminence of spiritual ties over ethnic ones: "From the canonical or, it is better to say, the religious point of view, I find the Greeks to be correct. One should not *distort* Christianity even for the noblest of goals. In other words, one should not consider Orthodoxy . . . a secondary matter."[106] This divergence in the views of two prominent Pan-Slavists points to a larger rift among Russian intellectuals.

The majority of them, particularly the Pan-Slavists, for whom the rebirth of the Bulgarian people was a cherished dream, not only sided with the Bulgarians but also lauded their autocephalous church as a historic achievement: "Ever since the Bulgarian national consciousness was awakened," observed Ivan Aksakov, "the Bulgarians started to struggle for their own church heads, for their own exarchate, for their own schools—to free themselves from the spiritual yoke of the Greeks or, to put it more precisely, from the yoke of the patriarchate."[107] Katkov also praised the Bulgarians, and for him the schism posed no conundrum, given his inclination to downplay the religious aspect of national identity: "We call this issue the Greek–Bulgarian church conflict, but strictly speaking, the church aspect here is just a pretext. . . . It is the principle of nationality that dominates our age," he pronounced ecstatically. "It is to be found at the bottom of every current problem. It is now the driving force behind each historical event. Now national movements create and destroy powerful states."[108] Yet an increasingly vocal group of Russian thinkers began to criticize the Bulgarians for violating church canon and repudiating ecclesiastical unity, a tendency that, they believed, held the potential to undermine the ecumenical orientation of the Orthodox church. In addition to Dostoevsky, two other prominent thinkers forcefully supported this alternative position: Konstantin Leont'ev, cited earlier, and Tertii Filippov, a folklorist, writer, and influential statesman.[109] To the indignation of many Pan-Slavists, they both acknowledged and accepted the patriarch's decision to proclaim the Bulgarians schismatic. Filippov and Leont'ev were most vehement in condemning the idea of gaining national freedom at the expense of ecclesiastical unity.

This is not to say that this second group approved of the Hellenization of the Slavic population in the Balkans. Four years after rejecting Pogodin's article, Dostoevsky envisioned a future Russian conquest of Constantinople in his *Diary of a Writer*. The picture he drew of the Greek–Slavic relations that would develop under such circumstances makes it clear that Dostoevsky regarded the Greeks' national ambitions as a source of endless tension in the Orthodox world: "The Greeks will look upon the new Slavic elements in Constantinople jealously and hate and fear the Slavs more intensely than they ever did the Mohammedans. The recent controversy between the Bulgarians and the patriarchal throne may serve as an example of the future."[110] There is no contradiction between this quotation and Dostoevsky's previous opinion. In the letter to Pogodin, he praised the Greeks as guardians of ecclesiastical tradition. In *Diary of a Writer*, he excoriated them as a people whose national interests prevailed over religious ones. In both quotations, Dostoevsky was speaking of the "Greeks," but in the first case, he took the Greeks as advocates of church unity, in the second as cunning politicians who used the authority of the Constantinople patriarchate to implement their own national project. In both of Dostoevsky's statements, there is a juxtaposition of national and religious goals, with the latter always taking precedence. In Dostoevsky's view, Orthodoxy constitutes the defining principle of Russian national identity and the most powerful unifying force of the empire. Only Russia could capture and control Constantinople, he believed, and the nation would defend the true dogma of the faith and unite all the Orthodox nationalities under its aegis, regardless of ethnicity. In this way, Russia would fulfill the role of supranational ecumenical center that the Greeks had betrayed.[111] With his censure of the Bulgarians in their dispute with the patriarchate, Dostoevsky in essence criticized the intrusion of nationalism into the sphere of religion. He sought to justify the Russian Empire as the only true bearer of the Orthodox church's universalist orientation, a position Russia could not compromise even to support its Slavic brothers.

Dostoevsky's views overlapped in part with those of Leont'ev, who devoted several articles to the Greek–Bulgarian quarrel. Leont'ev was among the first Russian thinkers to publicly break with the Pan-Slavists by denouncing the independent Bulgarian church. In the 1860s and 1870s he dealt with this issue in real life, working in the Russian embassy to the Ottoman Empire (where he opposed the diplomacy of Ambassador Ignatiev, who supported the Bulgarians). At the very beginning of the 1870s Leont'ev predicted that the Bulgarians would rebel against Russian authority if the Russian Empire continued to protect them. Furthermore, in his famous book *Byzantinism and Slavdom* (1875), Leont'ev introduced into popular usage a new image of the Bulgarians—new in comparison with the stereotype created by the Pan-Slavists and widely accepted in Russia. Instead of depicting the Bulgarians as a people insulted, humiliated, and suffering under the double pressure of the political and the ecclesiastical "yoke," Leont'ev presented them as heavily influenced by the Greeks and driven by the same harsh "tribal" nationalism that led the Greeks to suppress them. The Bulgarians, he asserted, were simply mimicking Western European national movements, with their subversive and egalitarian implications. "The face of this nation is excessively democratic," Leont'ev wrote disapprovingly, and "its habits and ideals are excessively emancipatory."[112] Fearing that this liberal contagion might spread to Russia and contribute to its disintegration, he ultimately rejected the idea of Slavic unity.

Dostoevsky, Leont'ev, and Filippov understood that to side with the Bulgarians in their struggle against Orthodox authority was quite different than supporting the Bulgarians in their struggle against the Ottomans. If the Russians were to choose in favor of the Bulgarians in their clash with the patriarchate, it would mean that the Russians approved of breaking ecclesiastical law in the name of national aspirations. But such a position would subordinate faith to ethnicity and therefore undermine the conflation of Orthodoxy and nationality as a defining principle of Russian national self-understanding. Moreover, such a position would endorse the division of the Orthodox world along ethnic lines and therefore call into question the integrity of the Romanov empire: it would run counter to the imperial policies employed inside Russia with regard to its ethnically diverse Orthodox population.[113] Finally, this approach would render religious ties secondary to ethnic ones in the nation-making process and thus weaken the territorial claims that Russians legitimized through the myth of the people's spiritual pedigree.

Leont'ev and Dostoevsky established a symbolic projection of the Greek–Bulgarian schism onto Russian soil. They viewed the church as the best grounds for national consolidation and contemplated discarding the ethnic aspect of Russian national identity in favor of the religious one, all of which brought them closer to Tiutchev's vision of Russia's imperial mission (discussed in chapter 4). Leont'ev dreamt of a mighty theocratic state that would unite peoples of many different origins. Dostoevsky yearned for the secular state to become so closely integrated with the church that ultimately nothing but the church would remain. As Ivan says in *The Brothers Karamazov*, "according to the Russian hope and understanding, the state must ultimately reach a point where it becomes pure church and nothing else."[114] In *The Brothers Karamazov*, the monks in the monastery and particularly the Elder Zosima endorse this idea—a sign that it is among Dostoevsky's most cherished beliefs.

Though they both subscribed to the concept of pan-Orthodox unity, Dostoevsky's project differed significantly from Leont'ev's. While Dostoevsky viewed the church as a union of love and an embodiment of brotherhood, Leont'ev understood the uniting power of religious ties to be based on force and spiritual fear. Both realized, however, that ethnic aspirations bore strong subversive implications and had to be subordinated to a higher principle—to Orthodoxy and church law, or (as Leont'ev paradoxically concluded at the end of his life) to socialist ideology. He believed that socialism—like religion—could serve as a powerful protective force, an antidote to the possible ethnic fragmentation of the Russian Empire. It is difficult to overestimate the significance of this belief in a uniting principle superior to ethnic sentiments for Russian nationalist discourse of the twentieth century.

If Leont'ev and Dostoevsky are responsible for the symbolic projection of the Greek–Bulgarian conflict onto Russian soil, a second group of Russian intellectuals is responsible for the symbolic projection of a living Bulgarian church—a church with the potential to lead a national revival—onto the Russian church. The support of the Bulgarians on the part of this group bespoke the spirit of religious populism so central to the 1870s and 1880s. Vladimir Solov'ev and Ivan Aksakov demanded more freedom for the church, but at the same time they realized that the Russian church lacked the inner resources to serve as a basis for national consolidation. For these thinkers, the prominence of the clergy and church institutions in the Bulgarian national movement seemed to point the way to revitalizing the Russian nation by releasing the church from the state's control and restoring its pre-Petrine independence. They saw in the Bulgarians' struggle the model of a fruitful strategic alliance between religion and nationalism, wherein the church would become an instrument of nation-building.

The Slavic myth of the birth of the Russian people, like all the previous myths examined in this book, served as both charter and justification for a program of national transformations conceived under the influence of Europeans blueprints. Like all the other myths, this narrative also symbolically resolved those domestic problems of Russian nationhood that the government could not or would not address. While perennial tensions between the imperial, the national, and the religious dogged tsarist policy and impeded the nation-making process, this myth reconciled all those aspects of Russianness. Moreover, it supplied Russian nationalists with powerful arguments for the expansion of the empire and for its legitimization on nationalistic terms. The myth of spiritual descent not only emphatically removed the nation from the shadow of empire (by denying them any common origin) but also offered a new basis for their interaction. Within this charmed space, the empire neither suppressed the nation (as it did in reality) nor appeared as a "necessary evil" (as it did for the Slavophiles), but instead stood ready to lead the nation onward to ultimate salvation.

Yet such a synthesis of the religious, the national, and the imperial could survive only as long as the doctrine remained untested by national realities. The dilemma Russian intellectuals faced in their discussions of the Greek–Bulgarian schism arose from a contradiction implicit in the persistent attempts to ground Russian national distinctiveness in Orthodoxy, with its universalistic and inclusive stance. The Greek–Bulgarian church conflict revealed this contradiction and provided a testing ground for competing visions of the nation. Leont'ev relied on the imperial and religious components of Russianness and stigmatized ethnicity as "tribal nationalism." Katkov, on the contrary, discounted religion as an instrument of cohesion and proposed building imperial integrity on the basis of ethnic secular culture (first and foremost through the spread of the Russian language). Vladimir Solov'ev and Ivan Aksakov offered a third way to solve the problem of national identity. They expected a reformed Orthodox church to consolidate the nation.

The persistence of religious motifs in nineteenth-century Russian nationalism should not be understood simply as a result of the pervasiveness of Orthodoxy in Russian culture. Under a regime that had closed all avenues to mass participation in political life, religious myth offered an ideal epic space for the God-bearing people to take center stage. Like the memories of war, the people's commitment to Orthodoxy became a symbolic substitute for mass engagement.

In Place of a Conclusion

The Legacy
of Reform-Era Nationalism

Reform-era thinkers recast historical mythology to accommodate a dramatic shift in national self-perception—the growing understanding of the nation as a political construct—that marked the 1850s and 1860s. Under the traumatic impact of the Crimean defeat, writers of divergent ideological persuasions sought to chart Russia's future by exploiting the tale of the founding of the state, legends of Cossack independence, memories of popular wars, and the story of the Russian people's spiritual birth. These narratives, with their aura of antiquity, helped foster a sense of the nation's immutable nature. By invoking pivotal events of the past, they also helped to justify emerging projects of national transformation as a return to deeply ingrained ways of life. Once the reforms were set in motion, defining the nation through collective memories made it possible to absorb innovations while maintaining a sense of national continuity. Moreover, new renditions of basic historical myths proved instrumental in the dialogue between the public and the government in the context of

183

the unfolding transformations. As we have seen, intellectuals refashioned the past in an effort to press the authorities to alter traditional imperial policies—to shore up the Russian people's position as the "reigning nationality," unify the heterogeneous population of the empire on the basis of allegiance to its ethnic core, and enlist the ruler in the Russian cause.

Articulated by thinkers from across the political spectrum, these projects competed with one another, converging at only a few points. But these points of agreement disclose the overarching tendencies of reform-era nationalism. What brought all these writers together was their effort to reconsider the empire-nation dichotomy. They approached empire as an ongoing process, with the nation as its central topos and main agent. Employing national mythology, a broad group of intellectuals based the nation's claim to greatness on its status as the builder and defender of empire, as an emblem of hope for the Slavs and for the entire Orthodox world.

This understanding of the empire-nation nexus, expressed in various forms of cultural production, found its most systematic articulation toward the end of the reform era in Nikolai Danilevsky's *Russia and Europe* (1869). Serialized initially in the journal *Zaria*, the work was regarded by Dostoevsky, who avidly followed its installments, as "the future handbook [*nastol'naia kniga*] for all Russians."[1] Most of the other protagonists of my study also welcomed *Russia and Europe* or even, like Nikolai Strakhov, propagated it. Though each of them, including Dostoevsky, could or did suggest something to add, alter, or correct in it, the book united reform-era nationalists more than it divided them. Danilevsky forcefully synthesized the major nationalist arguments then in circulation and put forward a vision of the empire as an "organic" outgrowth of Rus'—as an ever-expanding stage where the Russian people's historical drama continued to unfold. *Russia and Europe* might be considered the compendium of the principal ideas of reform-era nationalism. Subsequent generations of Russian thinkers regularly referred to this source, either to agree with or refute it. For this reason, a brief discussion of its main points provides a logical coda to my study.

In the 1840s Danilevsky, like Dostoevsky, had belonged to the radical Petrashevskii circle, a group of young intellectuals who advocated the socialistic ideas of Fourier. In 1849, also like Dostoevsky, he was arrested and imprisoned, though for a much shorter period and under much less severe conditions. In prison, again like Dostoevsky, he reread the Bible and repudiated his previous atheistic and socialist views.[2] During his relatively short exile and over the next several decades, Danilevsky distinguished himself by producing major studies in statistics, ecology, and biology.[3] In *Russia and Europe*, he mobilizes his professional knowledge and skills to buttress nationalist ideology with scientific argument.

Danilevsky applies the assumptions of natural science to history in order to produce a theory of "cultural-historical types" that provide the conceptual framework for his vision of humanity's future. He draws extensive parallels between the evolution of species and that of "cultural-historical types" (or "civilizations") to claim that the distinctive traits of each "type" — a combination of racial, social, political, and artistic characteristics — constitute the basis of its development, a process similar to evolution in the natural world. At first glance, his approach may seem to reflect a typical nineteenth-century need to sound scientific in an age when positivism was transforming Europe's intellectual landscape. Danilevsky's views, however, took shape in direct opposition to this movement. He found his main source of inspiration in the strain of Romanticism that saw nations through the prism of organic metaphor.[4] Subject to the laws of nature, each "cultural-historical type" appears as an organic whole, growing to realize its individuality and assume its unique place in world history.

Danilevsky discusses the distinct traits of ten civilizations (from Egyptian and Chinese to Romano-Germanic) to claim that no universal goal and no single historical trajectory can exist for mankind as a whole. In his typical "scientific" manner, he observes that neither the palm tree, nor the cypress, nor any other species can fully implement the idea and task of the vegetable kingdom: various species embody different aspects of the world of plants. In the same way, Danilevsky asserts, humanity expresses itself in distinct "types" — through multiple, diverse, and frequently incompatible cultures. Each civilization, he claims, evolved in pursuit of its own ultimate end.[5] It is on the basis of this conception that Danilevsky denounces the notion of a common, all-embracing historical progress that, he emphasizes, conceals the divergent evolutionary pathways of humanity.

These views arose out of Danilevsky's critique of Darwin.[6] The struggle for existence does play an important role in the evolution of species; Danilevsky has no doubts about that. But Darwin has exaggerated its significance and scope. Natural selection is not at work everywhere, and when it does occur, since it is interrelated with other environmental pressures, it does not necessarily lead to directional, or "teleological," development.[7] Danilevsky treats Darwin's theory as both a product and an accurate description of the Romano-Germanic civilization. It is no coincidence, he states, that Darwin—a representative of the strong Germanic nation—should come up with the concept of struggle for existence. Such an idea reflects the fundamental values that drive the Romano-Germanic "type," based as it is on conquest, domination, political contestation, and economic competition. While struggle for existence may adequately explain European history, the Slavic world, Danilevsky declares, is governed by different principles and does not fit the Darwinian scheme.

This statement leads Danilevsky to his most important point: Russia displays unique Slavic values that are inherently incompatible with those of Europe. As the only independent Slavic state, Russia represents an eleventh cultural-historical type, still emerging but destined to carve a new path in world history and eventually to supplant the Romano-Germanic type in world leadership.[8] All the pivotal developments in Russian history, Danilevsky asserts, are the result not of a tumultuous struggle of diametrically opposed interests, as is the case in the West, but of cooperative efforts carried out by the people in an atmosphere of unanimity. At appropriate times, through the deep workings of their collective consciousness, the Russian people gradually realize the necessity of change and prepare themselves for it, emerging in consensus when the critical moment finally arrives. This pattern manifests itself clearly in the way the Russian state was founded. Without a "struggle of parties" and without "quarrels among themselves," the Novgorodians sent envoys across the sea to invite the Varangians to rule over them.[9] In the familiar manner of reform-era writers, Danilevsky draws on historical myth to express his views and buttress his vision of the empire-nation nexus. Like Katkov, Danilevsky believes that "the Finnish tribes," together with the Slavs, participated in summoning the Varangians. This act of peaceful cooperation on the part of ethnically distinct groups confirms for Danilevsky the unique nature of the state, rooted since its inception in joint undertakings by diverse constituents. It also enshrines—and in this respect Danilevsky's views once again dovetail with Katkov's—the Russians' ruling status within the empire: it was under Russian leadership that "Latvians and Estonians laid the foundations of the Russian state."[10]

Danilevsky consistently fuses historical myths with scientific arguments. While, as Danilevsky reminds his readers, Darwin holds that organisms are packed tightly into every available space (and therefore need to compete for it), Russia's vast, complex environment makes it possible for various species—and for distinct nationalities—to coexist peacefully.[11] *Russia and Europe* describes the cultural and political assimilation of various tribes in terms of a natural process of absorption. In the same way that a mighty tree draws into its mass various foreign objects, the Slavs slowly assimilated Finnish tribes scattered across the territory of Russia. Over the course of Russian expansion, "weak, half-savage and entirely wild native peoples were not only not destroyed or wiped off the face of the earth, but they were not even deprived of their freedom and property, nor turned into serfs by their conquerors."[12] What France had given only to the French, Russia gave to all—on condition of political allegiance to the Russian people. In other words, Russia absorbed non-Slavic ethnic groups not to oppress, violate, or compete, but to protect them, to give them the freedom to flourish without fear of greedy neighbors. Thus, for Danilevsky, as for the wide group of intellectuals examined in this book, the Russian empire came into existence as the result of a "natural expansion" (*rasselenie*) of the Russian people, "almost without the involvement of the authorities."[13] Danilevsky views Russia as an indivisible entity that continues to grow, steadily drawing in other nationalities—the Estonians, the Tatars, the Armenians.[14] And if these groups have not yet been fully Russified, this is a consequence of government's wrong-headed supranational policies. Again, like most reform-era nationalists, Danilevsky sought to press the authorities to alter traditional imperial practices and embark on a new nation-building project.

Russia and Europe rightly enjoys the reputation of being the "Bible of Pan-Slavism." In keeping with the vision of Russia's future that was put forward at the Slavic Congress two years prior to the appearance of his book, Danilevsky highlights Russia's role as gatherer and protector of the Slavs. Though speakers at the congress held divergent views on the political outcome of Slavic integration, Russian participants of the gathering often drew parallels with the unifications of Germany and Italy. Danilevsky raises the stakes even higher. He advocates the creation of a Union of Slavic Lands, under Russia's hegemony, and claims that the projected political entity would be equal in scope and historical significance to the entire Romano-Germanic civilization: "Slavdom is a term that belongs to the same category as Hellenic, Latin, or European [civilizations]."[15] Like Europe and other long-lasting "historical types," the emerging Slavic civilization is distinguished by cultural heterogeneity. Danilevsky turns the ethnic and cultural diversity of the Slavic world—and of the Russian empire—into evidence of its power, asserting that, just as in nature, the more varied the component parts of a civilization, the more successful it is.[16] Thus, again using scientific argument, he neatly binds together the two themes that Russian nationalists had employed at the Slavic Congress: diversity and unification.

Like other Pan-Slavists, Danilevsky saturates the Russian imperial impulse with religious overtones. Reiterating Pogodin's arguments, he sees the confluence of the dates of the Russian state's founding and the beginning of Slavic Orthodoxy as proof of Russia's calling to protect, lead, and represent Slavdom.[17] Like Tiutchev and Dostoevsky, he envisions a Slavic union built on Christian brotherhood, love, and peace. While religious intolerance, usurpation of ecclesiastical authority, and rationalism constitute the distinctive features of European civilization, the Slavic type, he maintains, is governed by an all-encompassing Christian mindset and by a pure devotion to the church. And it is precisely these features that predestine Slavic civilization to express the true ecumenical spirit of Orthodoxy and bring about its ultimate triumph throughout the world. By ascribing exclusively to the Slavs the capacity to implement the Orthodox church's universalist orientation, Danilevsky attempts to overcome the antinomy between supranational Christian values and national particularism—an antinomy that, as we have seen, haunted reform-era thinkers. Outside the Orthodox church, declares Danilevsky, "there is no salvation for the nation even in the secular meaning of this word."[18] *Russia and Europe* is yet another project seeking to tie up in one package the concepts of religious, national, and imperial identity. And in doing so Danilevsky encounters the same imperative to reconcile the irreconcilable that determined the paradoxical character of many other reform-era nation-building constructs. Though *Russia and Europe* claims to discuss only political realities, it fuses the sacred and the secular and, like Tiutchev's poetry, merges them in the transcendental. While the book forcefully challenges the belief in a single goal for the whole of humanity, its author ends up proclaiming that Russia is predestined by Providence to bring salvation to the entire world.[19]

The theme of divine intervention in history reveals Danilevsky's affinities even with the author of *War and Peace*, though Tolstoy disapproved of the Pan-Slavic movement and ultimately condemned the imperial paradigm of nationalism. Like Tolstoy, Danilevsky manages to conflate the providential frame of reference with a focus on human instinct and blind self-interest as a driving force of historical developments. Both Tolstoy and Danilevsky ridicule the political rhetoric of altruistic morality and use biological metaphor to underpin their visions of the nation. Both, in their interpretations of the Patriotic War, hold it up as a victory of the Russian spirit and a sign of the Russians' moral supremacy. It is no coincidence that Danilevsky enthusiastically quotes *War and Peace* to support his own explanation of Russia's victory over Napoleon.[20]

In his use of war memories, however, Danilevsky displays more points of convergence with Katkov than with Tolstoy. By glorifying the nation as the main agent of empire-building, Danilevsky, like the editor of *Moskovskie vedomosti*, turns the cult of war into the dominant form of national mythmaking. He employs the same paradoxical mode of representing war as peace that was discussed in chapter 3. The Russian empire emerged as a peaceful amalgamation of ethnically divergent groups protected by the Russian people. Danilevsky sees Russia's expansion into the Slavic lands as a continuation of the same process: "Russia's fate is a happy one: to increase its own might, it must not conquer, not oppress," but rather "liberate and restore."[21] Yet since the Slavic Union would be the only counterweight to Europe's desire for world domination, Danilevsky predicts prolonged clashes and inevitable battles with Romano-Germanic civilization, which he advocates as "wars of liberation."[22] These coming wars, he asserts, would forge solidarity among the Slavs (a goal not readily achievable in peacetime), foster their sense of national identity (emancipating them from Western influences), and thus allow Slavic civilization to manifest itself fully.[23] Like Katkov, Aksakov, and Pobedonostsev during the Polish uprising, Danilevsky utilizes memories of the popular wars of 1612–13 and 1812 to present the Russian people as a decisive historical actor, to prove the nation's ability to unite across social divides and to enlist the ruler in the national cause.[24]

In the 1860s Danilevsky, like all the other protagonists of this book, welcomed the reforms.[25] Yet, at the end of his life, he drastically reevaluated Alexander II's reign, seeing it as having foiled the very expectations it first aroused. Danilevsky lost hope that the authorities would ever alter traditional imperial policies, promote allegiance to the Russian people on the part of nontitular nationalities of the empire, or firmly defend the interests of the Slavs abroad. Reflected in his articles and in the extensive notes he made around 1880 for a new edition of *Russia and Europe*, this deep disillusionment reinforced his advocacy of war as an instrument of nation-building.[26] Danilevsky's intellectual trajectory thus encapsulates the overarching tendency of reform-era nationalism to forge—and, as the era progressed, to reinforce—a profound linkage between advocacy of war and the empowerment of the Russian people.

The reform-era efforts to synthesize the imperial and the national that culminated in Danilevsky's *Russia and Europe* set the terms for future debates about the nation, profoundly contributing to the nationalist discourse of the twentieth and even the twenty-first centuries. As to its most immediate outcome, it laid the ground for the model of autocracy put forward by Alexander III (1881–94). Succeeding the reform era, his reign repudiated Alexander II's innovations and marked a turning point in the development of Russian official nationalism. As Wortman has revealed, the young tsar built a new mythical image of the monarchy: he claimed to revive its native origins and presented himself as "the highest embodiment of the Russian people."[27] It was the 1860s renditions of historical mythology that supplied Alexander III with the epic stage on which he could act as national leader, the role reform-era thinkers had yearned for their emperor to assume.[28] The tsar incorporated memories of pious Rus' into the imperial narrative to display the ethnic roots of the state. He made the Orthodox church into a visual expression of the ruler's spiritual union with the people and, by building old-style churches across the empire, asserted Russian domination of the borderlands. He celebrated the Cossacks as the incarnation of the Russian people's martial spirit, always at the ready to advance and defend the empire. He refashioned the autocracy's 1613 restoration as the new founding myth, and it symbolized, along with the memory of 1812, the timeless union of the people, the tsar, and the state.[29]

While employing all these cultural idioms of the 1860s, Alexander III changed their function dramatically. Born at the dawn of the reform era, these constructs sought to empower the Russian people and to assimilate the unfolding transformations into what was perceived as authentic Russian culture. As appropriated by Alexander III, these constructs came to reaffirm the tsar's unlimited authority and justify the use of force. His reign distinguished itself by harsh measures against the press and the universities, by counterreforms of the courts and the *zemstvos*, and by ethnic oppression and persecution. This brutal exercise of power was presented as an expression of Russianness.[30] It was the underlying aggression of reform-era national discourse, with its glorification of war memories, that provided nationalist legitimacy for the ruler's ruthless domination. Myth-based nationalism of the 1860s thus revealed its self-defeating nature. The very rhetoric designed to build up the Russian nation and recast the monarchical empire in nationalist terms now served to justify unlimited use of force by the Russian emperor.

Notes

Introduction

1. Pushkin, *Dnevniki*, 55, with reference to Karamzin, *Istoriia gosudarstva Rossiiskogo*.

2. *Den'*, no. 30 (July 27, 1863) (lead article); reprinted in Aksakov, *Pol'skii vopros*, 102. By "obscure" parts of Rus', Aksakov, in fact, meant Byelorussia, which he always conceived of as an integral part of Rus' (on the notion of a single all-Russian nation that included Ukrainians and Byelorussians, see note 22 in this chapter).

3. Dostoevsky, *Polnoe sobranie sochinenii*, 25:98. The quotation is from the April issue of his *Diary of a Writer* (1877).

4. Also, the ruling dynasty officially defined itself as Russian, though until the last quarter of the century the Romanovs preferred to justify their power through associations with the West. See Wortman, *Scenarios of Power*, esp. 1:3–10; 2:12–15.

5. On this terminological distinction and its roots and implications, see Hosking, *Russia*, xix. The nineteenth-century proposals to rename Russia "Petrovia" (in honor of its first emperor) represent a half-joking attempt to give onomastic priority to

Russia's imperial nature. See N. V. Riasanovsky, *Nicholas I and Official Nationality in Russia*, 139.

6. Hosking, *Russia*, xix, 41–42. The same approach is elaborated in Hosking and Service, *Russian Nationalism*. See also Rowley, "Imperial versus National Discourse."

7. Tolz, *Russia*, 10, 15, 155–81.

8. For a discussion of the challenges involved in defining Russia's heartland and of how the perception of Russia's core shifted over the nineteenth and early twentieth centuries, see Gorizontov, "The 'Great Circle' of Interior Russia." On the imperial character of Russian nationalism, see N. V. Riasanovsky, *Nicholas I and Official Nationality in Russia*, 137–38, 154–61; Bassin, *Imperial Visions*, 12–15.

9. For critical remarks on Hosking's and Tolz's views on the empire-nation dichotomy, see Becker, "Russia and the Concept of Empire"; Wortman, "Natsionalizm, narodnost' i rossiiskoe gosudarstvo"; Miller, *Romanov Empire and Nationalism*, 161–79; Norris, *War of Images*, 3, 193–94, notes 25 and 26; Dolbilov, "Russian Nationalism and the Nineteenth-Century Policy of Russification," esp. 141–44.

10. *Materialy dlia istorii*, 1:114. A year and a half after this speech, Alexander publicly announced his plan for the emancipation of the serfs in the Nazimov rescript (November 6, 1857). On the complex issue of what exactly impelled the emperor and his advisers to initiate the reforms, see Lincoln, *Great Reforms*, xiv; Wortman, *Scenarios of Power*, 2:58–59.

11. As Terence Emmons observes, "Measured by their collective impact on Russian life," the Great Reforms "constituted the most important episode in Russian history between the reign of Peter the Great and the Revolution of 1905." See Emmons, *Russian Landed Gentry*, vii. Already in the 1860s the parallel between Alexander's reforms and Peter's innovations circulated widely.

12. In recent years interest in this issue has emerged in the pioneering works of Theodore Weeks, Andreas Renner, Alexei Miller, Paul Werth, Mikhail Dolbilov, Darius Staliunas, and Andrei Zorin. The present study is particularly indebted to two monographs: Renner, *Russischer Nationalismus und Öffentlichkeit im Zarenreich*, and Miller, *Ukrainskii vopros*.

13. Nikitenko, *Dnevnik*, 1:423 (diary entry of October 16, 1855).

14. On the postwar exposé literature, see Kornilov, *Obshchestvennoe dvizhenie pri Aleksandre II*, 73–104, 118–31; Levin, *Ocherki po istorii russkoi obshchestvennoi mysli*, 293–404.

15. *Sovremennaia letopis'*, no. 1 (1862): 20 (lead article).

16. Aksakov, *Pol'skii vopros*, 67 (May 25, 1863). Because some of Aksakov's articles never actually appeared in print during the 1860s (they were banned by the censor), here and in later notes I provide only the dates of their composition as indicated in the collection I am citing, without reference to the newspaper issues.

17. It should be mentioned, however, that no matter how much Russian thinkers

owed to ideological trends developed in the neighboring empires, they construed Russia as its neighbors' "other." On the mutual influence of imperial policies among the Romanov, Hapsburg, Ottoman, and Hohenzollern empires and the interdependent development of nationalist ideologies across their borders, see Miller, *Romanov Empire and Nationalism*, 20–27. For insightful theoretical discussion of "areas of interaction" of empires and patterns of their reactions to common challenges, see Gerasimov et al., "In Search of New Imperial History," esp. 49–55. For a valuable discussion of how the Great Reforms, coupled with Russia's growing colonial enterprise, facilitated the inclination of some imperial administrators to promote, though only hesitantly, policies that diverged from the traditional non-national imperial model, see Werth, "Changing Conceptions of Difference," esp. 169–81. On how the empire-nation dichotomy took on a new urgency during the reforms, see Kaspe, "Imperial Political Culture and Modernization."

18. Field, "Kavelin and Russian Liberalism," 77–78; Rieber, "Interest-Group Politics," 63; Khristoforov, *Aristokraticheskaia oppozitsiia*, 22. Daniel Field discussed this issue in his review of the latter work in *Kritika*, 412. On the mixture of liberal and conservative attitudes among gentry opposition to Alexander II's policies, see Emmons, *Russian Landed Gentry*, 419.

19. For a discussion of the evolution of Pobedonostsev's views, see Polunov, "Konstantin Petrovich Pobedonostsev," 43–45.

20. On N. G. Chernyshevskii's position with regard to the Ukrainian and Polish questions, see Miller, *Ukrainskii vopros*, 82–83, 86.

21. For a general overview of Aksakov's position and its development, see Lukashevich, *Ivan Aksakov*, and Tsimbaev, *I. S. Aksakov v obshchestvennoi zhizni*. On Katkov's views, see Katz, *Mikhail N. Katkov*; Tvardovskaia, *Ideologiia poreformennogo samoderzhaviia*.

22. On the notion of a single all-Russian nation, see Weeks, *Nation and State in Late Imperial Russia*, 64–68; Gorizontov, *Paradoksy imperskoi politiki*, 7; Miller, *Ukrainskii vopros*, 31–41.

23. On Kostomarov and his polemic with Katkov and Aksakov, see Miller, *Ukrainskii vopros*, 83–95, 106–11, 117–25; Saunders, "Mikhail Katkov and Mykola Kostomarov." For a discussion of how Kostomarov's political views shaped his historical inquiries, see Prymak, "Mykola Kostomarov as a Historian."

24. For insightful discussion of Russian public nationalism as a challenge to the autocratic system and to official imperial patriotism, see Kappeler, *Russian Empire*, 241; Suny, "Empire Strikes Out," esp. 56–57; Renner, "Defining a Russian Nation," esp. 663; Weeks, "Official and Popular Nationalism."

25. On official nationality as a doctrine grounded in the monarchical vision of nationhood, see N. V. Riasanovsky, *Nicholas I and Official Nationality in Russia*. For more recent inquiries into the issue, critically important for the present study, see

Wortman, *Scenarios of Power*, 1:297–332, 379–81; Knight, "Ethnicity, Nationality, and the Masses," 54–60; Zorin, *Kormia dvuglavogo orla*, 337–74. To avoid obscuring certain continuities in the development of Russian nationalism, we should note that even in the time of Nicholas I, adherents of this doctrine diverged in their understanding of "nationality": in addition to the strictly dynastic interpretation of the notion, some writers, including Tiutchev and Pogodin, viewed it in terms of romantic nationalism and ascribed to "the Russian people" the role of historical actor in the divine plan of salvation (see N. V. Riasanovsky, *Nicholas I and Official Nationality in Russia*, 124, 137–38). Alexei Miller, however, exaggerates the continuity between nationalism in the time of Nicholas I and that of the reform era, presenting Uvarov's program as the first attempt to modernize the empire in nationalist terms and thus to initiate developments that had already begun to take shape in Europe at that time (see Miller, *Romanov Empire and Nationalism*, 139–59). For a critique of this interpretation, see my review of Miller's book.

26. In the course of preparations for emancipation, this position was forcefully expressed by leaders of the landed gentry (Emmons, *Russian Landed Gentry*, 98, 252–60, 312, 328, 331–32). A large segment of the reform-era press also openly denounced the bureaucracy. Even Katkov shared this attitude, though he envisioned the state's administrative apparatus as the main instrument for transforming the heterogeneous empire into a single nation. He argued that the government should cultivate nationally aware administrators to implement the russification of subject nationalities of the empire.

27. On expansion of the public sphere during and after the reforms, see Clowes, Kassow, and West, *Between Tsar and People*. The formative role played in reform-ear national discourse by increased production and circulation of the daily press has been thoroughly researched in Renner, *Russischer Nationalismus und Öffentlichkeit im Zarenreich*.

28. In the 1860s, among the most visible critics of the introduction of representative institutions were the Westernizers K. D. Kavelin and B. N. Chicherin and the Slavophiles Iu. F. Samarin, I. S. Aksakov, and V. A. Cherkasskii.

29. For Anthony Smith's concept of antecedent collective cultural identities as one of the determining factors in the nation-making process, see Smith, *Nationalism*, 57–58. For an extensive explication of his theory of ethno-symbolism, see Smith, *National Identity*.

30. On the formative role of myths in shaping national self-understanding, see Hosking and Schopflin, *Myths and Nationhood*; Smith, *Myths and Memories of the Nation*. On myths as vehicles of national identity in Russia, see Franklin and Widdis, *National Identity in Russian Culture*.

31. For incisive discussion of the role of collective memories in fostering a sense of national identity, see Confino, *Germany as a Culture of Remembrance*.

32. Balibar, "Nation Form," 140.

33. Hroch, *Social Preconditions of National Revival in Europe.* On the two basic types of nation-forming, see Hroch, "Real and Constructed," esp. 94–95; Smith, *National Identity*, 54–70; Smith, *Nationalism*, 87–92.

34. Kappeler, *Russian Empire*, 157–62; Suny, "Empire Strikes Out," 56–57; Becker, "Russia and the Concept of Empire," 329–42.

35. Kimitaka Matsuzato applies the term "ethnic Bonapartism" to the Russian authorities' strategy of supporting "weaker" national movements against the influence of "strong" nationalities that were seen as disloyal. For his thorough analysis of discrepancies in the application of imperial policy to various regions and on how that diversified approach depended on territorial context, see Matsuzato, "General-gubernatorstva v Rossiiskoi imperii." For theoretical insights into the principles of differentiated governance, see Burbank, von Hagen, and Remnev, *Russian Empire*, esp. 1–29; Staliunas, *Making Russians*, esp.13–14, 27–41; Miller, *Romanov Empire and Nationalism*, 53–54.

36. On the inconsistency of the Romanov empire's nationality policies, see Gorizontov, *Paradoksy imperskoi politiki*; Weeks, *Nation and State in Late Imperial Russia*, 14–15; Staliunas, *Making Russians*, 13–22.

37. Kappeler, *Russian Empire*, 157–62; Lieven, *Empire*, 253–59.

38. With the inclusion of Ukrainians and Byelorussians, the Russian nation amounted to nearly two-thirds of the empire's population. See Weeks, *Nation and State in Late Imperial Russia*, 67, 214n70.

39. Dolbilov, "Kul'turnaia idioma vozrozhdeniia Rossii."

40. Regarding the thesis that Russia does not fit into either of the two types of nation-building, see Hosking, *Russia*, xxiv–xxv, 40–41; Wortman, "Natsionalizm, narodnost' i rossiiskoe gosudarstvo"; Renner, "Defining a Russian Nation," 663.

41. Wortman, *Scenarios of Power*, 2:24.

42. Quoted in Dolbilov, "Emancipation Reform of 1861," 209.

43. Katkov, *Sobranie peredovykh statei "Moskovskikh vedomostei": 1867 god*, 313 (lead article from no. 133 [June 18, 1867]). In the original Russian text, Katkov uses the term "Russkaia natsional'naia politika" to designate what is translated here as "a policy that defends the interests of the Russian people." Literal translation of this expression into English—"Russian national policy"—does not fully convey the meaning of a term that was designed to function as the antonym of "supranational policy." In the same lead article (and in many others), Katkov explains the term as encompassing "a defense of the interests, honor, and privileges of the Russian people" (313–14). For more on Katkov's concept of the Russian nation, see chapter 2. When citing Katkov's lead articles, I provide the date when each text actually appeared in the newspaper. In the multivolume collection I cite here and elsewhere, each article is preceded both by issue number and the date when it was written rather than when it was published.

44. Aksakov, *Pol'skii vopros*, 49 (May 4, 1863).

45. *Sovremennaia letopis'*, no. 14 (1862): 11 (lead article).

46. On "Russification" during and after the reform era, see Thaden, *Russification in the Baltic Provinces and Finland*; Staliunas, *Making Russians*, 13–16, 43–70; Werth, "Changing Conceptions of Differences." See also a useful deconstruction of the term "Russification" that yields a more nuanced picture of imperial nationality policies in Miller, *Romanov Empire and Nationalism*, 45–65.

47. On the fluctuating official policies with regard to gentry involvement in the preparation of the emancipation, see Emmons, *Russian Landed Gentry and the Peasant Emancipation*, 61–68.

48. Wortman, *Scenarios of Power*, 2:39, 43, 46–48, 80–91. On Alexander's conciliatory policy after the promulgation of the emancipation of the serfs, see Emmons, *Russian Landed Gentry and the Peasant Emancipation*, 308, 328–30.

49. Katkov, "Chto nam delat' s Pol'shei," 496–504. The same manifesto encouraged P. A. Valuev, at that time the interior minister, to submit to the tsar his proposal for incorporating a limited number of *zemstvo* representatives into the State Council. See Chernukha, *Vnutrenniaia politika tsarizma*, 31–40.

50. Tsimbaev, *Slavianofil'stvo*.

51. Emmons, *Russian Landed Gentry and the Peasant Emancipation*, 350–93; Chernukha, *Vnutrenniaia politika tsarizma*, 15–135.

52. Howard, "War and Nations," 255. On the impact of war in shaping a sense of national belonging, see Smith, "War and Ethnicity"; Colley, *Britons*; Sanborn, *Drafting the Russian Nation*.

53. Emmons, *Russian Landed Gentry and the Peasant Emancipation*, 410–11; Chernukha, *Pravitel'stvennaia politika v otnoshenii pechati*, 8.

54. In this approach I build on Irina Paperno's research, which has revealed that various groups from across Russian society sometimes converged in their perceptions of the peasant emancipation, seeing it through the prism of Christian symbolism. See Paperno, "Liberation of the Serfs."

55. Duara, *Rescuing History from the Nation*, 8. On the understanding of nationalism as a dialogical process, see Eley, *Reshaping the German Right*, 11.

56. See chapters 2 and 3.

57. Weeks, *Nation and State*, 9.

58. See Renner, *Russischer Nationalismus und Öffentlichkeit im Zarenreich*, 196–273; Renner, "Defining a Russian Nation," 663, 674.

59. On the developmental character of national mythology, see Smith, *Myths and Memories of the Nation*.

60. Danilevsky, *Rossiia i Evropa*, 21–22, 211 (originally serialized in 1869). For similar assertions, see Katkov, *Sobranie peredovykh statei "Moskovskikh vedomostei": 1864 god* [hereafter cited as Katkov, *SPS 1864*], 295 (no. 109 [May 17, 1864]); 319 (no. 118 [May 28, 1864]). On the ways that S. M. Solov'ev and popular historiography elaborated the same cliché, see Becker, "Russia between East and West," 50.

61. Wortman, *Scenarios of Power*, 1:298–99, 2:3–6, 12.

62. See Tartakovskii, *1812 god i russkaia memuaristika*; Martin, *Romantics, Reformers, Reactionaries*, 123–42; Zorin, *Kormia dvuglavogo orla*, 239–66; Norris, *War of Images*, 11–35.

63. On how state officials faced the same need to decouple faith and ethnicity during and after the reform era, see Geraci, *Window on the East*, 223–63; Weeks, "Religion and Russification"; Werth, "Changing Conceptions of Difference," esp. 181–88.

64. On the "Russian party" as the formative source of Alexander III's policies and efforts to Russify the empire, see Wortman, *Scenarios of Power*, 2:161–95.

Chapter 1. A Shifting Vision of the Nation

1. On the Crimean War and the international situation that led to the war, see Goldfrank, *Origins of the Crimean War*; Curtiss, *Russia's Crimean War*; Tarle, *Krymskaia voina*. Sardinia also took part in this war against Russia.

2. Religious motifs reinforced this twofold juxtaposition, serving to express Russianness vis-à-vis both Muslim and non-Orthodox Christian enemies.

3. See Tartakovskii, *1812 god i russkaia memuaristika*; Rebekkini, "Russkie istoricheskie romany."

4. Tolz, *Russia*, 158–61; Ely, *This Meager Nature*, 95–97, 115–22; Widdis, "Russia as Space."

5. According to Steven Norris, the images created by artists during the 1812 war established the wintry Russian landscape as a source of national identity and linked it most indelibly with the victory over Napoleon. See Norris, *War of Images*, 17.

6. On the distinction between imperial patriotism and Russian public nationalism, see Renner, "Defining a Russian Nation," esp. 663; Weeks, "Official and Popular Nationalism." For an insightful overview of the various interpretations of "patriotism" and "nationalism," see Viroli, *For Love of Country*, 2–9, 169–82.

7. Viroli, *For Love of Country*, 140–60.

8. The Russo-Turkish campaign began in October 1853; England and France joined the war in March 1854. By the time Tiutchev composed the poem, the run-up to war had already begun: Russia had occupied the Danube principalities of Moldavia and Walachia and the combined navy of England and France had entered the Dardanelles.

9. Tiutchev, *Polnoe sobranie stikhotorenii*, 186–87.

10. On the pronouncement of the Second Empire, the struggle over Louis Napoleon's title, and his policy of appealing to the accomplishments of his great uncle, see Tarle, *Krymskaia voina*, 117–30; Curtiss, *Russia's Crimean War*, 50–57; Goldfrank, *Origins of the Crimean War*, 17, 32, 92, 102–3. On the Russian perception of the Second Empire's continuity with respect to the First, see Tartakovskii, *1812 god i russkaia memuaristika*, 230.

11. Aksakov, *Biografiia Fedora Ivanovicha Tiutcheva*, 234, 240–241.

12. Letter from S. P. Shevyrev to M. P. Pogodin (December 25, 1853), in Barsukov, *Zhizn' i trudy M. P. Pogodina*, 13:18–19.

13. M. P. Pogodin, "Nastoiashchaia voina v otnoshenii k russkoi istorii," in *Sochineniia*, 4:143–44 (this article was written in June 1854 and then circulated in manuscript); M. P. Pogodin, "Chtenie poslednego manifesta," 13:202; G. Titov, "Krestovye pokhody i Vostochnyi vopros," *Russkii invalid*, no. 127 (June 8, 1854); no. 128 (June 9, 1854); no. 131 (June 12, 1854); no. 132 (June 13, 1854). Shortly after Titov's brochure was serialized in the newspaper and advertized in its bibliographic section, it appeared as a separate publication (G. Titov, *Krestovye pokhody i Vostochnyi vopros*). What also gave impetus to parallels between the Crimean War and the Crusades was a stunning "anniversary": the year 1853 marked exactly four hundred years since the capture of Constantinople by the Turks. Poets of divergent views—Tiutchev, A. N. Maikov, K. S. Aksakov—depicted this momentous date as a symbolic threshold auguring the rebirth of an Orthodox East under Russia's leadership. See Tiutchev, "Prorochestvo" (1850), in *Polnoe sobranie stikhotvorenii*, 162; A. N. Maikov, "Pamiati Derzhavina," in *Polnoe sobranie sochinenii*, 7th ed. (1901), 4:284; Maikov, "Klermonskii sobor," in *Polnoe sobranie sochinenii*, 6th ed. (1893), 2:32. The poem "Orel Rossii (1453–1853)" ("Russia's Eagle") written by the famous Slavophile K. S. Aksakov also highlighted the symbolic dates, but, unlike Tiutchev and Maikov, he did not craft a thematic motif of Russia's imperial mission.

14. For a selection of testimony to the popularity of such a perception of the Crimean War, see Barsukov, *Zhizn' i trudy M. P. Pogodina*, 13:9, 35, 95, 120, 139, 202–3; Druzhinin, "Moskva v gody Krymskoi voiny"; Shtakenshneider, *Dnevnik i zapiski*, 470; M. F. A. A., "Otgoloski kavkazskoi poezii," *Russkii invalid*, no. 132 (June 13, 1854); Colonel Lebedev, "Diadia i plemiannik," *Russkii invalid*, no. 153 (July 11, 1854); Dubrovin, *Istoriia Krymskoi voiny i oborony Sevastopolia*, 1:317; Aksakov, *Ivan Sergeevich Aksakov v ego pis'makh*, 3:89.

15. Quoted in Barsukov, *Zhizn' i trudy M. P. Pogodina*, 13:40–41. On October 16, 1854, Nicholas I instructed Prince A. S. Menshikov, then in command of the Crimean army: "It is highly desirable that we prove in the eyes of our foreign enemies and even of Russia itself, that we are still the same Russians of 1812—of Borodino and Paris!" (Dubrovin, *Istoriia Krymskoi voiny i oborony Sevastopolia*, 2:114).

16. Norris, *War of Images*, 55, 68–69, 72–73.

17. Ia. Psarev, "Russkie-spartantsy," *Russkii invalid*, no. 150 (July 8, 1854). Another contributor wrote: "Now Odessa is our native land" (Dm. B., "Pis'mo iz Voronezhskoi gubernii," *Russkii invalid*, no. 155 [July 14, 1854]). P. A. Viazemskii in his poem "Odessa," also published in this newspaper, depicted how Odessa acquired Russian spirit under fire (*Russkii invalid*, no. 143 [June 27, 1854]).

18. Innokentii [I. A. Borisov], *Sochineniia*, 2:551–54; Pogodin, "Chtenie

poslednego manifesta," 13:199. For further examples, see Norris, *War of Images*, 66–68. For the formation of this myth, see Plokhy, "City of Glory." For Nicholas's concept of the national empire, see Wortman, "Simvoly imperii," 414–21. For official nationalism during Nicholas's reign, see N. V. Riasanovsky, *Nicholas I and Official Nationality in Russia*; Wortman, *Scenarios of Power*, 1:297–332, 379–81; Knight, "Ethnicity, Nationality, and the Masses," 54–60.

19. It was all the more important to do so, since some of the Crimean Tatars had gone over to the enemy's side. See Barsukov, *Zhizn' i trudy M. P. Pogodina*, 13:144–45.

20. "Nastavlenie nizhegorodskogo voennogo imama Zamiga Khatyba," *Russkii invalid*, no. 181 (August 14, 1854).

21. Innokentii, "Slovo pri poseshchenii pastvy," in *Sochineniia*, 2:448–49. This sermon, preached in Simferopol's Alexander Nevskii Cathedral on September 14, 1854, first appeared in *Odesskii vestnik*, no. 118 (1854) and then in *Russkii invalid*, where all Innokentii's wartime sermons were printed. Later it was included in Dubrovin, *Materialy*, 3:168–69.

22. Ely, *This Meager Nature*, 13–14.

23. To insert Crimea into Russian history, Archbishop Innokentii utilized other myths in addition to the memories of 1812, promoting the belief that the exotic peninsula represented the "cradle of Russian Christianity"; see Innokentii, *Sochineniia*, 1:498–502, 2:553. On the development of this legend, see Kozelsky, "Ruins into Relics."

24. Petr G.o.v.e.n., "Na nyneshniuiu voinu," *Russkii invalid*, no. 116 (May 25, 1854). The identity of the pseudonymous author remains unknown.

25. In 1831 "To the Slanderers of Russia" ("Klevetnikam Rossii"), along with another poem of Pushkin's written almost simultaneously, "The Anniversary of Borodino" ("Borodinskaia godovshchina"), and V. A. Zhukovskii's "The Russian Song of the Taking of Warsaw" ("Russkaia pesn' na vziatie Varshavy"), which at that time was titled "An Old Song in a New Key" ("Staraia pesn' na novyi lad"), were published in the officially sanctioned brochure *Na vziatie Varshavy* (On the taking of Warsaw). During the Crimean War *Russkii invalid* often cited "To the Slanderers of Russia" to raise confidence in Russia as a unified empire (see, for example, I. Mogilevich, "Golos s Urala," *Russkii invalid*, no. 152 [July 10, 1854]; Colonel Lebedev, "Diadia i plemiannik," *Russkii invalid*, no. 153 [July 11, 1854]). For a discussion of Pushkin's poem in a broader literary context, see Fedotov, "Pevets imperii i svobody," esp. 250–51; Ospovat, "Pushkin, Tiutchev i pol'skoe vosstanie 1830–1831 godov"; Dixon, "Repositioning Pushkin."

26. In contrast to Spain, which also defeated the French, but where the anti-Napoleonic movement was so closely connected with anti-absolutism that the monarchy preferred to ignore this war (see Alvarez Junco, "Formation of Spanish Identity," 16–20, 26–27), official ideology in Russia succeeded in adapting the victory

over Napoleon to its own ends. In Nicholas Riasanovsky's precise formulation, "it was above all 1812, the *annus mirabilis* that cast its long shadow over the thought and the writings of Official Nationality" (*Nicholas I and Official Nationality in Russia*, 120). Throughout Nicholas's reign, his interpretation of Russia's triumph over Napoleon was fostered by carefully crafted public ceremonies and a historiography controlled by the tsar himself. On public commemorations of the Patriotic War, see Wortman, *Scenarios of Power*, 1:316–21, 384–86. On historiography, see Tartakovskii, *1812 god i russkaia memuaristika*, 199–212.

27. An imperial manifesto, December 14, 1854. Quoted in Barsukov, *Zhizn' i trudy M. P. Pogodina*, 13:197–98 (here and in later citations, the italics are in the original unless otherwise stated).

28. On the promulgation of the manifesto, see Pogodin, "Chtenie poslednego manifesta," 13:202–3. During the war, this article circulated in manuscript.

29. On January 29, 1855, under dismal military circumstances, Nicholas I issued an imperial manifesto, "O prizvanii k gosudarstvennomu opolcheniiu" (On the summoning of a national militia), in which he employed, though implicitly, the parallel with the militia of 1812 to raise confidence in Russia's victory: "More than once already, Russia has faced and been overtaken by difficult, sometimes cruel, trials. But it has always been saved by humble faith in Providence and the strong, unshakeable bond of the Tsar with His subjects, His devoted children. Be it so even now." In the "Polozhenie o gosudarstvennom opolchenii" (Statement on the national militia) that accompanied the manifesto, the government specifically referred to the "example of the 1812 militia" as the model to emulate (*Sankt-Peterburgskie vedomosti*, no. 25 [February 1, 1855]). Within a few months a brochure was published: "The general militia of Russia for faith, tsar, and fatherland, or the Russian soldiers at the time of the Emperor Alexander and the currently reigning Alexander II" (Moscow, 1855); it contained the text of Alexander I's manifestos and the history of the militia of 1812. On this brochure, see Druzhinin, "Moskva v gody Krymskoi voiny," 758.

30. Bogdanovich, *Vostochnaia voina*, 4:141. See also Dubrovin, *Istoriia Krymskoi voiny i oborony Sevastopolia*, 3:427–28.

31. Bogdanovich, *Vostochnaia voina*, 4:141. Alexander II issued this order to the army on his name day, August 30, 1855. Seconding the tsar's words in his orders to the army, Gorchakov portrayed surrendered Sevastopol—by analogy with Moscow abandoned in 1812—as a redeeming sacrifice, portent of the resurrection of Russia (ibid.).

32. Alexander II's official visit to Moscow following the surrender of Sevastopol also evoked memories of 1812. It was staged, as Richard Wortman has observed, "as a repeat performance of Alexander I's dramatic appearance after Napoleon's invasion" (*Scenarios of Power*, 2:25).

33. On the prominent role of the image of Ivan Susanin during Nicholas's time, see Kiseleva, "Stanovlenie russkoi national'noi mifologii"; Wortman, *Scenarios of Power*, 1:390–95.

34. "Vnutrennie izvestiia," *Russkii invalid*, no. 153 (July 11, 1854).

35. For the theme of Orthodoxy during the Crimean War, see Norris, *War of Images*, 63–66; Kozelsky, "Ruins into Relics."

36. M. P. Pogodin, "Neskol'ko myslei po prochtenii solovetskogo doneseniia," *Russkii invalid*, no. 195 (September 1, 1854).

37. Ia. Psarev, "Russkie-spartantsy," *Russkii invalid*, no. 150 (July 8, 1854).

38. On how Nikitin's poetry mingled praise for Russia's military glory with descriptions of Russia's distinctive landscape, see Ely, *This Meager Nature*, 121.

39. The missive appeared, under the signature "I. N.," in *Russkii invalid*, no. 181 (August 14, 1854). The authoritative edition of I. S. Nikitin's verse erroneously indicates that this missive was first published in 1912. See I. S. Nikitin, *Polnoe sobranie stikhotvorenii*, 166–68, 580. It should be stated, however, that the original poem differs from the newspaper version. For publication in *Russkii invalid* the censor muted the theme of the Russian people's love of freedom and foregrounded faithfulness to the dynasty and the defense of thrones—even foreign ones—as a distinctive national trait. Nonetheless, both versions of the poem glorify the very same national qualities that were staples of official war rhetoric. On the use of Cossacks as an embodiment of the Russian spirit since the 1812 war, see Norris, *War of Images*, 20, 202.

40. Eikhenbaum, *Lev Tolstoy*, 1:147.

41. Tolstoy, "Zapiska ob otritsatel'nykh storonakh russkogo soldata i ofitsera," in *Polnoe sobranie sochinenii*, 4:291. On this tract of Tolstoy's, intended for submission to one of Nicholas I's sons and inspired by hopes of army reform, see Gusev, *Lev Nikolaevich Tolstoy*, 528–32.

42. Orwin, "Tolstoy and Patriotism," 56. On Tolstoy's patriotic mood at the beginning of the Crimean War, see also Christian, *Tolstoy*, 59–60.

43. Tolstoy, *Polnoe sobranie sochinenii*, 3:43. Tolstoy, however, admits in this story that he also knows those who "command badly."

44. Ibid., 4:16.

45. Ibid.

46. Ibid. These lines contrast sharply with the episode in *War and Peace* where the author, through Nikolai Rostov, ridicules the comparison of Raevskii's bravery with the legendary heroism of the Greeks at Thermopylae (ibid., 11:55–56).

47. In besieged Sevastopol, every soldier goes about his work "calmly, assuredly, coolly, as though all this were happening somewhere in Tula or Saransk" (ibid., 4:5). The author mentions towns in Russia's heartland not only because they are far from danger. Apart from this obvious reason, the comparison also asserts the unchanging character of Russians in any corner of the empire. It is characteristic that the

sketch should conclude with the claim that not only will Sevastopol not be taken by the enemy, but it is impossible "to shake the power of the Russian people, *wherever they may be*" (ibid., 4:16; italics mine).

48. *Russkii invalid*, no. 122 (June 5, 1855); Tolstoy, *Polnoe sobranie sochinenii*, 4:385.

49. In "The Woodfelling," Tolstoy explicitly followed "The Singers," by I. S. Turgenev (and dedicated the story to him), defining the national character through folk songs. For a discussion of how Turgenev's approach to the Russian true self influenced "The Woodfelling," see Orwin, "Tolstoy and Patriotism," 57.

50. The censor's corrections of the Sevastopol stories are reflected in the versions of the texts that appeared in *Sovremennik* (see them in Tolstoy, *Polnoe sobranie sochinenii*, 4:173–278).

51. The defeatist approach is reflected in memoirs by the famous historian S. M. Solov'ev, the Slavophile A. I. Koshelev, and the journalist E. M. Feoktistov: Solov'ev, *Zapiski*, 150; Koshelev, *Zapiski*, 81–82; Feoktistov, *Za kulisami politiki i literatury*, 105.

52. On the government's sharply negative reaction to this poem of Khomiakov's, see Bodianskii, "Vyderzhki iz dnevnika," 123–24 (entry of June 19, 1854).

53. M. P. Pogodin, "Pis'mo k grafine Bludovoi, v dekabre mesiatse 1855," in *Sochineniia*, 4:78–80. Though Pogodin contributed to the development of the official nationality doctrine, he became increasingly disappointed with Nicholas's unwillingness to turn the war into a campaign for the liberation of the Slavs suffering under Ottoman rule—a campaign that, he believed, would mobilize the entire Russian nation. Pogodin's articles criticizing the course of the war were not published at that time, but they circulated in educated society and even reached the Winter Palace (see Tiutcheva, *Pri dvore dvukh imperatorov*, 1:146–48; Levin, *Ocherki po istorii russkoi obshchestvennoi mysli*, 324).

54. Aksakova, *Dnevnik*, 102–3, 126 (entries of April 10 and September 3, 1855).

55. Levin, "Gertsen i Krymskaia voina," 172–83, 195–97. As mentioned in the introduction, in the 1850s Herzen tended to work some Slavophile ideas into his revolutionary schemes.

56. Dostoevsky, *Polnoe sobranie sochinenii*, 8:409–16. For analysis of the literary sources of this fragment of *The Idiot*, see Martinsen, *Surprised by Shame*, 78–82.

57. Gertsen, *Sobranie sochinenii*, 8:15–23.

58. Obolenskii, *Zapiski*, 91 (diary entry of August 29, 1855).

59. Shtakenshneider, *Dnevnik i zapiski*, 40.

60. Filaret [V. M. Drozdov], "Beseda v den' pamiati sviatitelia Aleksiia," in *Sochineniia*, 5:302–3. For a discussion of how Filaret positioned himself with regard to official ideology, see Maiorova, "Mitropolit Moskovskii Filaret."

61. B. N. Chicherin, "Vostochnaia voina s russkoi tochki zreniia" (1855), quoted in Levin, *Ocherki po istorii russkoi obshchestvennoi mysli*, 330. In 1855 this tract circulated in manuscript (ibid., 323–30). On Chicherin, see Hamburg, *Boris Chicherin and Early Russian Liberalism*.

62. Valuev, "Duma russkogo vo vtoroi polovine 1855 goda."

63. Tolstoy, *Polnoe sobranie sochinenii*, 17:7. On the progression of Tolstoy's views after his return from Sevastopol, see Feuer, *Tolstoy and the Genesis of "War and Peace,"* 135–67.

64. For Tolstoy's comparisons with "biblical legends," see Tolstoy, *Polnoe sobranie sochinenii*, 47:146 (diary entry of July 23, 1857). During recent decades scholars have put forward a number of innovative interpretations of *The Cossacks*, analyzing this text from the standpoint of such diverse paradigms as the cultural myth about the Cossacks (Kornblatt, *Cossack Hero in Russian Literature*, 91–96), European adventure narratives in the age of imperialism (Anemone, "Gender, Genre, and the Discourse of Imperialism"), the literary construction of the Caucasus (Layton, *Russian Literature and Empire*, 233–51; Hokanson, *Writing at Russia's Border*, 198–223), and problems of the relationship between nature and morality (Orwin, *Tolstoy's Art and Thought*, 86–93). While I take into account the results of these important studies, this chapter analyzes the novella within the context of the profound changes that affected the national discourse in Russia following the Crimean War.

65. Kornblatt, *Cossack Hero in Russian Literature*, 4–5, 13–20; Norris, *War of Images*, 19–21, 34–35, 57–58, 202.

66. Tolstoy, *Polnoe sobranie sochinenii*, 6:15–16. For a concise account of the Greben Cossacks' history, see Barrett, "Crossing Boundaries." For an insightful discussion of their obscure origins, multiethnic composition, and evolving relationship to the Russian state, see Barrett, *At the Edge of Empire*, 13–55.

67. Tolstoy, *Polnoe sobranie sochinenii*, 47:10 (diary entry of July 9, 1854).

68. Ibid., 6:16, 51. The draft is published in Tolstoy, *Kazaki*, 163–67.

69. Tolstoy, *Polnoe sobranie sochinenii*, 6:51–52.

70. Ibid., 6:16, 39–40.

71. For insightful observations about Tolstoy's emphasis on the affinities between the two ethnic groups, see Layton, *Russian Literature and Empire*, 236, 245. For a historical account of the cultural exchange between the Cossacks and the native peoples of the Caucasus, see Barrett, "Crossing Boundaries," 228–29, 233–44. I find very helpful the term "poetics of marginalization" that Katya Hokanson coins to analyze Tolstoy's and some of his contemporaries' tendency to approach the issue of Russianness by depicting the characters' encounter with marginalized ethnic and social groups (Hokanson, *Writing at Russia's Border*, 200–201, 212). As I try to show in this chapter, the very marginality of the Cossacks helps Tolstoy to (re)position the nation with regard to the state.

72. Eastern courage, the narrator in "The Woodfelling" asserts, unlike Russian courage, is based on "a quickly flaring and quickly cooling enthusiasm" (Tolstoy, *Polnoe sobranie sochinenii*, 3:70–71).

73. Ibid., 6:15 (quotation); L. D. Opul'skaia, "Povest' L. N. Tolstogo *Kazaki*," in Tolstoy, *Kazaki*, 348n11.

74. On the literary tradition of portraying the Cossack hero as a combination of opposites (nature-civilization, Russian-foreign, primordial-modern), see Kornblatt, *Cossack Hero in Russian Literature*, esp. 13–20, 94–96.

75. Although I concur with Anthony Anemone regarding the ambiguous character of the nature-culture dichotomy in the novella, I find it difficult to agree that the concept of the noble savage is not applicable to Tolstoy's vision of the Cossack community. Tolstoy presents his Greben settlers as an embodiment of authentically Russian traits that the coercive state has stifled in the rest of the Russian population. This is why his Cossacks are closer to the savage world than are the rest of the Russians. I also disagree with the thesis that Tolstoy's purpose was to present Cossacks as an alternative to—rather than the true incarnation of—Russian civilization (see Anemone, "Gender, Genre, and the Discourse of Imperialism," 55–60).

76. Mel'gunov, "Mysli vslukh," 130–31.

77. Russkii liberal [K. D. Kavelin and B. N. Chicherin], "Pis'mo k izdateliu," *Golosa iz Rossii* 1 (1856): 22–23.

78. Iu. F. Samarin, "O krepostnom sostoianii i o perekhode iz nego k grazhdanskoi svobode," in *Sochineniia*, 2:18. The article was written in 1856.

79. Mel'gunov, "Mysli vslukh," 118–20; N. A. Mel'gunov, "Priiatel'skii razgovor," *Golosa iz Rossii* 2 (1856): 25.

80. For a selection of the novel's scenes where Turgenev emphasizes the passivity of his Russian male characters in comparison with Insarov, see his *Polnoe sobraniie sochinenii i pisem: Sochineniia*, 6:167–69, 219–22. For public criticism of the regime on the grounds that it robs its subjects of initiative, see "Tsirkuliar ministerstva vnutrennikh del," 39; Chicherin, "O krepostnom sostoianii," 130–31, 139, 159.

81. Tolstoy, *Polnoe sobranie sochinenii*, 6:15–16.

82. Kornblatt, *Cossack Hero in Russian Literature*, 48–49.

83. Barrett, *At the Edge of Empire*, 14–15.

84. Kornblatt, *Cossack Hero in Russian Literature*, 5, 41, 96.

85. While Pushkin in *The Captain's Daughter* depicts the Cossacks of the eighteenth century, the heroes of Gogol's *Taras Bulba* live in "unbounded time," transgressing the temporal barrier (ibid., 71–90).

86. Tolstoy, *Polnoe sobranie sochinenii*, 6:57, 82–83, 108. For a different interpretation of the morality of the killing, see Orwin, *Tolstoy's Art and Thought*, 86–93.

87. Tolstoy, *Polnoe sobranie sochinenii*, 6:38.

88. Turgenev, *Polnoe sobraniie sochinenii i pisem: Sochineniia*, 6:167–69, 201, 298. For the ambiguity of Russian patriotic sentiments as reflected in Turgenev's novel, see Wortman, "Natsionalizm, narodnost' i rossiiskoe gosudarstvo."

89. On Turgenev's delight at the Italian liberation movement as the antithesis of Russian life, see also his letter to Countess E. E. Lambert of June 12 [24], 1859 (Turgenev, *Polnoe sobranie sochinenii i pisem: Pis'ma*, 4:51).

90. Tolstoy, *Polnoe sobranie sochinenii*, 47:204 (entry of April 1 [13], 1857).

91. For Kostomarov's views on the Cossacks, see a selection of his articles that were published in the late 1850s and the 1860s and were recently reprinted in a book titled *Kazaki*. Kostomarov's understanding of the Russian nation is discussed in chapter 2. The quotation from Herzen appears in *Byloe i dumy* (*My Past and Thoughts*); see Gertsen, *Sobranie sochinenii*, 9:148–49.

92. Mel'gunov, "Mysli vslukh," 110–11.

93. Since the Old Believers were persecuted (and especially severely during Nicholas's reign), revolutionary intellectuals placed great hope in the putative power of their discontentment and considered them the bulwark of the coming revolution. For the revolutionary approach to the Old Believers, see Kel'siev, *Sbornik pravitel'stvennykh svedenii o raskol'nikakh*. The historian A. P. Shchapov interpreted the Old Believers' communities as a source of national revival and "a continuation of the communal, Russian, Zemstvo manner of life" (see Paperno, "Liberation of the Serfs," 422). N. S. Leskov's story "The Sealed Angel" (1873) reflects another approach to the Old Believers, advocated by M. N. Katkov (it was not a coincidence that the story first appeared in *Russkii vestnik*, a journal edited by Katkov). It treats the Old Believers as potential allies of the regime (if only the government would show them tolerance) and looks to their reunion with the official church as a source of national consolidation. Intellectuals across the political spectrum thus identified the Old Believers—for good or ill—as a powerful force in national life.

94. Solov'ev, *Zapiski Sergeia Mikhailovicha Solov'eva*, 158.

95. Samarin, "Uprazdnenie krepostnogo prava i ustroistvo otnoshenii mezhdu pomeshchikami i krest'ianami v Prussii," in *Sochineniia*, 2:193–400 (quotations on 236, 239). In this work, first published in the journal *Sel'skoe blagoustroistvo* (1858), Samarin focuses on the activities of Freiherr von Stein, whom he considered the architect of reform after Prussia's defeat by Napoleon's troops in 1807.

96. Bell, "Unbearable Lightness of Being French."

97. Russkii liberal [K. D. Kavelin and B. N. Chicherin], "Pis'mo k izdateliu," 32.

98. Saltykov-Shchedrin, "Gubernskie ocherki," in *Sobranie sochinenii*, 2:12–13, 79.

99. In *On the Eve*, Turgenev also places in the mouth of one of his central characters the comparison of Russia with a swamp (Turgenev, *Polnoe sobranie sochinenii i pisem: Sochineniia*, 6:277).

100. Mel'gunov, "Mysli vslukh," 123, 142.

Chapter 2. The Varangian Legend

1. Cross and Sherbowitz-Wetzor, *Russian Primary Chronicle*, 59.

2. Miliukov, *Glavnye techeniia russkoi istoricheskoi mysli*, 76, 104–12; Rubinshtein, *Russkaia istoriografiia*, 81, 96–97.

3. Lomonosov, *Polnoe sobranie sochinenii*, 6:19 –80. For a discussion of the eighteenth-century debates about the Norman theory, see Miliukov, *Glavnye teche-niia russkoi istoricheskoi mysli*, 77, 111–12; V. A. Riasanovsky, *Obzor russkoi kul'tury*, 1: 161–63; Klein, *Spor o variagakh*, 15 –24; A. V. Riasanovsky, "Ideological and Political Extensions," 335 –38; Khlevov, *Normanskaia problema v otechestvennoi istoricheskoi nauke*.

4. Already for Bayer, the creator of the Norman theory (1736), Scandinavian domination framed the Russian past in terms familiar from the history of Europe-an monarchies, which traced their origins to Viking conquerors. See A. V. Riasa-novsky, "Ideological and Political Extensions," 335 –36.

5. Rubinshtein, *Russkaia istoriografia*, 81.

6. Whittaker, "Idea of Autocracy," 43 –44.

7. Reyfman, "Zametki A. N. Radishcheva po russkoi istorii," esp. 231–32.

8. Only a small group of skeptics denied the legend's accuracy outright. The most famous among them were M. T. Kachenovskii, in the first half of the nine-teenth century, and D. I. Ilovaiskii, in the second.

9. Katkov, *SPS 1864*, 290 (lead article from no. 108 [May 15, 1864]). For debates about the Varangian question in the 1860s, see Klein, *Spor o variagakh*, 26 –33.

10. Smith, *Myths and Memories of the Nation*, 61.

11. Karamzin, *Istoriia gosudarstva Rossiiskogo*, 1:26.

12. Rubinshtein, *Russkaia istoriografiia*, 81, 160, 164 –65.

13. Karamzin, *Istoriia gosudarstva Rossiiskogo*, 1:67.

14. Pogodin, *Istoriko-kriticheskie otryvki*, 1:64. For a discussion of Pogodin's interpretation of the summoning in the broader context of his historical views, see Rubinshtein, *Russkaia istoriografiia*, 261–67.

15. Pogodin, *Istoriko-kriticheskie otryvki*, 1:42, 63 –64.

16. Pogodin, "Otvet P. V. Kireevskomu," 50. Drevliane and Radimichi are ancient names for Slavic tribes in the vicinity of Kiev.

17. Pogodin, *Istoriko-kriticheskie otryvki*, 1:62.

18. Ibid.

19. Ibid.

20. Kireevskii, "O drevnei russkoi istorii (Pis'mo k M. P. Pogodinu)," 17.

21. Ibid.

22. Ibid., 28. On A. S. Khomiakov's interpretation of the Varangian legend, see N. V. Riasanovsky, *Russia and the West*, 76 –77.

23. Pogodin, "Otvet P. V. Kireevskomu," 54 –56.

24. It was a tenet of Slavophile ideology shared by many thinkers. See, for instance, Gil'ferding, "Chem podderzhivaetsia pravoslavnaia vera u iuzhnykh slavian," 15.

25. Solov'ev, *Istoriia Rossii s drevneishikh vremen*, 1:90; Solov'ev, *Sochineniia*, 1:119–23, 293–95.

26. Wortman, *Scenarios of Power*, 1:298–99.

27. Solov'ev, *Istoriia Rossii s drevneishikh vremen*, 1:91. He reinforced the argumentation of the historian F. I. Krug, who much earlier had proposed redating the "summoning" on the basis of indirect evidence (ibid., 1:91). Some publications, including official ones, initially endorsed Solov'ev's recalculation. In 1852 an anonymous contributor to *Zhurnal Ministerstva vnutrennikh del* (The journal of internal affairs) subscribed to the new dating, concluding with a grandiloquent congratulation to readers on the millennium that had "passed from the time when the first seeds of statehood were sown on Russian soil" ("Tysiacheletie Rossii," *Zhurnal Ministerstva vnutrennikh del*, no. 1 [1852]: 8).

28. Pogodin, "Kogda Russkomu gosudarstvu ispolnitsia tysiacha let?" 53. See also Barsukov, *Zhizn' i trudy M. P. Pogodina*, 12:65–66.

29. Pogodin, "Kogda Russkomu gosudarstvu ispolnitsia tysiacha let?" 53.

30. Ibid.; Barsukov, *Zhizn' i trudy M. P. Pogodina*, 12:65. See also Ustrialov, "Zapiska."

31. *Sbornik postanovlenii po ministerstvu narodnogo prosveshcheniia*, col. 1386; Barsukov, *Zhizn' i trudy M. P. Pogodina*, 12:67. Apart from Pogodin, two other specially invited historians (N. G. Ustrialov and Ia. I. Berednikov) contributed to the formation of the official opinion.

32. *Zhurnal Ministerstva narodnogo prosveshcheniia*, no. 11 (1852): 20 (official section). The order was issued on August 21, 1852.

33. On the ambiguity of the concept of the nation expressed in the ceremony, see Wortman, *Scenarios of Power*, 2:78–88.

34. Quoted in Zakharenko, "Istoriia sooruzheniia pamiatnika, 54–55.

35. Ibid., 55.

36. Otto and Kupriianov, *Biograficheskie ocherki*, i; "Neskol'ko slov o pamiatnike tysiacheletiia Rossii," *Severnaia pchela*, no. 204 (July 30, 1862).

37. Valuev, *Dnevnik*, 1:158 (entry of April 10, 1862).

38. Ibid., 1:178 (entry of June 18, 1862).

39. Dmitrii Tolstoi, the director of the police department at the Ministry of Internal Affairs, arriving in Petersburg from the provinces shortly before the commemoration, was struck by the uneasy atmosphere that reigned in both capitals: "People were so unsettled that they were predicting the inevitable and imminent fall of the government and even counting its remaining days" (D. N. Tolstoi, "Zapiski," 37). For similar contemporary accounts of the political atmosphere that enveloped Russian society on the eve of the commemoration, see Miliutin, *Vospominaniia*, 304–5; Nikitenko, *Dnevnik*, 2:271 (entry of April 29, 1862).

40. Eval'd, "Vospominaniia," 78.

41. On the eve of his trip to Novgorod, the tsar wrote to his brother, "I hope for God's mercy that the day will go well despite all gloomy predictions" (*Dela i dni*, no. 3 [1922]: 79).

42. "Letter from our first correspondent," *Syn otechestva*, no. 218 [September 11, 1862]. For a similar observation, see Ar[kadii] Eval'd, "Prazdnik Tysiacheletiia Rossii (Ot nashego korrespondenta)," *Sankt-Peterburgskie vedomosti*, no. 196 (September 8, 1862).

43. [Valuev], "8-e sentiabria 1862 goda," 6.

44. Wortman, *Scenarios of Power*, 2:78 –88.

45. "Opisanie pamiatnika tysiacheletiiu Rossii," 71; Otto and Kupriianov, *Biograficheskie ocherki*, ii; B . . . ov, *Beseda u pamiatnika tysiacheletiia*, 45; "Neskol'ko slov o pamiatnike tysiacheletiia Rossii," *Severnaia pchela*, no. 204 (July 30, 1862).

46. Iversen, *Medali, vybitye v tsarstvovanie imperatora Aleksandra II*, 17 –18.

47. Maslova, *Pamiatnik Tysiacheletiiu Rossii*, 59.

48. The popular brochure recommended that "the literate Russian" walk around the monument with the brochure in hand "and observe it closely," starting with Peter (B . . . ov, *Beseda u pamiatnika tysiacheletiia*, 1).

49. Semenovskii, *Pamiatnik tysiacheletiiu Rossii*, 8 –9.

50. N. V. Riasanovsky, *Nicholas I and Official Nationality in Russia*, 105 –15; Wortman, *Scenarios of Power*, 1:380.

51. B . . . ov, *Beseda u pamiatnika tysiacheletiia*, 43. P. A. Valuev quoted this passage from the brochure approvingly in his article in *Severnaia pochta* (reprinted in *Moskovskie vedomosti*, no. 200 [September 13, 1862]).

52. *Syn otechestva*, no. 216 (September 8, 1862).

53. Semenovskii, *Pamiatnik tysiacheletiiu Rossii*, 17. Groups are presented in just this order in official descriptions of the monument.

54. Lyttelton, "National Question in Italy," 72–73.

55. Mikeshin had to appeal personally to the emperor for permission to place Gogol on the monument. See Mikeshin, "Vospominaniia khudozhnika," 160.

56. Ibid., 160–61.

57. The head of the Holy Synod conveyed Alexander's wishes to Filaret (see *Pis'ma dukhovnykh i svetskikh lits*, 583). For the text of the prayers, see Filaret [V. M. Drozdov], *Sobranie mnenii i otzyvov*, 1:262. This service had a profound effect even on Alexander himself. Upon his return to Petersburg, he wrote to Great Prince Konstantin Nikolaevich, then governor of the Kingdom of Poland: "The ceremony consecrating the monument was itself splendid and highly moving, in particular the three final prayers, written specially for the occasion by Filaret at my request" (*Dela i dni*, no. 3 [1922]: 82).

58. Originally given as a public lecture, the article "O znachenii Velikogo

Novgoroda v russkoi istorii" was published in *Otechestvennye zapiski* in 1862 (for details, see Kostomarov, *Avtobiografiia*, 199, 202–3). Kostomarov articulated the same interpretation of Novgorod in his monograph, which appeared a year later (Kostomarov, *Severnorusskie narodopravstva*).

59. The speech Pavlov delivered differed significantly from its published version (P. V. Pavlov, "Tysiacheletie Rossii"). The speech caused an uproar and led to the professor's exile from St. Petersburg.

60. On the earlier attempts to incorporate the symbolism of Novgorodian liberty into the imperial narrative, see Whittaker, "Idea of Autocracy," 45 –46.

61. Ar[kadii] Eval'd, "Prazdnik Tysiacheletiia Rossii (Ot nashego korrespondenta)," *Sankt-Peterburgskie vedomosti*, no. 201 (September 16, 1862). The monument could also be associated with Monomakh's hat; its shape easily lent itself to both "readings." Some data suggest that in Mikeshin's original design the monument was, in fact, identified with Monomakh's hat, which may provide additional motivation for the cross on top of the structure (see Zakharenko, "Istoriia sooruzheniia pamiatnika," 58). Yet all interpretations, official and unofficial, compared the monument exclusively to a bell, a pointed reminder of *veche* freedom.

62. Eval'd, "Prazdnik Tysiacheletiia Rossii . . . ," *Sankt-Peterburgskie vedomosti*, no. 201. In fact, the *veche* did not always assemble on Sophia Square. This space assumed such crucial symbolic connotations for the commemorations that its organizers did not hesitate to relocate a monument to the militia of 1812 that had previously stood on the square and replace it with the bell structure.

63. Eval'd, "Prazdnik Tysiacheletiia Rossii . . . ," *Sankt-Peterburgskie vedomosti*, no. 196.

64. B . . . ov, *Beseda u pamiatnika tysiacheletiia*, 14 –15.

65. For a discussion of these historical figures, see chapter 3.

66. Eval'd, "Prazdnik Tysiacheletiia Rossii . . . ," *Sankt-Peterburgskie vedomosti*, no. 201.

67. Semenovskii, *Pamiatnik tysiacheletiiu Rossii*, 91.

68. Wortman, *Scenarios of Power*, 2:17 –157.

69. V. Ch., "Pis'mo nashego vtorogo korrespondenta," *Syn otechestva*, no. 217 (September 10, 1862).

70. [Valuev], "8-e sentiabria 1862 goda," 7.

71. I. K-v, "Neskol'ko slov o pamiatnike tysiacheletiia Rossii," *Sankt-Peterburgskie vedomosti*, no. 164 (July 29, 1862); "Vnutrennie izvestiia," *Russkii mir*, no. 29 (July 28, 1862). These articles announced that G. R. Derzhavin and Nicholas I would be included on the monument. As Mikeshin later recalled, Alexander at first fully supported his plan to "forget" Nicholas but later changed his mind (Mikeshin, "Vospominaniia khudozhnika," 162).

72. Dostoevsky, *Polnoe sobranie sochinenii*, 10:374 –75.

73. *Sovremennaia letopis'*, no. 37 (August 12, 1862): 12–13.

74. P. Polevoi, "Iz Novgoroda Velikogo: Neskol'ko slov o Novgorodskikh drev-nostiakh," *Den'*, no. 33 (August 26, 1862); see also Aksakov, *Polnoe sobranie sochinenii*, 5:3–4. Although the censor forbade the publication of Aksakov's article, readers could find almost all its arguments against the commemoration scattered in other publications of his newspaper. See A. Gil'ferding, "Sud'ba prezhnikh slavianskikh gosudarstv," *Den'*, no. 36 (September 8, 1862); *Den'*, no. 39 (September 29, 1862) (lead article).

75. *Den'*, no. 39 (September 29, 1862) (lead article); Gil'ferding, "Sud'ba prezh-nikh slavianskikh gosudarstv." Some other Slavophiles' reactions to the celebration are discussed in Wortman, *Scenarios of Power*, 2:84–85, 87–88.

76. "Vse ili nichego," *Otechestvennye zapiski*, no. 2 (1862): 52.

77. A. K. Tolstoi, "Istoriia gosudarstva Rossiiskogo ot Gostomysla do Tima-sheva," in *Sobranie sochinenii*, 1:384–400. Tolstoi drew on earlier renditions of the myth in satirical poetry, in particular on M. A. Dmitriev's "Kogda nash Novgorod Velikii," *Golosa iz Rossii* 4 (1857): 44. Tolstoi's poem appeared in print only in 1883, but it circulated widely before that in manuscript copies (see A. K. Tolstoi, *Sobranie sochinenii*, 1:762–63).

78. A. K. Tolstoi, "Istoriia gosudarstva Rossiiskogo."

79. Saltykov-Shchedrin, "Sovremennaia idilliia," in *Sobranie sochinenii*, vol. 15, pt. 1, 70–73. The chapter was first published in 1883.

80. Ibid.

81. On the concept of a single all-Russian nation, see introduction, 10, and 195n22.

82. On Kostomarov's views and his construction of Ukrainian identity, see Prymak, "Mykola Kostomarov as a Historian"; Miller, *Ukrainskii vopros*, 76–115.

83. Kostomarov, "Nachalo Rusi."

84. For a detailed account of the debate, see Barsukov, *Zhizn' i trudy M. P. Pogo-dina*, 17:272–301.

85. "Publichnyi disput 19 marta 1860 goda o nachale Rusi mezhdu gospodami Pogodinym i Kostomarovym," *Sovremennik*, no. 3 (1860): 257–92; Barsukov, *Zhizn' i trudy M. P. Pogodina*, 17:293–98.

86. N. A. Dobroliubov, "Normanskii period russkoi istorii," *Sovremennik*, no. 1 (1860): 104–8 (reprinted in Dobroliubov, *Sobranie sochinenii*, 6:39–43); N. A. Do-broliubov, "Nauka i svistopliaska," *Sovremennik*, no. 3 (1860): "Svistok" (a satirical supplement bound with the journal *Sovremennik*, no. 4), 1–24 (reprinted in Dobro-liubov, *Sobranie sochinenii*, 7:394–417); N. G. Chernyshevskii, "Zamechanie na 'Pos-lednee slovo gospodinu Pogodinu' Kostomarova," *Sovremennik*, no. 5 (1860): 84–88.

87. Barsukov, *Zhizn' i trudy M. P. Pogodina*, 17:283.

88. Saltykov-Shchedrin, "Glupov i glupovtsy," in *Sobranie sochinenii*, 4:202–10. The sketch was written in 1862.

89. Nikitenko, *Dnevnik*, 2:113 (entry of March 27, 1860).

90. For other contemporaries' accounts of the debate, see Barsukov, *Zhizn' i trudy M. P. Pogodina*, 17:272–323.

91. N. I. Kostomarov, "Predaniia pervonachal'noi russkoi letopisi v soobrazheniiakh s russkimi narodnymi predaniiami," in *Raskol*, 3–130. The article was first published in *Vestnik Evropy*, no. 1–2 (1873). Its central points had already been articulated by Kostomarov in 1861, in his work "Mysli o federativnom nachale Drevnei Rusi," which first appeared in *Osnova*, no. 1 (1861).

92. N. I. Kostomarov, "Tysiacheletie," *Sankt-Peterburgskie vedomosti*, no. 5 (January 9, 1862).

93. Ibid.

94. N. I. Kostomarov, "Nachalo edinoderzhaviia v drevnei Rusi," in *Raskol*, 141, 158 (first published in *Vestnik Evropy*, no. 11–12 [1870]).

95. Ibid., 131–61.

96. Ibid., 157.

97. Kostomarov, "Nachalo Rusi," 20–23. For further statements of this kind, see Kostomarov, "Predaniia pervonachal'noi russkoi letopisi v soobrazheniiakh s russkimi narodnymi predaniiami," 35–36.

98. Kostomarov, "Nachalo Rusi," 20–21. Kostomarov included this part of the article in his monograph *Severnorusskie narodopravstva vo vremena udel'novechevogo uklada* (1863). See the recent republication of this study under the title *Russkaia respublika* (the quotations are from pages 13–14).

99. The idea for the book first came to him, as he recalled, in 1846 (Gedeonov, *Variagi i Rus'*, 1:xviii). For the sections of the book published in 1862–63, see S. A. Gedeonov, "Otryvki iz issledovanii o variazhskom voprose."

100. Gedeonov, *Variagi i Rus'*, 1:v.

101. Pogodin, "Gedeonov i ego sistema o proiskhozhdenii variagov i Rusi," 3. Other generally positive responses from famous scholars who, however, did not fully subscribe to Gedeonov's position include Kunik, "Zamechaniia"; Fortinskii, "*Variagi i Rus'*: Istorichiskoe issledovanie S. Gedeonova"; Sreznevskii, "Zamechaniia o knige S. A. Gedeonova *Variagi i Rus'*."

102. Gedeonov, *Variagi i Rus'*, 1:48, 308.

103. Ibid., 1:308

104. Like many anti-Normanists before him, Gedeonov reiterated the claim that the theory of Riurik's Scandinavian origins was in itself a malicious fabrication by German scholars seeking to denigrate the Russians. On the defensive nature of Russian nationalism, see Becker, "Russia between East and West," esp. 49–50.

105. Gedeonov, *Variagi i Rus'*, 1:94–100, 130–32.

106. Ibid., 1:56.

107. Ibid., 1:307–58.

108. Gedeonov attacked Solov'ev's theory that the Varangians introduced the Slavs to a higher level of social development with almost the same fury that he attacked Schlözer's assertion of their "savagery."

109. Gedeonov, *Variagi i Rus'*, 1:94–100, 130–32.

110. Ibid., 1:102–4, 127.

111. Ibid., 1:xiv, 104.

112. Ibid., 1:59–66.

113. Thus, from Gedeonov's point of view, Russia's position between East and West contributed immensely to its high level of education and culture.

114. Ostrovskii, *Polnoe sobranie sochinenii*, 14:158–61, 164–66, 168–82, 187, 189, 192–95, 221. Gedeonov and Ostrovskii coauthored the play *Vasilisa Melent'eva*. N. A. Rimskii-Korsakov composed the opera-ballet *Mlada* on the basis of Gedeonov's play of the same name, which features the themes central to *The Varangians and Rus'*. It is set in the ninth and tenth centuries in the Wendish territory along the Elba river and depicts the Slavic gods, demons, and pagan rituals. The play also highlights the motif of German aggression against the Slavs. For the libretto of the opera, see *Mlada: Opera-balet v 4-kh deistviiakh* (Petersburg: Tipografiia A. S. Marksa, 1891). For a discussion of Gedeonov's work as director of the Hermitage, see Miasoedova, "S. A. Gedeonov i imperatorskii Ermitazh."

115. Sreznevskii, "Zamechaniia o knige S. A. Gedeonova *Variagi i Rus'*."

116. Kuz'min, "Ob etnicheskoi prirode variagov"; Fomin, *Variagi i Variazhskaia Rus': K itogam diskussii po variazhskomu voprosu.*

117. Katkov, *SPS 1864*, 292–95 (lead article from no. 109 [May 17]).

118. Katkov, *SPS 1864*, 346 (lead article from no. 125 [June 6]).

119. Ibid., 318 (lead article from no. 118 [May 28]).

120. Ibid., 319.

121. Ibid., 318–20.

122. Ibid., 346 (lead article from no. 125 [June 6]).

123. Only those minor ethnic groups that lacked advanced culture or their own history did Katkov consider doomed to complete absorption by Russian culture. He presciently warned that it would be dangerous to cultivate and support the cultures of "ethnographic scraps" and "fragments" that might later begin to harbor dreams of independence. See Katkov, *SPS 1864*, 136 (lead article from no. 51 [March 5]), 201–2 (lead article from no. 75 [April 3]).

124. On the introduction of Russian language in Catholic Church services and Katkov's role in establishing this policy, see Staliunas, *Making Russians*, 159–80. On Katkov's vision of the empire, see Renner, "Defining a Russian Nation."

125. On the development of Russian nationalist ideology as a reaction to similar pressures faced by the Ottoman, Romanov, and Hapsburg empires, see Miller, *Romanov Empire and Nationalism*, 20–27.

126. Katkov, *SPS 1864*, 334 (lead article from no. 122 [June 3]).

127. Ibid., 201 (lead article from no. 75 [April 3]).

128. For Katkov's comments on Russian science, see ibid., 385 (lead article from no. 139 [June 24]); for his comments on Russian literature, see ibid., 334 (lead article from no. 122 [June 3]), 380 (lead article from no. 138 [June 23]); Katkov, *Sobranie peredovykh statei "Moskovskikh vedomostei": 1865 god* [hereafter cited as Katkov, *SPS 1865*], 169 (lead article from no. 64 [March 23]), 214 (lead article from no. 76 [April 10]); on the superiority of the German language, see Katkov, "Chto nam delat' s Pol'shei," in *1863 god*, 1:225–26 (first published in *Russkii vestnik*, no. 3 [1863]); Katkov, *SPS 1864*, 294 (lead article from no. 109 [May 17]).

129. Katkov, *SPS 1864*, 95–96 (lead article from no. 35 [February 12]), 291 (lead article from no. 108 [May 16]).

130. Ibid., 201 (lead article from no. 75 [April 3]), 259 (lead article from no. 97 [May 2]), 346 (lead article from no. 125 [June 6]).

131. Smith, *National Identity*, 99–122.

132. Becker, "Russia and the Concept of Empire."

133. On "exchanges of imperial experience" between empires of different types, and for a discussion of the scholarly literature on this subject, see Miller, *Romanov Empire and Nationalism*, 32–33.

134. Katkov, *SPS 1864*, 319 (lead article from no. 118 [May 28]), 286 (lead article from no. 106 [May 14]).

135. Ibid., 319, 286.

136. On Katkov's concept of the "political nation," see Renner, "Defining a Russian Nation."

137. It was exactly this understanding of the Russian people that guided the efforts of D. I. Ilovaiskii, one of the leading historians of the reform era, to prove the Varangian legend's total improbability. In the ninth century, the Slavs were too strong, energetic, and self-reliant, he claimed, to be conquered by alien forces, let alone to submit voluntarily to rulers from abroad. Like Gedeonov, Ilovaiskii asserted that in 862 the institution of princely rule had already existed in Rus' for so long that it had become one of the most powerful states of the time (Ilovaiskii, "O mnimom prizvanii variagov"). Ilovaiskii included this article, along with his other anti-Normanist works, in his book *Razyskaniia o nachale Rusi*.

138. Wortman, *Scenarios of Power*, 2:24.

139. M. P. Pogodin, "O publichnom dispute v zale Peterburgskogo universiteta," Manuscript Division of the Russian State Library (OR RGB), fond 231/I, folder 9, document 12, p. 6.

Chapter 3. War as Peace

1. Dostoevsky, *Polnoe sobranie sochinenii*, 22:122–26. On the paradoxicalist as an outlet for Dostoevsky's own views on war, see Frank, *Dostoevsky*, 273–79.

2. Aksakov, *Polnoe sobranie sochinenii*, 1:244.

3. Ibid., 1:251–52.

4. Geyer, *Russian Imperialism*, 70–85.

5. Crook, *Darwinism, War, and History*. For a general discussion of concepts of war and violence in nineteenth-century thought, see Pick, *War Machine*, 75–87.

6. Vucinich, *Darwin in Russian Thought*.

7. Initially these beliefs in the Russian people's meekness and propensity to peace were inspired by Johann Herder's vision of the Slavs. See Kohn, *Pan-Slavism*, x. On the development of these ideas by Russian thinkers, see Walicki, *Slavophile Controversy*, 136; N. V. Riasanovsky, *Nicholas I and Official Nationality in Russia*, 147–48, 154–55.

8. On wars as a means of shaping national identity, see Smith, "War and Ethnicity," esp. 376–77; Smith, *National Identity*, 27; Smith, "'Golden Age' and National Renewal," 42. For a discussion of war-bound national self-definitions in the imperial context, see Colley, *Britons*, 283–319. Use of the war theme in Russian nationalism has recently begun to attract scholars' attention. See Martin, *Romantics, Reformers, Reactionaries*, 123–42; Zorin, *Kormia dvuglavogo orla*, 157–86; Norris, *War of Images*. On how the theme of conquest determined the key components of the official vision of the nation, see Wortman, *Scenarios of Power*, esp. 2:6–7, 10–15, 524–528. On the militaristic rhetoric of proponents of official nationality, see N. V. Riasanovsky, *Nicholas I and Official Nationality in Russia*, 120–23, 137–38. On nationalism and the role of war in the later period, see Sanborn, *Drafting the Russian Nation*; Lohr, *Nationalizing the Russian Empire*.

9. For general discussion of Russian perceptions of Poland and of the long-term impact of the mutually hostile national stereotypes, see Weeks, *Nation and State in Late Imperial Russia*, esp. 92–94; Gorizontov, *Paradoksy imperskoi politiki*; Weeks, "Slavdom, Civilization, Russification," esp. 225–32; Ransel and Shallcross, *Polish Encounters, Russian Identity*, esp. 1–19 (introduction). On Pushkin's "To the Slanderers of Russia," see chapter 1, note 25. On Polish nationalist conceptualizations of Russian-Polish relations, see Porter, *When Nationalism Began to Hate*.

10. Kappeler, *Russian Empire*, 239. On the connection between the November rebellion and the articulation of official nationalism, see N. V. Riasanovsky, *Nicholas I and Official Nationality in Russia*, 227; Tartakovskii, *1812 god i russkaia memuaristika*, 192–93; Zorin, *Kormia dvuglavogo orla*, 340. On Russian intellectuals' response to the November uprising, see Ospovat, "Pushkin, Tiutchev i pol'skoe vosstanie 1830–1831 godov."

11. Weeks, *Nation and State in Late Imperial Russia*, 93–94; Gorizontov, *Paradoksy imperskoi politiki*, 7; Miller, *Ukrainskii vopros*, 31–41.

12. On the Polish question in the context of the peasant reform, see Gorizontov, "Pol'skii aspect podgotovki krest'ianskoi reformy v Rossii"; Dolbilov and Miller, *Zapadnye okrainy Rossiiskoi imperii*, 134–39.

13. Leslie, *Reform and Insurrection in Russian Poland*, 46.

14. Tatishchev, *Imperator Aleksandr Vtoroi*, 1:233–34.

15. Alexander amnestied the 1830 insurgents, rescinded laws that discriminated against the Polish nobility in the western borderlands, suspended military recruiting, and opened a medical academy in Warsaw with Polish as the language of instruction. But he undertook firm repressive measures as soon as the Poles voiced their demands for independence. For a detailed account of Alexander II's policies in Poland and the western borderlands before the uprising, see Thaden, *Russia's Western Borderlands*, 154–56; Dolbilov and Miller, *Zapadnye okrainy Rossiiskoi imperii*, 127–37, 152–55, 161–72.

16. Leslie, *Reform and Insurrection in Russian Poland*, 219–24; Weeks, *Nation and State in Late Imperial Russia*, 94–96; Dolbilov and Miller, *Zapadnye okrainy Rossiiskoi imperii*, 179–84.

17. See Aksakov, *Pol'skii vopros*, 19–21, 47 (February 2 and May 4, 1863). The full quotation from Katkov reads as follows: "On paper, the compass draws a map; on earth, the sword. Only its line is firm, only its line constitutes a border" (Katkov, *1863 god*, 1:215, first published in *Russkii vestnik*, no. 3 [1863]).

18. Aksakov, *Pol'skii vopros*, 104 (July 27, 1863); Katkov, *Sobranie peredovykh statei "Moskovskikh vedomostei": 1863 god* [hereafter cited as Katkov, *SPS 1863*], 167 (lead article from no. 79 [April 13]). For a discussion of Katkov's inclusive concept of the nation, see Renner, "Defining a Russian Nation" and the final section of chapter 2.

19. For a general analysis of these publications' coverage of the January uprising, see Tvardovskaia, *Ideologiia poreformennogo samoderzhaviia*, 24–73; Durman, *Time of the Thunderer*, 54–69, 486; Renner, *Russischer Nationalismus und Öffentlichkeit im Zarenreich*, 210–44; Walicki, "Slavophile Thinkers and the Polish Question," esp. 92–98.

20. On Aksakov's and the Pan-Slavists' gradual drift toward Katkov's position, see Petrovich, "Russian Pan-Slavists and the Polish Uprising"; Durman, *Time of the Thunderer*, 486n39; Wortman, *Scenarios of Power*, 2:162–64; Walicki, "Slavophile Thinkers and the Polish Question," 94–98.

21. "The Polish nation," wrote Katkov, "seeks not freedom but dominance and dominion [over Russia]" (Katkov, *SPS 1863*, 151 [lead article from no. 71 (April 4)]). The Slavophile Iurii Samarin seconded Katkov: "In the name of its nationality, Poland demands for itself political sway over other nations" (Samarin, "Sovremennyi ob"em pol'skogo voprosa," in *Sochineniia*, 1:342; first published in *Den'*, no. 38 [September 21, 1863]).

22. Geyer, *Russian Imperialism*, 52

23. Aksakov, *Pol'skii vopros*, 65 (May 25, 1863).

24. Katkov, *SPS 1863*, 143 (lead article from no. 68 [March 28]), 209 (lead article from no. 96 [May 4]).

25. Ibid., 59 (lead article from no. 23 [January 29]). See Aksakov's similar statement in *Polnoe sobranie sochinenii*, 2:251–52 (November 28, 1864).

26. Pogodin, "Pis'mo k izdateliam," *Moskovskie vedomosti*, no. 117 (May 31, 1863).

27. Shtakenshneider, *Dnevnik i zapiski*, 329 (diary entry of May 9, 1863).

28. Strakhov, "Rokovoi vopros," in *Bor'ba s Zapadom v nashei literature*, 2:91–105. Though Strakhov praises the Poles for their "highly advanced civilization," he views it as an aristocratic culture that repudiated folk traditions and therefore was fundamentally unhealthy, less original, and less promising than the Russian culture. This article, first published in the April 1863 issue of the journal *Vremia* (Time), elicited widespread indignation from public and government alike and led to the closing of the journal. See Nechaeva, *Zhurnal M. M. i F. M. Dostoevskikh "Vremia,"* 305–6; Walicki, "Slavophile Thinkers and the Polish Question," 90–92.

29. On the historical rhyme between 1612 and 1812 in poetry and political rhetoric at the beginning of the nineteenth century, see Gasparov, *Poeticheskii iazyk Pushkina*, 82–84; Zorin, *Kormia dvuglavogo orla*, 159–86.

30. The November uprising of 1830 was also perceived through the prism of the Patriotic War (see Tartakovskii, *1812 god i russkaia memuaristika*, 190–92). The press of 1863 therefore relied on an established tradition of mythologizing disturbances in Poland. But 1830 Poland had its own army and launched full-scale military operations against Russia, while in 1863 the Russian troops met only with undisciplined bands of fighters who used guerilla tactics and were not in a position to take control of important strategic objectives. Thus in the 1830s the very nature of the situation gave more justification for associations with enemy attack.

31. Katkov, *SPS 1863*, 207 (lead article from no. 95 [May 3]). Katkov himself, as well as at least two other contributors to the patriotic press of 1863 (M. P. Pogodin and Iu. F. Samarin), wrote or edited some of these letters to the tsar. See Tvardovskaia, *Ideologiia poreformennogo samoderzhaviia*, 50–52; Barsukov, *Zhizn' i trudy M. P. Pogodina*, 21:84–85; Samarin, *Sochineniia*, 1:299–300. Alexander Herzen condemned the campaign as a fraud ("Protest," *Kolokol*, no. 168 [August 1, 1863]: 1387; Gertsen, *Sobranie sochinenii*, 17:154, 418). What helped the journalists to present this influx of missives as a sincere expression of nationwide enthusiasm was the fact that during the uprising the letters were coming from all strata of society, including former serfs, who before 1861 were prohibited from addressing the ruler directly (on these restrictions, see Nardova, "Zakonodatel'nye dokumenty").

32. "Vsepoddanneishee pis'mo ot malorossiiskikh kazakov Prilukskogo i Piriatinskogo uezdov Poltavskoi gubernii," *Moskovskie vedomosti*, no. 132 (June 18, 1863). A comparison of the Polish crisis with the Patriotic War also figured in the letters of the Nizhnii Novgorod and Vologda nobility and the letter of the Vologda city council (*Moskovskie vedomosti*, no. 86 [April 23, 1863], no. 88 [April 25, 1863], no. 104 [May 15, 1863]). The motif of putting aside the "sickle and plow" in order to take up

arms goes back to the rhetoric of 1812 (see Glinka, *Pis'ma russkogo ofitsera*, 46). For a discussion of the rhetoric utilized in the letter-writing campaign, see Maiorova, "Obraz natsii i imperii v vernopoddanneishikh pis'makh."

33. Aksakov, *Polnoe sobranie sochinenii*, 2:149 (June 29, 1863).

34. Ibid., 2:145 (June 8, 1863). Katkov also drew parallels between 1612, 1812, and the Polish uprising. See Katkov, *SPS 1863*, 175 (lead article from no. 83 [April 19]).

35. Katkov, *SPS 1863*, 276 (lead article from no. 116 [May 30]).

36. Ibid., 342 (lead article from no. 142 [June 29]). Here Katkov drew on the vision of the Patriotic War articulated by conservatives who lived through 1812. For incisive accounts of how they mythologized the war, see Martin, *Romantics, Reformers, Reactionaries*, 123–42; Mazur, "Iz istorii formirovania russkoi natsional'noi ideologii."

37. Aksakov, *Pol'skii vopros*, 51 (May 11, 1863).

38. Ibid., 49 (May 4, 1863), 53–54 (May 11, 1863), 79 (July 6, 1863).

39. On this diplomatic campaign, see Revunenkov, *Pol'skoe vosstanie 1863 goda*; Leslie, *Reform and Insurrection in Russian Poland*, 170–202.

40. Samarin, *Sochineniia*, 1:332. The article was first published in *Den'*, no. 38 (September 21, 1863).

41. A. V. Nikitenko, *Dnevnik*, 1:317–84; Odoevskii, "Tekushchaia khronika i osobye proisshestviia," 165–73; Del'vig, *Moi vospominaniia*, 3:229–30.

42. Katkov, *SPS 1863*, 152 (lead article from no. 72 [April 5]).

43. "We can openly say . . . that there would not have been a Polish uprising at all, were it not for French incitement" (Katkov, *SPS 1863*, 169 [lead article from no. 80 (April 14)]); for similar observations, see ibid., 246 [no. 107 (May 18)]).

44. Ibid., 168 (lead article from no. 80 [April 14]), 174–75 (lead article from no. 83 [April 19]).

45. Katkov wrote that Poland always was and would be "the certain ally of any enemy of Russia" (Katkov, *1863 god*, 1:45 [lead article from no. 57 (March 14)]). Aksakov also saw in Poland "the *bulwark* of Europeanism against the development and strengthening of the Slavic element" (Aksakov, *Pol'skii vopros*, 85 [July 13, 1863]). Poland's "treachery" has been a theme of Russian historiography at least since N. M. Karamzin (see Gorizontov, *Paradoksy imperskoi politiki*, 8; Renner, *Russischer Nationalismus und Öffentlichkeit im Zarenreich*, 189; Zorin, *Kormia dvuglavogo orla*, 165).

46. Aksakov, *Polnoe sobranie sochinenii*, 2:143 (June 8, 1863), 2:223 (October 17, 1864); see also *Moskovskie vedomosti*, no. 85 (April 21, 1863) (lead article).

47. Katkov, *SPS 1863*, 213 (lead article from no. 97 [May 5]). Katkov meant the Poles' demand for the restoration of the Polish-Lithuanian Commonwealth within its 1772 borders.

48. Katkov, *SPS 1863*, 145 (lead article from no. 69 [March 29]).

49. An interesting example of the combination of "treason" and "conquest" in a single context is the Moscow nobility's letter of allegiance, in which Russia's rights to Poland are asserted through references to "the Russian blood shed more than once in defense against Polish *lust for power* and Polish *treason*" (*Moskovskie vedomosti*, no. 109 [May 22, 1863]; italics mine).

50. This is how the uprising was presented by Russian revolutionary propaganda (especially on the pages of Herzen's *Kolokol*).

51. Aksakov, *Polnoe sobranie sochinenii*, 2:153 (June 29, 1863).

52. Katkov, *SPS 1863*, 141–42 (lead article from no. 67 [March 27]). The entire passage is a reference to the Poles' projects, which at some points won the support of Alexander I. According to these projects, the western borderlands were to be returned to Poland, thus reinventing the Polish-Lithuanian Commonwealth as an autonomous kingdom under the auspices of Russia and under the rule of its emperor. Alexander I also considered the unification of the Kingdom of Poland with Lithuania under the authority of his brother Grand Duke Konstantin Pavlovich (see Thaden, *Russia's Western Borderlands*, 64–65, 71–76). In addition to these historical references, Katkov alluded to the demands of the Polish nobility in the *Zapadnyi krai*, voiced prior to the 1863 uprising, that some districts of the region be administratively attached to the Kingdom of Poland. Katkov condemned not only these requests but also Alexander II's conciliatory policy implemented during the years immediately preceding the January uprising. Finally, the emperor's brother Grand Duke Konstantin Nikolaevich, viceroy to Poland in 1862–63, elicited sharp criticism from the patriotic press for his concessions to the Poles.

53. Both journalists often called the empire *Russkaia derzhava* (state), *Russkoe tsarstvo* (kingdom), and *Russkaia zemlia* (land). See Katkov, *SPS 1863*, 109, 141–42, 152, 167, 175; Aksakov, *Pol'skii vopros*, 51, 57.

54. Aksakov, *Pol'skii vopros*, 51 (May 11, 1863), 65 (May 25, 1863).

55. Katkov, *SPS 1863*, 167 (lead article from no. 79 [April 13]). In speaking about a "map with many-colored borders," Katkov employed the language of irredentism, popular across Europe at the time, implying that substantial parts of Russian ancestral land remained beyond the borders of the Romanov Empire. In this context he often mentioned Galicia, which was part of Austria but regarded by Russian nationalists as a portion of the original national territory that had been split off from Russia.

56. Katkov, *SPS 1863*, 167 (lead article from no. 79 [April 13]); Aksakov, *Polnoe sobranie sochinenii*, 2:218–19 (October 3, 1864).

57. Aksakov, *Pol'skii vopros*, 67 (May 25, 1863). Mikhail Koialovich, a contributor to *Den'*, expressed the same demand in his article "Vernopoddannichestvo poliakov Zapadnoi Rossii" (*Den'*, no. 39 [September 28, 1863]).

58. Katkov, *SPS 1864*, 200–201 (lead article from no. 75 [April 3]); for similar assertions by Katkov, see ibid., 342–46 (lead article from no. 125 [June 6]). For the shift of loyalty from the ruler to the nation proposed by the Russian nationalists, see Kappeler, *Russian Empire*, 239. On Katkov's interpretation of this notion, see Renner, "Defining a Russian Nation," 676 –77.

59. Suny, "Empire Strikes Out," 23 –28.

60. "The struggle with the mutinous [Polish] officials, landowners, and priests," wrote Katkov, "has assumed the character of a rebirth of Orthodox Rus', suppressed and downtrodden by Polonism and Latinity. The Polish mutineers raised the banner of freedom, meaning by freedom their own dominion, and unwittingly made themselves the instrument of the liberation of Rus' from the Polish yoke" (Katkov, *SPS 1863*, 425 [lead article from no. 169 (August 3)]). Aksakov also viewed the rebellion as a watershed, offering at long last an outlet for the anger of the "oppressed" Russian nationality (Aksakov, *Pol'skii vopros*, 52–53 [May 11, 1863]).

61. After describing the painful condition of the oppressed Byelorussians, Aksakov made this appeal: "To their aid, Russian people! . . . Let us extend a brotherly hand to them, offer them the gift of our brotherly love, and assist them with all our social resources, material and spiritual!" (*Pol'skii vopros*, 78 [June 22, 1863]). Katkov also enthusiastically informed his readers that in the Russian core, groups of volunteers were forming up to "move into the Western regions" to defend "the unity of the Russian land" (Katkov, *SPS 1863*, 284 [lead article from no. 119 (June 2)]).

62. Aksakov, *Pol'skii vopros*, 67 (May 25, 1863).

63. "Iz dal'nego ugla S.-Peterburgskoi gubernii," *Moskovskie vedomosti*, no. 134 (June 20, 1863).

64. "Oblastnoi otdel: Izvestiia iz Kazani," *Den'*, no. 17 (April 27, 1863).

65. *Moskovskie vedomosti*, no. 90 (April 24, 1864).

66. On the representation of the Russian (not just Polish) nobility of the western provinces as traitors to Russian national interests, see Dolbilov, "Kul'turnaia idioma vozrozhdeniia Rossii," 236 –37. To present the region's nobility as the main actor of the uprising, Russian nationalists ignored evidence that contradicted this vision. The patriotic press never discussed, for example, the fact that Lithuanian peasants in the Kovno area were among the most active supporters of the uprising. On the Lithuanian aspect of the complex situation in the northwestern region, see Weeks, "Russification and the Lithuanians"; Staliunas, *Making Russians*, 48 –91, 109 –20, 233 –69; Dolbilov and Miller, *Zapadnye okrainy Rossiiskoi imperii*, 248 –49.

67. The official newspaper *Severnaia pochta* laid it out very clearly, and *Moskovskie vedomosti* hastened to reprint the main point made by the official newspaper:

"Local authorities . . . are required to take strong measures against that very segment of the population which . . . cooperates with the government in preserving the general order, and at the same time is forced to take strong measures, as it were, for the benefit of those figures who either openly participate in the disorders or at the very least do not offer cooperation or even sympathy for putting an end to them" ("Izvestiia iz Vil'no," *Moskovskie vedomosti*, no. 49 [March 5, 1863], article published with reference to *Severnaia pochta*).

68. On this decree, see Thaden, *Russia's Western Borderlands*, 138; Dolbilov and Miller, *Zapadnye okrainy Rossiiskoi imperii*, 229.

69. *Severnaia pochta*, no. 100 (April 17, 1863).

70. These pictures were reprinted and discussed in Dolbilov, "Russification and the Bureaucratic Mind," 262–64. I want to express my gratitude to Mikhail Dolbilov and Darius Staliunas for helping me to obtain high-quality copies of the caricatures and to the Lithuanian State Historical Archive (LVIA) for permission to reprint them here.

71. Indeed, the local authorities were afraid of the peasants. One gendarme informed his superiors that he could not cross the territory of Dinaburg district without a convoy of Cossacks (see *Vosstanie v Litve i Belorussii: 1863–1864* [Moscow: "Nauka," 1965], 496–500).

72. "Poslednie telegraficheskie izvestiia o delakh pol'skikh," *Severnaia pochta*, no. 103 (April 20, 1863).

73. Katkov, *1863 god*, 1:135 (lead article from no. 92 [April 30]). The article is also reprinted in Katkov, *SPS 1863* (199–201). Katkov urged the government to join the people in their anger and thus prevent the popular movement from becoming overwhelmingly destructive. For a discussion of Katkov's program of introducing government control over popular resistance to the Poles, see Tvardovskaia, *Ideologiia poreformennogo samoderzhaviia*, 45–47, 53–55.

74. M. O. Koialovich, "Narodnoe dvizhenie v Zapadnoi Rossii," *Russkii invalid*, no. 91 (April 27, 1863). In the same year, this article was reprinted as a separate brochure (St. Petersburg: Voennaia tipografia, 1863).

75. *Den'*, no. 18 (May 4, 1863), 7.

76. Katkov, *1863 god*, 1:137 (lead article from no. 92 [April 30]).

77. Katkov, *SPS 1864*, 272 (lead article from no. 102 [May 8]).

78. Katkov, *SPS 1863*, 303 (lead article from no. 128 [June 13]).

79. Katkov, "Chto nam delat' s Pol'shei."

80. M. N. Katkov, "Mnimoe i deistvitel'noe," in *1863 god*, 1:515–17 (first published in *Russkii vestnik*, no. 5 [1863]).

81. Katkov, *SPS 1863*, 479–81 (lead article from no. 185 [August 24]).

82. Aksakov, *Polnoe sobranie sochinenii*, 2:219–20 (October 3, 1864). See also Aksakov, *Pol'skii vopros*, 115 (August 17, 1863).

83. Katkov, *SPS 1863*, 398 (lead article from no. 161 [July 24]), 427–28 (lead article from no. 169 [August 3]); Aksakov, *Pol'skii vopros*, 52 (May 11, 1863).

84. Glinka, *Pis'ma russkogo ofitsera*, 43; Dostoevsky, *Polnoe sobranie sochinenii*, 25:98 (*Diary of a Writer*, April 1877). Tolstoy also has Alexander speak these words in *War and Peace*, but to completely different effect (for a discussion of how Tolstoy uses the phrase, see chapter 4, p. 146).

85. Aksakov, *Polnoe sobranie sochinenii*, 2:148 (June 29, 1863). Aksakov often repeated this phrase in the aftermath of the Polish uprising. See, for example, ibid., 1: 93 (January 4, 1867).

86. In early 1862 the Holy Synod issued a decree abolishing the performance of special services on the days of all military victories except for the Battle of Poltava, on the grounds that they "held significance only for their own times" (Filaret [V. M. Drozdov], *Sobranie mnenii i otzyvov*, vol. 5, pt. 2, 163–64). Thus the government relegated the Battle of Borodino to the rank of a secondary historical event, a move that drew criticism from *Moskovskie vedomosti* (lead article from no. 70 [March 28, 1864]).

87. Tatishchev, *Imperator Aleksandr Vtoroi*, 1:568–74.

88. Sovremennik 12-ogo goda [S. A. Maslov], "Vospominanie Borodinskoi bitvy v 1864 godu," *Sovremennaia letopis'*, no. 34 (1864): 2–3.

89. On the official interpretation of Alexander's role in the victory over Napoleon, see Tartakovskii, *1812 god i russkaia memuaristika*, 184–85, 202–6.

90. Nikitenko, *Dnevnik*, 2:423 (entry for March 19, 1864).

91. "Piatidesiatiletie vziatiia Parizha," *Moskovskie vedomosti*, no. 68 (March 22, 1864).

92. As *Moskovskie vedomosti* reported, the dinner for higher-ranking officers "was held in the Alexander hall, decorated with a portrait of the Sovereign Emperor Alexander I . . . and paintings of battles from the wars of 1813–1814." The lower ranks—"112 men who participated in the battle of Paris in 1814"—dined in the portrait gallery of Alexander I's generals. "During the dinner, the emperor, expressing his gratitude to the veterans for their faithful and courageous service to the fatherland, raised a toast 'to the health of the brave Russian army.' After a loud *hurrah* and the customary flourish, the band struck up the march to whose strains our troops had entered Paris in 1814" (ibid.). Thus the arrangement of this event promoted the symbolic equation of the two emperors.

93. P. A. Valuev, *Dnevnik*, 1:274 (entry for March 16, 1864).

94. The Russian court agreed to recognize the title that the French emperor had assumed personally but not to acknowledge it as a heritable title. In this way, Nicholas demonstrated his uncompromising loyalty to the decisions of the Congress of Vienna. On the diplomatic conflict over the French emperor's title and how he should be addressed, see Tarle, *Krymskaia voina*, 119–25; Curtiss, *Russia's Crimean War*, 53–57.

95. Wortman, *Scenarios of Power*, 1:193–243.

96. Katkov, *SPS 1864*, 164 (lead article from no. 63 [March 19]). For similar assertions, see S. M. Liubetskii, "Prazdnestva i uveseleniia v Moskve po sluchaiu vziatiia Parizha soiuznymi voiskami v 1814 godu marta 19-go," *Sovremennaia letopis'*, no. 15 (1864): 5.

97. Stephen Norris has shown that from the time of the Patriotic War, popular prints tended to represent the conflict as both a people's victory and as Alexander I's personal achievement (Norris, *War of Images*, 27). While these two visions of the war did indeed coexist in some cultural expressions, the reform-era press bridged them by endowing the nation and the tsar with the same features.

98. Pobedonostsev and Babst, *Pis'ma o puteshestvii*. For an incisive account of the heir's tour, see Wortman, *Scenarios of Power*, 2:104–8.

99. Pobedonostsev and Babst, *Pis'ma o puteshestvii*, 41.

100. Ibid., 86; the missives to the tsar handed to Nicholas are discussed in ibid., 39, 125.

101. Ibid., 85.

102. Ibid., 87, 99, 102, 111.

103. Ibid., 153. Pobedonostsev and Babst deplored the Kostroma monument to Susanin, but they criticized its "tasteless design and lack of artistic inspiration" only to contrast it with the exuberant Susanin-like feelings exhibited by the crowds around them.

104. Ibid., 55.

105. Ibid., 126.

106. Zorin, *Kormia dvuglavogo orla*, 161–65.

107. Pobedonostsev and Babst, *Pis'ma o puteshestvii*, 87. This shift in emphasis in interpretation of the Time of Troubles resembles the evolution of the Varangian legend during the reform era: in both cases, the imperial theme came to saturate the historical myths in order to justify Russians' dominant position within the empire.

108. Ibid., 42.

109. Ibid., 86.

110. Ibid., 428.

111. Ibid., 470.

112. Ibid., 508.

113. See chapter 1.

114. Pobedonostsev and Babst, *Pis'ma o puteshestvii*, 433–36.

115. Ibid., 434. On the concept of the empire as expressed in the *Letters*, see Wortman, "Simvoly imperii," 420–21.

116. Pobedonostsev and Babst, *Pis'ma o puteshestvii*, 356–57.

117. Some phrases in the *Letters* (in particular those discussing the imperial awareness of the Russian people) sound very much like Katkov's editorials. It is

possible that Katkov not only influenced the main concept of the report but also added his own phrases to the text (as was his usual editorial practice; see Tvardovskaia, *Ideologiia poreformennogo samoderzhaviia*, 29).

118. Pobedonostsev and Babst, *Pis'ma o puteshestvii*, 373.

119. Ibid., 264, 361.

120. Wortman, *Scenarios of Power*, 2:107.

121. For a discussion of Pobedonostsev's influence on Grand Duke Alexander Aleksandrovich after the death of Nicholas Aleksandrovich, see Maiorova, "Mitropolit Moskovskii Filaret," esp. 615–20.

122. On Alexander III's model of autocracy and his appeal to the Time of Troubles, see Wortman, *Scenarios of Power*, 2:159–306.

123. "Korrespondentsii iz Peterburga," *Moskovskie vedomosti*, no. 72 (April 7, 1866). Popular booklets that targeted a less educated readership also repeated this phrase of the tsar's (see *O chudesnom izbavlenii zhizni gosudaria imperatora*; Izvol'skii, *Slava vsevyshnemu Bogu!*). For an official account of the event, see Tatishchev, *Imperator Aleksandr Vtoroi*, 2:5–10. On Karakozov and the revolutionary group to which he belonged (the Ishutin circle), see Gleason, *Young Russia*, 324–30; Verhoeven, *The Odd Man Karakozov*.

124. For a discussion of the public perception of Karakozov's attack, see Shilov, *Karakozov i pokushenie 4 aprelia 1866 goda*, 11; Bukhshtab, "Posle vystrela Karakozova," 70–75; Maiorova, "Tsarevich-samozvanets," 221–28; Wortman, *Scenarios of Power*, 2:110–14.

125. *Moskovskie vedomosti*, no. 77 (April 13, 1866) (lead article).

126. Ibid., no. 71 (April 6, 1866) (lead article). *Moskovskie vedomosti* made similar assertions with regard to Karakozov's presumed Polish origins in the lead article of April 8 (no. 73) and in "Korrespondentsii iz Peterburga" (no. 74 [April 9]).

127. *Moskovskie vedomosti*, no. 85 (April 22, 1866) (lead article).

128. In 1867 a real Pole, Anton Berezovskii, did shoot at Alexander II, this time in the very center of the "European contagion," in Paris. However, Berezovskii's attempt was the second, and it did not produce such a thunderous effect as the first.

129. Izvol'skii, *Slava vsevyshnemu Bogu!* 9. See similar statements in other popular booklets published within a few weeks of Karakozov's assassination attempt: *O chudesnom izbavlenii zhizni gosudaria imperatora*, 9; *Novyi Susanin*. Alexander II himself endorsed the parallel Susanin-Komissarov in his rescript that granted Komissarov hereditary nobility (April 9, 1866). The rescript is quoted and discussed in Maiorova, "Tsarevich-samozvanets," 226.

130. Iversen, *Medali v chest' russkikh gosudarstvennykh deiatelei i chastnykh lits*, 304.

131. *Moskovskie vedomosti*, no. 76 (April 12, 1866).

132. Ibid.

133. Ibid.

134. Ibid.

135. On the significance of this opera for the official ideology of Nicholas I's era, see Wortman, *Scenarios of Power*, 1:391–94; Kiseleva, "Stanovlenie russkoi natsional'noi mifologii."

136. See "Vyrazhenie narodnykh vernopoddanicheskikh chuvstv po povodu pokusheniia na zhizn' Gosudaria Imperatora," *Russkii invalid*, no. 86 (April 6, 1866).

137. *Moskovskie vedomosti*, no. 71 (April 6, 1866) (lead article).

138. *Sankt-Peterburgskie vedomosti*, April 10, 1866. A typical depiction of Komissarov as the tsar's savior and the embodiment of the mystical union between the ruler and his people appeared in N. A. Nekrasov's poem "Osipu Ivanovichu Komissarovu" (1866) and A. N. Maikov's "4 Aprelia 1866 goda" (1866). For insightful findings regarding the role of emerging media technologies and nascent capitalism in the production, distribution, and consumption of Komissarov's image, see Verhoeven, *The Odd Man Karakozov*, 72–78.

139. *Moskovskie vedomosti*, no. 85 (April 22, 1866) (lead article).

140. Dostoevsky, *Polnoe sobranie sochinenii*, 25:94–102 (April 1877 issue of *Diary of a Writer*).

141. See Barooshian, *V.V. Vereshchagin*, 125–42; V. M. Garshin's stories "The Four Days" (1877), "From the Reminiscences of Private Ivanov" (1883), and "The Red Flower" (1883), in Garshin, *From the Reminiscences of Private Ivanov*.

Chapter 4. Literary Representations of a Nation at War

1. Leskov, *Soboriane*, 4:225.

2. Leskov envisions that the Old Believers will be reunited with the official church within the framework of the fundamental changes brought about by the reforms. The author sees the same process at work during the 1860s as in 1812, when the enemy's invasion prompted the Old Believers of Old Town—Russia's epitome in the chronicle—"to overcome all kinds of quarrels with our common mother the Russian Church" in order to save the country. This version of the novel was published under the title "Chaiushchie dvizheniia vody: Romanicheskaia khronika." See *Otechestvennye zapiski*, no. 3 (1867): 182.

3. Leskov, "Bozhedomy," 120. This work is an early draft for *Cathedral Folk*.

4. Ibid., 120–21.

5. *Starina i novizna* 2 (1916): 208. In the words of Ernestina Tiutcheva, her husband was very pleased with his Moscow trip, "because he was constantly in the company of Katkov, Aksakov, and all of that group" (Dinesman et al., "Tiutchev v pis'makh i dnevnikakh," 342).

6. For more details, see Tiutchev's correspondence with I. S. Aksakov and A. F. Aksakova in Tiutchev, "Pis'ma k moskovskim publitsistam," 258–380.

7. Quotation from Tiutchev's letter to A. I. Georgievskii, October 6 [18], 1864 (ibid., 382). Upon his return to Petersburg, Tiutchev described the editor of *Moskovskie vedomosti* in most flattering terms: "In Katkov, courage and penetrating intellect touchingly combine with an excellent disposition" (Tiutchev, "Pis'ma k rodnym," 462 [letter to Ekaterina Tiutcheva, October 26, 1863]). For a discussion of Tiutchev's attitude toward Katkov and for their correspondence, see Tiutchev, "Pis'ma k moskovskim publitsistam," 412–21.

8. In a letter to his wife, Tiutchev judged his Moscow mission "no more useless than many others." In fact, the attempt at influencing Katkov came almost to nothing.

9. Tiutchev, *Polnoe sobranie stikhotvorenii*, 209.

10. At the very beginning of the uprising, Aksakov wrote: "By all accounts, priests with crosses in hand appear everywhere at the head of the mutinous gangs, bless the bloody, bestial orgies, and whip up the fanatical crowds, performing brutal murders like some holy rite" (Aksakov, *Pol'skii vopros*, 17 [February 2, 1863]). Katkov presented the Polish clergy in much the same spirit: "Who can find a word of pardon for these priests who turned from servants of a religion of peace into leaders of mutinous gangs, conspirators, and murderers?" (Katkov, *SPS 1863*, 310 [lead article from no. 130 (June 15)]).

11. As an example of this reading of the poem, common to the scholarly literature, see A. A. Nikolaev's notes in Tiutchev, *Polnoe sobranie stikhotvorenii*, 405.

12. Moreover, at the time the poem was composed the English and Austrian notes had not yet been presented. See Revunenkov, *Pol'skoe vosstanie 1863 goda*, 316.

13. Both the notes themselves and the Russian government's answering dispatches were hotly debated in society and the press. See Revunenkov, *Pol'skoe vosstanie 1863 goda*, 288–301; Valuev, *Dnevnik*, 1:229, 232, 404; Katkov, *1863 god*, 1:269–73, 343–62. In regard to the prospect of war, already in February 1863, a month after the first news of the bloody events in Warsaw, A. V. Nikitenko wrote in his diary: "In Polish affairs we are threatened by the meddling of Europe, which in its monstrous, incomprehensible hatred seems ready to tear Russia to shreds" (Nikitenko, *Dnevnik*, 2:319 [entry of February 19, 1863]). A little later, on March 10, 1863, Prince V. F. Odoevskii reported talk around Moscow about the possibility of Russia's being dragged into war over Poland: "Alarming rumors of war with France" (Odoevskii, "Tekushchaia khronika i osobye proisshestviia," 165).

14. Nikitenko, *Dnevnik*, 2:333 (entry of May 21, 1863). In late September 1863, however, Nikitenko observed that Tiutchev was no longer so strongly convinced of the nearness and inevitability of war (ibid., 367–68).

15. In the first version of the poem these dead men were called *teni*, "shades."

16. Two works are particularly interesting in this connection: A. S. Khomiakov's poem "Pole mertvymi kostiami" (1859) and Dostoevsky's story "Bobok" (1873).

17. Dolbilov, "Kul'turnaia idioma vozrozhdeniia Rossii," 237.

18. Tiutchev, "Pis'mo doktoru Gustavu Kol'bu, redaktoru *Vseobshchei gazety*," 216. Discussing Poland in this article, Tiutchev does not, however, name the country directly.

19. Pogodin, *Pol'skii vopros*, 48.

20. Katkov, *SPS 1863*, 459 (lead article from no. 180 [August 18]).

21. Ibid., 240 (lead article from no. 105 [May 16]).

22. Ibid., 427 (lead article from no. 169 [August 3]).

23. Aksakov, *Pol'skii vopros*, 114 (August 10, 1863).

24. *Kolokol*, no. 155 (February 1, 1863): 1286.

25. A. I. Gertsen, "Prestupleniia v Pol'she," *Kolokol*, no. 157 (March 1, 1863): 1303.

26. As Aksakov wrote in the lead article of *Den'*: "The Messianism . . . so eloquently preached by Mickiewicz . . . is not merely the poetic incarnation of Poland as a Messiah-nation, which suffered and was crucified for the sins of the nations, for whose garments the other nations cast lots, and which is to be resurrected for the salvation and social welfare of mankind. It is not merely the lyrical outpouring of the Polish patriot's wounded soul, but a whole mystical doctrine, with its own inspired, uncommonly talented prophets and disciples" (Aksakov, *Pol'skii vopros*, 109–10 [August 10, 1863]).

27. Roman Leibov's reading of Tiutchev's poem "Over Russian Vilno" ("Nad russkoi Vil'noi") (1870) supports my idea of the infernal nature of the Polish "risen corpses" in "A horrid dream" (see Leibov, *"Literaturnyi fragment" F. I. Tiutcheva*, 61–68).

28. Katkov, *SPS 1863*, 391 (lead article from no. 159 [July 20]), 401 (lead article from no. 161 [July 24]). By "nightmare," Katkov also meant the policy of placating the Poles, toward which Alexander II inclined at the beginning of his reign.

29. Aksakov, *Pol'skii vopros*, 68 (June 15, 1863). The patriotic press pinpointed the chronology of the "awakening," connecting it with the appointment of Count M. N. Murav'ev as governor general of the northwestern provinces (May 1863). Famed for his harsh suppression of the November uprising, he also brutally crushed the 1863 rebels, earning himself the name "Hangman Murav'ev." This appointment marked a change in policy toward the insurgents. On M. N. Murav'ev's policies in the *Zapadnyi krai*, see Weeks, *Nation and State in Late Imperial Russia*, 96–98; Weeks, "Monuments and Memory: Immortalizing Count M. N. Murav'ev"; Dolbilov, "Kul'turnaia idioma vozrozhdeniia Rossii."

30. For an analysis of the "living-dead" dichotomy in Tiutchev's lyrics as a whole, see Leibov, *"Literaturnyi fragment" F. I. Tiutcheva*.

31. Pogodin, *Pol'skii vopros*, 146. As the tragic events unfolded, Pogodin continued to exploit vampiric associations: "The Poles intend . . . to wrest our history from us, rip our tongue from our mouths, extract the blood from our veins, and pour in their mixture of Finn and Tatar" (ibid., 124). The words about "the mixture

of Finn and Tatar" refer to Frantiszek Duchinski's theory about the Turanic ethnic substrate in the Russian people.

32. Katkov, *SPS 1863*, 459 (no. 180 [August 18]).

33. A. N. Maikov, "Kniaziu Drutskomu-Liubetskomu," in *Polnoe sobranie proizvedenii* (6th ed.), 2:395. On how the press made the conversion of Prince A. I. Drutskii-Liubetskii into a showcase of the local nobility's "return" to its native Russian roots, see Staliunas, *Making Russians*, 137.

34. Verdery, *Political Lives of Dead Bodies*, 110. On the vampire in literature as a tool for ostracizing certain ethnic or social groups, see Halberstam, "Technologies of Monstrosity."

35. Verdery, *Political Lives of Dead Bodies*, 106.

36. The first alarming accounts from Warsaw already reported: "The revolutionary party decided to conduct a St. Bartholomew's night massacre between January 10 [22] and 11 [23]. At midnight in every province, simultaneous attacks were launched on various cities and on detachments of troops quartered in towns and villages. The mutineers attacked the soldiers while they slept, strangling them in their beds" (*Golos*, no. 13 [January 15, 1863]). This report was reprinted in full in *Den'* (no. 3 [January 19, 1863]). The comparison of the events that signaled the beginning of the uprising with the St. Bartholomew's Day massacre (the assassination of Protestants in Paris in 1572) circulated widely in 1863. See Katkov, *SPS 1863*, 37–38, 55; Odoevskii, "Tekushchaia khronika i osobye proisshestviia," 162.

37. Pogodin, *Pol'skii vopros*, 77.

38. Del'vig, *Moi vospominaniia*, 3:230.

39. For an analysis of Karamzin's poem "Osvobozhdenie Evropy i slava Aleksandra I" and of depictions of Napoleon in the poetry of contemporaries of the Patriotic War, see Gasparov, *Poeticheskii iazyk Pushkina*, 91–93.

40. Ospovat, "Pushkin, Tiutchev i pol'skoe vosstanie 1830–1831 godov."

41. Tiutchev, *Polnoe sobranie stikhotvorenii*, 119–20.

42. Tiutchev, "Russkaia geografiia," in *Polnoe sobranie stikhotvorenii*, 152.

43. For a detailed analysis of this concept, see Ospovat, "Elementy politicheskoi mifologii Tiutcheva."

44. Hollingsworth, *Poetics of Hive*, 21.

45. Tolstoy, *Polnoe sobranie sochinenii*, 12:211.

46. Ibid., 11:327–28.

47. Ibid., 12:211.

48. Strakhov, "*Voina i mir*: Sochinenie grafa Tolstogo," 130. Other literary critics of Tolstoy's time made similar points, supported by some veterans of 1812 who accused Tolstoy of distorting the truly heroic atmosphere of the war. For insightful discussions of this criticism, see Eikhenbaum, *Lev Tolstoy*, 2:388–97; Ungurianu, *Plotting History*, 109–20.

49. Aksakov, *Polnoe sobranie sochinenii*, 1:244. Tolstoy wrote about his reading of *War and Peace* to Aksakov in a letter to S. A. Tolstaia on December 11, 1864 (Tolstoy, *Polnoe sobranie sochinenii*, 83:93).

50. See Orwin, *Tolstoy's Art and Thought*, 99–140.

51. Tolstoy, *Polnoe sobranie sochinenii*, 48:52–53 (entry of March 3, 1863).

52. For more on Tolstoy's views at the time he worked on the novel, see Feuer, *Tolstoy and the Genesis of "War and Peace,"* 168–206.

53. Orwin, *Tolstoy's Art and Thought*, 100–107.

54. Tolstoy, *Polnoe sobranie sochinenii*, 12:211.

55. Ibid., 81. As Garry Morson has shown, the novel's battle scenes represent the reign of diffusion and chaos. See Morson, *Hidden in Plain View*, 97–98.

56. Tolstoy, *Polnoe sobranie sochinenii*, 11:342. This statement is one of the instances when Tolstoy's famous scorn for the "cult of great men" in history shapes his vision of the nation at war.

57. Ibid., 11:173.

58. In the novel, the emperor pronounces these words with Napoleonic grandiosity, a testament to the author's sarcasm. Moreover, he says them in French (ibid., 12:12). On the use of this phrase in the patriotic press, see chapter 3, pp. 112–13, 223n84.

59. Ibid., 11:54–55, 174.

60. As for characters less dear to the author, some of them experience no patriotic feelings whatsoever (Boris, Berg, Hélène), while the mood of others (Anatole Kuragin, Dolokhov) goes unmentioned.

61. In 1812 many called these provinces Polish, since they were relatively recently annexed to Russia. For the Russian public's typical perception of the western borderlands, see chapter 3. The poet Fedor Glinka, for instance, called Smolensk "the gates of Russia," thus denying the status of Russian territory to the area west of Smolensk. See Glinka, *Pis'ma russkogo ofitsera*.

62. Tolstoy, *Polnoe sobranie sochinenii*, 11:55. The novel dates the beginning of the guerilla war to the capture of Smolensk by the French (ibid., 12:120).

63. Ibid., 12:123.

64. Ibid., 11:184. As Victor Shklovskii has demonstrated, Tolstoy intentionally ignores the fact that Kutuzov consciously chose Borodino as the site of the battle for strategic reasons (Shklovskii, "M. I. Kutuzov i Platon Karataev").

65. It is Tolstoy's preoccupation with this ethnocentric story that explains why the novel does not depict the Russian army's foreign campaign of 1813–15. In her book *Imperial knowledge*, Ewa Thompson analyzes *War and Peace* as a typical example of nineteenth-century European novels that translated "imperial outreach into artistic resourcefulness." Resting on "the bedrock of imperialism," the novel satisfied, according to Thompson, social demand for a literature that reflected

victorious imperial growth. To support this claim, Thompson argues that the novel delivers a "dramatic glorification of Russian nationhood" and rejects "any doubt about the empire's legitimacy or Russia's ethnic borders." In this argument Thompson lumps Russian national and imperial identities under the same rubric and takes *War and Peace* out of the context of nineteenth-century national discourse that sought to distinguish between Russian ancestral territory and imperial space (see Thompson, *Imperial Knowledge*, 85–108). Though in the 1860s Tolstoy was by no means the full-fledged anti-imperialist he would become later, the novel clearly demonstrates the predominance of the Russian nation over the Romanov Empire in the author's imagination.

66. On organic consolidation as the focal point of the novel, see Christian, *Tolstoy's "War and Peace,"* 105–12. Christian, however, calls the process "sublimation of the self" and focuses on the characters' moral development, rather than on how Tolstoy defines the nation.

67. Tolstoy, *Polnoe sobranie sochinenii*, 9:328.

68. Ibid., 11:189.

69. As Jeff Love has concisely put it, the novel reveals the timeless patterns "behind time-bound narrative progressions" (Love, *Overcoming of History in "War and Peace,"* 95). On repetitions in the novel, see also Christian, *Tolstoy's "War and Peace."*

70. Tolstoy, *Polnoe sobranie sochinenii*, 11:101.

71. Ibid., 12:81.

72. Ibid., 11:4 (italics mine).

73. On this tension between the forces of present and past in the novel, see Love, *Overcoming of History in "War and Peace,"* 105.

74. Tolstoy, *Polnoe sobranie sochinenii*, 9:4, 12:119.

75. Benedict Anderson sees the opening out of the internal time of novels as one of the basic instruments of imagining national community. See Anderson, *Imagined Community*, 22–36.

76. Tolstoy, *Polnoe sobranie sochinenii*, 12:36.

77. Ibid., 12:37.

78. Since the appearance of *War and Peace*, literary critics have discussed Tolstoy's tendency to ascribe to the beginning of the nineteenth century thoughts and sentiments that developed only later. Critics have labeled these transplantations anachronisms, ignoring their important role in highlighting the nation's unity across generational divides (for a discussion of critics' perception of Tolstoy's anachronisms, see Ungurianu, *Plotting History*, 114–16). On Tolstoy's opposition to the view that the Great Reform era represented a break with the past, see Feuer, *Tolstoy and the Genesis of "War and Peace,"* 168–79.

79. Tolstoy, *Polnoe sobranie sochinenii*, 12:98, 105–6, 158.

80. Ibid., 12:119–21.

81. Ibid., 12:165.

82. This does not mean that Tolstoy completely fails to show aggression on the Russian side, but he always surrounds scenes of violence with doubt about their acceptability. Thus, Nikolai Rostov commits what his commanders praise as a heroic act in the affair near the town of Ostrovna, but after leading the attack he feels "morally nauseated" (Tolstoy, *Polnoe sobranie sochinenii*, 11:65).

Chapter 5. The Myth of Spiritual Descent

1. For a general discussion on the relation between the sacred and the profane in nationalist ideologies, see Smith, *Chosen Peoples*. For an incisive overview of the role ascribed to religion in Russian national self-definitions, see Franklin, "Identity and Religion."

2. See chapter 2, p. 78.

3. Kliuchevskii, *Sochineniia*, 1:122–24. Kliuchevskii utterly scorned the vision of the Varangian legend as a starting point of Russian history. Arguing that the story reflected neither the origins of the nation nor the foundation of the state, he treated it as a compilation made in the twelfth century merely to legitimate the institution of princely power (ibid., 1:117, 152–56).

4. Pogodin, *K slavianam*, 10. The missive was first published in the newspaper *Nashe vremia* (no. 96 [1862]). It is extensively quoted in Barsukov, *Zhizn' i trudy M. P. Pogodina*, 19:74–83.

5. Pogodin, *K slavianam*, 11.

6. See chapter 2, pp. 56–58.

7. Pogodin, *K slavianam*, 1.

8. Cross and Sherbowitz-Wetzor, *Russian Primary Chronicle*, 62–63.

9. On two types of foundation myths—those that elaborate biological ties with presumed ancestors and those that trace ideological kinship, see Smith, *Myths and Memories of the Nation*, 57–95.

10. Russian thinkers subscribed to the view that the Poles were superficially tainted by Latinism, which ran counter to their national soul, while the Czechs had long yearned for deliverance from the Catholic "yoke." The latter contention—far-fetched as it may seem—relied on a view originated by the Slavophiles, who understood the Hussite movement as a semiconscious attempt on the part of the Czechs to return to their Orthodox roots. During and after the 1863 uprising in Poland, Russian Pan-Slavists began to view Poles as hopelessly Catholicized. On the Slavophiles' approach to the issue see, Walicki, "Slavophile Thinkers and the Polish Question," 92.

11. Pogodin, *K slavianam*, 1.

12. Smolich, *Istoriia russkoi tserkvi*, 2:12–13.

13. Miller, *Ukrainskii vopros*, 102–4.

14. Pogodin, *K slavianam*, 11.

15. Iu. F. Samarin and N. Ia. Danilevsky contributed greatly to this combination.

16. Pogodin, *K slavianam*, 5 –6.

17. *Den'*, no. 33 (May 26, 1862).

18. A. Gil'ferding, "O Kirille i Mefodii," *Den'*, no. 25 (March 31, 1862). His subsequent articles under the same title appeared in *Den'*, no. 29 (April 28, 1862), no. 30 (May 5, 1862), no. 31 (May 12, 1862).

19. A. Gil'ferding, "O Kirille i Mefodii," *Den'*, no. 29 (April 28, 1862).

20. On the empress's sympathy toward the Pan-Slavic projects, see Barsukov, *Zhizn' i trudy M. P. Pogodina*, 19:83; S. A. Nikitin, *Slavianskie komitety*, 40, 195.

21. Filaret [V. M. Drozdov], *Sobranie mnenii i otzyvov*, vol. 5, pt. 1, 242 (letter of A. P. Akhmatov to Filaret, April 12, 1862).

22. Ibid., 243.

23. Ibid., 244; Barsukov, *Zhizn' i trudy M. P. Pogodina*, 19:83 –86. Though the government agreed with Filaret, nevertheless in September 1862, in connection with the celebration of the Millennium of Russia, Alexander II issued a decree granting Russian military decorations to some prominent Slavs—activists, scholars, journalists, and politicians. The list of their names appeared in several newspapers, including *Den'* (see no. 38 [September 22, 1862]: 14 –15). Pogodin's project was not the only attempt to connect the two millennium celebrations. In 1855 S. P. Shevyrev had come up with a similar plan, but, unlike Pogodin, he proposed to commemorate both dates with a single ceremony (on Shevyrev's project, see Kotliarevskii, *Sochineniia*, 2:442).

24. Pogodin relied on the date put forward by O. M. Bodianskii in his book *O vremeni proiskhozhdeniia slavianskikh pis'men*.

25. Quoted in Barsukov, *Zhizn' i trudy M. P. Pogodina*, 19:82.

26. In September 1862 *Den'* reprinted from the Viennese journal *Ost und West* an article by the Croatian professor Imbro (Emeric) Tkalac, "An Invitation to Slavic Scholars to a Meeting on the Occasion of the Millennium of the Mission of the Apostles to the Slavs Cyril and Methodius in 1863": "It is to be hoped that all branches of the Slavic peoples," wrote Tkalac, "regardless of confession, will participate most actively in this celebration. And what occasion could be more auspicious for a brotherly convocation of Slavic scholars than this Christian and national celebration" (*Den'*, no. 38 [September 22, 1862]).

27. Barsukov, *Zhizn' i trudy M. P. Pogodina*, 19:82.

28. *Pravoslavnoe obozrenie*, no. 5 (1862): 3.

29. Knight, "Imperiia napokaz."

30. [Popov], *Vserossiiskaia etnograficheskaia vystavka*, 22–23. This book is a compilation of newspaper reports concerning the ethnographic exhibition and the Slavic Congress.

31. *Moskva*, no. 20 (April 25, 1867) (lead article).

32. On how the Pan-Slavists, the majority of whom were members of the Moscow Slavic Benevolent Committee (1858–76), came to influence the concept of the exhibition and use it to disseminate their message, see Petrovich, *Emergence of Russian Panslavism*, 199–201; S. A. Nikitin, *Slavianskie komitety*, 167–69; Milojković-Djurić, *Panslavism and National Identity*, 76–77. A collection of correspondence addressed to M. F. Raevskii, the priest of the Russian embassy's church in Vienna from 1842 to 1884, demonstrates that the Russian Pan-Slavists mobilized their entire network of contacts with Slavs abroad to generate the broad range of contributions to the exhibition. See *Zarubezhnye slaviane i Rossiia*, esp. 44, 45, 146, 169–71, 240, 257, 268, 480–82.

33. *Moskva*, no. 20 (April 25, 1867) (lead article).

34. S. A. Nikitin, *Slavianskie komitety*, 169.

35. Knight, "Imperiia napokaz," 130n65.

36. Though only donors of exhibits were to receive invitations to Moscow, the Pan-Slavists (including Pogodin) exceeded this limitation and issued invitations to a wider group of Slavs from abroad; see S. A. Nikitin, *Slavianskie komitety*, 169, 181; *Zarubezhnye slaviane i Rossiia*, 268 (letter of V. I. Lamanskii to Raevskii, November 1, 1866), 486–87 (letter of K. J. Erben to Raevskii, April 11, 1867).

37. S. A. Nikitin, *Slavianskie komitety*, 192–193.

38. Deeply ingrained in Russian history, this theme came to occupy an increasingly important place in Russian national self-perception in the nineteenth century. Russian intellectuals always referred with special reverence to the Treaty of Küçük Kaynarca (1774), signed after the Russian victory in the Russo-Turkish War of 1768–74. In this document, Russia claimed the right to defend the religious interests of the Orthodox Christians of the Ottoman Empire and, as one of the congress's reports stated, thus "first gave the Slavs the hope of deliverance" ("Slavianskii obed v zale Peterburgskogo Dvorianskogo sobraniia," *Russkii invalid*, no. 130 [May 12, 1867]).

39. "Iz Varshavy," *Russkii invalid*, no. 127 (May 9, 1867).

40. For this interpretation of the Pan-Slavist project, see Bassin, *Imperial Visions*, 13. See also Kohn, *Pan-Slavism*, 123–227.

41. Knight, "Imperiia napokaz," 116–23.

42. M. P. Pogodin, "Neskol'ko myslei o vstreche slavian," *Russkii*, May 1, 1867, 193.

43. Disagreements arose most often between hosts and guests. The participants' visions of future relations among the Slavs differed dramatically. Some guests sought military assistance from Russia. Others proposed a federation of independent Slavic states under Russia's protection; still a third group feared any form of

Russian political involvement and stood for only cultural contacts. The Czechs in particular were wary of falling under the sway of the Russian Empire. The Russian hosts were at odds among themselves as well. For an insightful account of the various positions expressed at the congress, see S. A. Nikitin, *Slavianskie komitety*, 156–259.

44. "Obed 11 maia v Peterburgskom Dvorianskom sobranii," *Moskovskie vedomosti*, no. 105 (May 14, 1867).

45. "K brat'iam slavianam" (To the Slavic brethren), *Russkii*, May 1, 1867, 197.

46. N. A. Sergievskii, "Slovo na 11 maia 1867 goda v den' sviatykh Kirilla i Mefodiia," *Russkii*, May 15, 1867, 203.

47. *Den'*, no. 33 (May 26, 1862).

48. "Slavianskii obed v zale Peterburgskogo Dvorianskogo sobraniia."

49. "Obed 11 maia v Peterburgskom Dvorianskom sobranii."

50. V. Andreev, "Slavianskie gosti v Peterburge," *Russkii invalid*, no. 128 (May 10, 1867), no. 129 (May 11, 1867). The correspondent for *Moskovskie vedomosti*, describing the greeting of the Slavic guests as they first arrived in Moscow, also claimed that "in many places a friendly exchange of native tongues was heard: to the common Slavic '*slava*,' which in this festive moment the Russian people called up from their ancient ritual poetry, the guests responded with the Russian '*zdravstvuite*'!" ("O vstreche slavian v Moskve," *Moskovskie vedomosti*, no. 107 [May 17, 1867]).

51. "Ozhidaniia v Moskve slavian," *Russkii*, May 15, 1867, 230. The rector of Moscow University also supported this project. In his speech before the Slavic guests, he noted "the urgent need for ... a single language, comprehensible to all educated Slavs and used by all in mutual dealings" (*Moskovskie vedomosti*, no. 109 [May 19, 1867]).

52. "Ozhidaniia v Moskve slavian," 229–30.

53. On the use of alphabet policies by the Hapsburg and Romanov empires and on events in Galicia during the 1850s and 1860s, see Miller, *Romanov Empire and Nationalism*, 74–75.

54. N. A. Popov, "Vopros ob obshcheslavianskoi azbuke," *Sovremennaia letopis'*, no. 39 (1865): 5–9. On the eve of the congress, the Russian scholar S. P. Mikutskii also assured Raevskii that "the brave and noble Croatian people" would soon adopt Cyrillic (*Zarubezhnye slaviane i Rossiia*, 294).

55. "Pis'mo chekha k redaktoru," *Russkii*, April 3, 1867, 109. In his letter to Raevskii (1862), A. F. Gil'ferding introduced Jezbera as "a tireless fighter for Church Slavonic and the Russian alphabet" (*Zarubezhnye slaviane i Rossiia*, 134). It was the Czech delegates, however, who most adamantly refused such calls. František Rieger, a Czech deputy, asserted in one of his speeches: "The Slavic tongues are so close among themselves that, had it been the will of God, we would now be a people united in writing and language. ... Many, perhaps, would prefer to converge into a single unit, body and soul, but a thousand years of history cannot disappear

without a trace" ("Slavianskie gosti v Moskve," *Moskovskie vedomosti*, no. 112 [May 23, 1867]; see similar statements by other guests in "Sokol'nitskii banket v chest' slavianskikh gostei," *Moskovskie vedomosti*, no. 113 [May 24, 1867]).

56. "Slavianskii obed v zale Peterburgskogo Dvorianskogo sobraniia."

57. Newspapers and popular brochures discussed the menu and provided a detailed description of it for the general public. See ibid.; "Obed 11 maia v Peterburgskom Dvorianskom sobranii"; *Russkii Slavianin: Pervyi vseslavianskii s"ezd v Rossii, ego prichiny i znachenie* (Moscow, 1867), 31.

58. "Slavianskii obed v zale Peterburgskogo Dvorianskogo sobraniia." Leading Russian scholars, including V. I. Lamanskii, took part in locating and selecting the flags and banners that represented the various Slavic peoples at this dinner (see the letter of A. V. Freigang to Raevskii, March 9, 1867, in *Zarubezhnye slaviane i Rossiia*, 450).

59. [Popov], *Vserossiiskaia etnograficheskaia vystavka*, 348–49, 371.

60. Ibid., 368.

61. *Moskovskie vedomosti*, no. 113 (May 24, 1867) (lead article).

62. *Moskva*, no. 10 (January 13, 1867) (lead article).

63. [Popov], *Vserossiiskaia etnograficheskaia vystavka*, 340.

64. "Inostrannye izvestiia: Iz Belgrada," *Russkii invalid*, no. 130 (May 12, 1867).

65. M. P. Pogodin, "Pribytie slavian v Moskvu," *Russkii*, May 22, 1867, 269.

66. G. E. Shchurovskii greeted the Slavic guests with the words: "Here the feeling of kinship has triumphed over physical impediments" ("Vnutrenie izvestiia," *Russkii invalid*, no. 138 [May 20, 1867]).

67. M. P. Pogodin, "Poslanie T'eru" (Missive to Thiers), *Russkii*, March 20, 1867, 35–36.

68. M. P. Pogodin, "Lektsiia o slavianakh, chitannaia v etnograficheskom obshchestve," *Russkii*, April 10, 1867, 135.

69. *Moskva*, no. 20 (April 25, 1867) (lead article).

70. [Popov], *Vserossiiskaia etnograficheskaia vystavka*, 299–300, 374. On the position of the Czech delegation, see S. A. Nikitin, *Slavianskie komitety*, 197, 202, 209–10, 215. See also note 55 of this chapter.

71. Hobsbawm, *Nations and Nationalism since 1780*, 31–45 (quotation on 33). See also Knight, "Imperiia napokaz," 120–21.

72. *Moskovskie vedomosti*, no. 110 (May 20, 1867) (lead article).

73. The speech by V. I. Lamanskii was published as a part of the following report: "V dopolnenie k opisaniiu slavianskogo obeda," *Russkii invalid*, no. 131 (May 13, 1867). Popov also included it in *Vserossiiskaia etnograficheskaia vystavka*, 203–6.

74. On the political background of the congress, see S. A. Nikitin, *Slavianskie komitety*, 158, 180–83; Petrovich, *Emergence of Russian Panslavism*, 202–4.

75. "Na obede v pervyi den' priezda slavianskikh gostei," *Russkii invalid*, no. 129 (May 11, 1867). Tiutchev used von Beust's motto in his poem "Slavianam," which was composed as a greeting to the Slavic guests. The work was read aloud by S. M. Sukhotin and I. S. Aksakov at one of the Moscow receptions for the Slavs, and was then published in *Moskovskie vedomosti* (no.113 [May 24, 1867]) and reprinted in *Vserossiiskaia etnograficheskaia vystavka*, 370.

76. "Ozhidaniia v Moskve slavian," *Russkii*, May 15, 1867, 229; "Moskovskie izvestiia: Pribytie slavian v Moskvu," *Russkii*, May 22, 1867, 268. For other reports that highlighted the unifying effect of the congress on the Russian public, see "Sokol'nitskii banket v chest' slavianskikh gostei 21 maia," *Moskovskie vedomosti*, no. 113 (May 24, 1867); [Popov], *Vserossiiskaia etnograficheskaia vystavka*, 210, 326–27, 369, 445.

77. V. Andreev, "Slavianskie gosti v Peterburge," *Russkii invalid*, no. 129 (May 11, 1867). Similar words by František Brauner, the Czech lawyer and politician, were enthusiastically quoted in *Moskovskie vedomosti* (M. [B. M. Markevich], "Obed u grafa D. A. Tolstogo 12 maia" [no. 106 (May 16, 1867)]).

78. [Popov], *Vserossiiskaia etnograficheskaia vystavka*, 347.

79. "Moskovskie izvestiia: Pribytie slavian v Moskvu," 269.

80. B. M. Markevich, letter to M. N. Katkov, May 15, 1867, Manuscript Division of Russian State Library (RGB), fond 120, folder 7, document 31, pp. 75–76.

81. S. A. Nikitin, *Slavianskie komitety*, 195–96; [Popov], *Vserossiiskaia etnograficheskaia vystavka*, 230–33.

82. A. A. Kireev, diary (entry from May 10, 1867), in Manuscript Division of Russian State Library (RGB), fond 126, folder 4a, pp. 36–39.

83. S. A. Nikitin, *Slavianskie komitety*, 196.

84. *Moskovskie vedomosti*, no. 116 (May 28, 1867).

85. Smith, *National Identity*, 37.

86. Tiutchev, *Polnoe sobranie stikhotvorenii*, 255.

87. It was not only the Pan-Slavists who expressed hopes that religious culture and Orthodox institutions would play a significant role in forging the Russian nation. With the beginning of the reform era, a portion of the press, ecclesiastical and lay alike, launched a campaign to advocate church reforms, with the expectation that the church would lend its strength to the nation-making process. These writers urged the government to release the church from state control and take steps toward reuniting the Old Believers with the majority of Russia's Orthodox population. Projects for restoring the church's independence found support not only from the leading periodicals of the 1860s (*Den'*, *Moskva*, *Pravoslavnoe obozrenie*, *Tserkovno-obshchestvennyi vestnik*) but also among some representatives of the ecclesiastical hierarchy (see Smolich, *Istoriia russkoi tserkvi*, 1:227–30, 374–77). They were not, however, implemented. On the Russian church's weakness with

respect to the state and its implication for the nation-making process, see Hosking, *Russia*, 225 –45. It was not only tsarist policies that hindered these projects. As we shall see later in the chapter, Russian independent thinkers also encountered serious difficulties in their attempts to construct a religion-based national identity that would make Christian values and religious ties into means of building the national community.

88. Though the last independent Balkan sees at Péc and Ohrid existed until the 1760s, they did not have political significance. For more on this issue, see Todorova, "Ottoman Legacy in the Balkans," 49.

89. Gerd, *Konstantinopol' i Peterburg*, 15 –26.

90. Arnakis, "Role of Religion," 134 –35.

91. For a detailed account of the Greek–Bulgarian church conflict, see Teplov, *Greko-bolgarskii tserkovnyi vopros*; Burmov, *Bŭlgaro-gŭrtskata tsŭrkovna raspria*; Meininger, *Ignatiev and the Establishment of the Bulgarian Exarchate*; Markova, *Bŭlgarkata ekzarkhiia*; Gerd, *Konstantinopol' i Peterburg*, 225 –308.

92. The Turks' grant of limited autonomy to the Principality of Serbia (1830) was followed by first partial (1832) and later complete (1879) release of the Serbs from the jurisdiction of the Constantinople patriarchate. The Greek Kingdom, after declaring its independence in 1830, established a Greek autocephalous church (1833), recognized by the Constantinople patriarchate only in 1850. In 1865 Romania declared its church autocephaly (recognized 1885). See Arnakis, "Role of Religion," 134 –35; Meininger, *Ignatiev and the Establishment of the Bulgarian Exarchate*, 14; Seton-Watson, *Rise of Nationality in the Balkans*, 78; Todorova, "Ottoman Legacy in the Balkans," 49; Gerd, *Konstantinopol' i Peterburg*, 30–32. For insightful analysis of the Bulgarian case and its significance for comparative study of the Ottoman, Hapsburg, and Russian empires, see Werth, "Georgian Autocephaly," 78 –80.

93. Quoted in Meininger, *Ignatiev and the Establishment of the Bulgarian Exarchate*, 83. On the policies of Patriarch Gregorios VI, see Gerd, *Konstantinopol' i Peterburg*, 234 –35. A supporter of the Pan-Slavist project, Ignatiev initially sought a compromise between the patriarchate and the Bulgarians. When he became convinced that compromise was not to be achieved, however, he helped the Bulgarians establish their independent church unilaterally. On Ignatiev's position and his strategy to avert the pronouncement of the schism, see Meininger, *Ignatiev and the Establishment of the Bulgarian Exarchate*, esp. 25 –30; Khevrolina, *Rossiiskii diplomat graf Nikolai Pavlovich Ignatiev*, 103 –7, 162 –81. On the Russian official position as explicated by the Russian Synod and by A. M. Gorchakov, the head of the Russian Foreign Ministry, and the tensions between Gorchakov and Ignatiev, see Mosse, *Alexander II and the Modernization of Russia*, 119; Meininger, *Ignatiev and the Establishment of the Bulgarian Exarchate*, 112–17; Gerd, *Konstantinopol' i Peterburg*, 230–38; Werth, "Georgian Autocephaly," 80–81.

94. Meininger, *Ignatiev and the Establishment of the Bulgarian Exarchate*, 177–81; Gerd, *Konstantinopol' i Peterburg*, 236.

95. The Holy Synod admitted that the Bulgarians' religious needs should be addressed by Constantinople, but it did not support the unilateral establishment of the Bulgarian church and advocated canonical resolution of the issue (see the incisive discussion of the official Russian position in Gerd, *Konstantinopol' i Peterburg*, 230–32). For the Russian government, the issue was potentially dangerous, as similar claims for autocephalous churches by the non–Russian Orthodox population of the Romanov empire could threaten the empire's integrity (see Werth, "Georgian Autocephaly," 81–83).

96. Barsukov, *Zhizn' i trudy M. P. Pogodina*, 19:74. It was a mid-nineteenth-century cliché to depict Bulgarians as "terrified and morally exhausted" (letter of L. V. Berezin to M. F. Raevskii, April 21, 1861, in *Zarubezhnye slaviane i Rossiia*, 32).

97. Pogodin, *Sobranie statei*, 133. This article was initially delivered as a speech to the Slavic Benevolent Committee in Moscow in 1873.

98. The typical Russian Pan-Slavist attitude toward the Bulgarians' struggle for their independent church was encapsulated in Nil Popov's speech to the Petersburg Slavic Benevolent Committee, delivered on May 11, 1872. See Popov, *Po povodu vosstanovleniia bolgarskogo ekzarkhata*.

99. Katkov, *Sobranie peredovykh statei "Moskovskikh vedomostei": 1871 god* [hereafter cited as Katkov, *SPS 1871*], 176–77 (lead article from no. 60 [March 19, 1871]).

100. Konstantin Leont'ev, "Vizantizm i slavianstvo" (1875), in *Vostok, Rossiia i slavianstvo*, 113.

101. Khomiakov, *Polnoe sobranie sochinenii*, 3:179 (original in French).

102. Ibid., 3:190–91 (original in French).

103. Ibid., 1:379–80. A broad group of Slavophiles signed this denunciation. For more details, see Barsukov, *Zhizn' i trudy M. P. Pogodina*, 16:451–60.

104. Pogodin, "Sviatye Kirill i Mefodii, " 1–2.

105. In his response to this article, the linguist and historian P. A. Lavrovskii criticized Pogodin precisely for downplaying the political significance of Russia's religious ties with the "Greeks." He bluntly stated: "The Greeks' current actions with respect to the Bulgarians . . . should not be taken as the yardstick . . . of the church question" (P. A. Lavrovskii, "Byli li Kirill i Mefodii slaviane ili greki: Otvet Pogodinu," in Manuscript Division of Russian State Library (RGB), fond 231/III, folder 7, document 26. The ecclesiastical press also responded disapprovingly to Pogodin's project. See *Dukhovnyi vestnik*, no. 2 (1866): 322–50.

106. Dostoevsky, *Polnoe sobranie sochinenii*, vol. 29, bk. 1, 263 (letter to M. P. Pogodin, February 26, 1873).

107. Aksakov, *Polnoe sobranie sochinenii*, 1:40 (May 30, 1864).

108. Katkov, *SPS 1871*, 175 (no. 60 [March 19, 1871]).

109. Filippov articulated his understanding of the conflict in a number of articles published in the newspaper *Grazhdanin* during the 1870s and later reprinted in his book *Sovremennye tserkovnye voprosy*. The recently published correspondence between Leont'ev and Filippov shows the substantial similarity of their views on the Greek–Bulgarian church controversy. See Fetisenko, "Brat ot brata pomogaem."

110. Dostoevsky, *Polnoe sobranie sochinenii*, 26:84 (November 1877 issue of *Diary of a Writer*).

111. Ibid., 26:85–87.

112. Leont'ev, *Vostok, Rossiia i slavianstvo*, 127.

113. For an insightful discussion of the implications of the schism for Russian imperial policies, see Werth, "Georgian Autocephaly," esp. 74–75, 78, 83.

114. Dostoevsky, *Polnoe sobranie sochinenii*, 14:58.

In Place of a Conclusion

1. Dostoevsky, *Polnoe sobranie sochinenii*, vol. 29, bk. 1, 30 (letter to Nikolai Strakhov, March 18, 1869). Several years later, in his *Diary of a Writer* (November 1877 issue), Dostoevsky took issue with Danilevsky on a few points, but again gave a highly enthusiastic overall assessment of the book (ibid., 26:83–87).

2. Robert MacMaster emphasizes, however, a certain continuity in Danilevsky's intellectual development before and after his imprisonment. In the views espoused by Danilevsky in the 1860s, MacMaster finds the leftist Hegelian overtones and traces of utopian socialism that defined the writer's outlook in the 1840s. See MacMaster, *Danilevsky: A Russian Totalitarian Philosopher*.

3. Thaden, *Conservative Nationalism in Nineteenth-Century Russia*, 102–4.

4. For the influence of German romantic and idealistic philosophy on Danilevsky, see ibid., 105–6.

5. Danilevsky, *Rossiia i Evropa*, 121–22, 124.

6. Danilevsky, *Darvinizm*. For insightful discussion of this study, see Todes, *Darwin without Malthus*, 41–43; Vucinich, *Darwin in Russian Thought*, 122–29. On the importance of Darwin's theory for *Russia and Europe*, see MacMaster, *Danilevsky: A Russian Totalitarian Philosopher*, 249.

7. Vucinich, *Darwin in Russian Thought*, 123–25; Todes, *Darwin without Malthus*, 41–42.

8. Danilevsky, *Rossiia i Evropa*, 139–71; Todes, *Darwin without Malthus*, 41–42.

9. Danilevsky, *Rossiia i Evropa*, 203–4.

10. Ibid., 26–27, 203–4, 239, 275, 319.

11. Todes, *Darwin without Malthus*, 42.

12. Danilevsky, *Rossiia i Evropa*, 201.

13. Ibid., 21–22.

14. Ibid., 238–40.

15. Ibid., 130.

16. Ibid., 105.

17. Ibid., 337–38.

18. Ibid., 234.

19. See MacMaster, *Danilevsky: A Russian Totalitarian Philosopher*, 226–27, 271–90.

20. Danilevsky, *Rossiia i Evropa*, 500–509, 550.

21. Ibid., 436.

22. Ibid., 451, 461–64.

23. Ibid., 410–27, 468–69; Thaden, *Conservative Nationalism in Nineteenth-Century Russia*, 111.

24. Danilevsky, *Rossiia i Evropa*, 411, 501–2.

25. Ibid., 300–301, 321, 425, 427, 535–37; Thaden, *Conservative Nationalism in Nineteenth-Century Russia*, 103.

26. Danilevsky made his additions to *Russia and Europe* in 1880–81. Nikolai Strakhov, his friend and follower, not only published the notes in posthumous editions of the book but also used bold print to bring them to readers' attention (see Danilevsky, *Rossiia i Evropa*, esp. 300–301, 379, 386–87, 392–93, 468).

27. Wortman, *Scenarios of Power*, 2:159–305, 525 (quotation).

28. For the influence on the tsar exerted by key figures of reform-era national discourse (Pobedonostsev and Katkov, above all), see Wortman, *Scenarios of Power*, 2:177–88.

29. Ibid., 178–79, 224–43, 251–55.

30. Ibid., 185, 237, 256–70.

Bibliography

Aksakov, I. S. *Biografiia Fedora Ivanovicha Tiutcheva.* Moscow: Tipografiia M. G. Volchaninova, 1886.

———. *Ivan Sergeevich Aksakov v ego pis'makh.* 4 vols. Moscow: Tipografiia M. G. Volchaninova, 1888 –96.

———. *Polnoe sobranie sochinenii.* 7 vols. Moscow: Tipografiia M. G. Volchaninova, 1886 – 87.

———. *Pol'skii vopros i zapadno-russkoe delo.*Vol. 3 of *Sochineniia.* St. Petersburg: Izdanie Imperatorskoi Publichnoi biblioteki, 1900.

Aksakova, V. S. *Dnevnik (1854–1855).* St. Petersburg: Ogni, 1913.

Alvarez Junco, Jose. "The Formation of Spanish Identity and Its Adaptation to the Age of Nations." *History and Memory* 14, no. 1/2 (2002): 13 –36.

Anderson, Benedict. *Imagined Community: Reflections on the Origin and Spread of Nationalism.* New York: Verso, 1991.

Anemone, Anthony. "Gender, Genre, and the Discourse of Imperialism in Tolstoy's *The Cossacks.*" *Tolstoy Studies Journal* 6 (1993): 47 – 63.

Arnakis, George G. "The Role of Religion in the Development of Balkan National-ism." In *The Balkans in Transition*, edited by Barbara and Charles Jelavich, 115 – 44. Berkeley: University of California Press, 1963.

Balibar, Étienne. "The Nation Form: History and Ideology." In *Becoming National: A Reader*, edited by Geoff Eley and Ronald Suny, 132 – 49. New York: Oxford University Press, 1996.

Barooshian, Vahan D. *V. V. Vereshchagin: Artist at War*. Gainesville: University Press of Florida, 1993.

Barrett, Thomas M. *At the Edge of Empire: The Terek Cossacks and the North Caucasian Frontier, 1700–1860*. Boulder, Colo.: Westview, 1999.

———. "Crossing Boundaries: The Trading Frontiers of the Terek Cossacks." In *Russia's Orient: Imperial Borderlands and Peoples, 1700–1917*, edited by Daniel R. Brower and Edward J. Lazzerini, 227 – 48. Bloomington: Indiana University Press, 1997.

Barsukov, N. P. *Zhizn' i trudy M. P. Pogodina*. 22 vols. St. Petersburg: Tipografiia M. M. Stasiulevicha, 1888 –1910.

Bassin, Mark. *Imperial Visions: Nationalist Imagination and Geographical Expansion in the Russian Far East, 1840–1865*. Cambridge: Cambridge University Press, 1999.

Becker, Seymour. "Russia and the Concept of Empire." *Ab Imperio* 3 – 4 (2000): 329 – 42.

———. "Russia between East and West: The Intelligentsia, Russian National Identity and the Asian Borderlands." *Central Asian Survey* 10, no. 4 (1991): 47 – 64.

Bell, David. "The Unbearable Lightness of Being French: Law, Republicanism, and National Identity at the End of the Old Regime." *American Historical Review: AHR Forum* 106, no. 4 (October 2001): 1215 –35.

Bodianskii, O. M. *O vremeni proiskhozhdeniia slavianskikh pis'men*. Moscow: Universitetskaia tipografiia, 1855.

———. "Vyderzhki iz dnevnika." In *Sbornik Obshchestva liubitelei rossiiskoi slovesnosti na 1891 god*, 109 –38. Moscow, 1891.

Bogdanovich, M. I. *Vostochnaia voina: 1853–1856 gody*. 4 vols. St. Petersburg: Tipografiia F. Sushchinskogo, 1876.

B . . . ov, V. *Beseda u pamiatnika tysiacheletiia russkoi zemli*. St. Petersburg: V. V. Kholmushin, 1862.

Bukhshtab, B. Ia. "Posle vystrela Karakozova." *Katorga i ssylka*, no. 5 (1931): 50 – 88.

Burbank, Jane, Mark von Hagen, and Anatolyi Remnev, eds. *Russian Empire: Space, People, Power, 1700–1930*. Bloomington: Indiana University Press, 2007.

Burmov, T. *Bŭlgaro-gŭrtskata tsŭrkovna raspria*. Sofia: Sv. Sinod na Bŭlgarskata tsŭrkva, 1902.

Chernukha, V. G. *Pravitel'stvennaia politika v otnoshenii pechati: 60-e-70-e gody XIX veka*. Leningrad: Nauka, 1989.

———. *Vnutrenniaia politika tsarizma s serediny 50-kh do nachala 80-kh godov XIX veka*. Leningrad: Nauka, 1978.

Chicherin, B. N. "O krepostnom sostoianii." *Golosa iz Rossii* 2 (1856): 139–250.

Christian, R. F. *Tolstoy: A Critical Introduction*. Cambridge: Cambridge University Press, 1969.

———. *Tolstoy's "War and Peace": A Study*. Oxford: Clarendon, 1962.

Clowes, Edith W., Samuel D. Kassow, and James L. West, eds. *Between Tsar and People: Educated Society and the Quest for Public Identity in Late Imperial Russia*. Princeton, N.J.: Princeton University Press, 1991.

Colley, Linda. *Britons: Forging the Nation, 1707–1837*. New Haven, Conn.: Yale University Press, 1992.

Confino, Alon. *Germany as a Culture of Remembrance: Promises and Limits of Writing History*. Chapel Hill: University of North Carolina Press, 2006.

Crook, David Paul. *Darwinism, War, and History: The Debate over the Biology of War from the "Origin of Species" to the First World War*. Cambridge: Cambridge University Press, 1994.

Cross, Samuel H., and Olgerd P. Sherbowitz-Wetzor, trans. and ed. *The Russian Primary Chronicle: Laurentian Text*. Cambridge, Mass.: Mediaeval Academy of America, 1953.

Curtiss, John Shelton. *Russia's Crimean War*. Durham, N.C.: Duke University Press, 1979.

Danilevsky, N. Ia. *Darvinizm: Kriticheskoe izsliedovanie*. St. Petersburg: Komarov, 1885–89.

———. *Rossiia i Evropa*. 1895. New York: Johnson Reprint, 1966.

Del'vig, A. I. *Moi vospominaniia*. 4 vols. St. Petersburg: Izdanie Imperatorskogo Moskovskogo i Rumiantsevskogo muzeia, 1913.

Dinesman, T. G., et al. "Tiutchev v pis'makh i dnevnikakh chlenov ego sem'ii i drugikh sovremennikov." In *Literaturnoe nasledstvo* 97 (*Fedor Ivanovich Tiutchev*), edited by S. A. Makashin, K. V. Pigarev, and T. G. Dinesman, 2:171–432. Moscow: Nauka, 1989.

Dixon, Megan. "Repositioning Pushkin and the Poems of the Polish Uprising." In Ransel and Shallcross, *Polish Encounters, Russian Identity*, 49–73.

Dobroliubov, N. A. *Sobranie Sochinenii*. 9 vols. Moscow: Khudozhestvennaia literatura, 1963.

Dolbilov, Mikhail. "The Emancipation Reform of 1861 in Russia and the Nationalism of the Imperial Bureaucracy." In *Construction and Deconstruction of National Histories in Slavic Eurasia*, edited by T. Hayashi, 205–35. Sapporo: Slavic Research Center at Hokkaido University, 2003.

———. "Kul'turnaia idioma vozrozhdeniia Rossii kak faktor imperskoi politiki v Severo-zapadnom krae v 1863–1865 gg." *Ab Imperio* 1–2 (2001): 227–68.

———. "Russian Nationalism and the Nineteenth-Century Policy of Russification in the Russian Empire's Western Region." In *Imperiology: From Empirical Knowledge to Discussing the Russian Empire*, edited by K. Matsuzato, 141–58. Sapporo: Slavic Research Center at Hokkaido University, 2007.

———. "Russification and the Bureaucratic Mind in the Russian Empire's Northwestern Region in the 1860s." *Kritika: Explorations in Russian and Eurasian History*, n.s., 5, no. 2 (2004): 245–71.

Dolbilov, M., and A. Miller, eds. *Zapadnye okrainy Rossiiskoi imperii*. Moscow: Novoe literaturnoe obozrenie, 2007.

Dostoevsky, F. M. *Polnoe sobranie sochinenii*. 30 vols. Leningrad: Nauka, 1973–90.

Druzhinin, N. M. "Moskva v gody Krymskoi voiny." In *Istoriia Moskvy*, edited by N. M. Druzhinin and M. K. Rozhkovaia, 3:728–83. Moscow: Izdatel'stvo Akademii nauk SSSR, 1954.

Duara, Prasenjit. *Rescuing History from the Nation: Questioning Narratives of Modern China*. Chicago: University of Chicago Press, 1995.

Dubrovin, N. F. *Istoriia Krymskoi voiny i oborony Sevastopolia*. 3 vols. St. Petersburg, 1900.

———, ed. *Materialy dlia istorii Krymskoi voiny i oborony Sevastopolia*. 5 vols. St. Petersburg, 1900.

Durman, Karel. *The Time of the Thunderer: Mikhail Katkov, Russian National Extremism, and the Failure of the Bismarckian System, 1871–1887*. East European Monographs 237. Boulder, Colo.: East European Monographs, 1988.

Eikhenbaum, B. M. *Lev Tolstoy*. 2 vols. Munich: Wilhelm Fink Verlag, 1968.

Eley, Geoff. *Reshaping the German Right: Radical Nationalism and Political Change after Bismarck*. New Haven, Conn.: Yale University Press, 1980.

Ely, Christopher. *This Meager Nature: Landscape and National Identity in Imperial Russia*. DeKalb: Northern Illinois University Press, 2002.

Emmons, Terence. *The Russian Landed Gentry and the Peasant Emancipation of 1861*. Cambridge: Cambridge University Press, 1968.

Eval'd, A. V. "Vospominaniia." *Istoricheskii vestnik*, no. 10 (1895): 43–85.

Fedotov, G. P. "Pevets imperii i svobody." In *Novyi Grad: Sbornik statei*, 243–68. New York: Izdatel'stvo imeni Chekhova, 1952.

Feoktistov, E. M. *Za kulisami politiki i literatury: 1848–1896; Vospominaniia*. Moscow: Novosti, 1991.

Fetisenko, O. L. "'Brat ot brata pomogaem': Iz neizdannoi perepiski K. N. Leont'eva i T. I. Filippova." *Nestor*, no. 1 (2000): 165–204.

Feuer, Kathryn B. *Tolstoy and the Genesis of "War and Peace."* Ithaca, N.Y.: Cornell University Press, 1996.

Field, Daniel. "Kavelin and Russian Liberalism." *Slavic Review* 32, no. 1 (1973): 59–78.

———. Review of *"Aristokraticheskaia" oppozitsiia Velikim reformam (konets*

1850—seredina 1870-kh gg.), by I. A. Khristoforov. *Kritika: Explorations in Russian and Eurasian History* 6, no. 2 (2005): 409 –16.

Filaret [V. M. Drozdov]. *Sochineniia Filareta, mitropolita Moskovskogoi Kolomenskogo: Slova i rechi.* 5 vols. Moscow: Tipografiia A. I. Mamontova, 1873 –85.

———. *Sobranie mnenii i otzyvov Filareta, mitropolita Moskovskogo i Kolomenskogo, po uchebnym i tserkovno-gosudarstvennym voprosam.* 5 vols. St. Petersburg: Sinodal'naia tipografiia, 1885 –87.

Filippov, T. I. *Sovremennye tserkovnye voprosy.* St. Petersburg: Tipografiia tovarishchestva "Obshchestvennaia pol'za," 1882.

Fomin, V. V. *Variagi i Variazhskaia Rus': K itogam diskussii po variazhskomu voprosu.* Moscow: Russkaia panorama, 2005.

Fortinskii, F. Ia. "*Variagi i Rus'*: Istorichiskoe issledovanie S. Gedeonova." In *Otchet o dvadtsatom prisuzhdenii nagrad grafa Uvarova* (supplement to *Zapiski Imperatorskoi Akademii nauk* 33 [1879]), 605 –51. St. Petersburg: Tipografiia Imperatorskoi Akademii nauk, 1878.

Frank, Joseph. *Dostoevsky: The Mantle of the Prophet, 1871–1881.* Princeton, N.J.: Princeton University Press, 2002.

Franklin, Simon. "Identity and Religion." In Franklin and Widdis, *National Identity in Russian Culture*, 95 –115.

Franklin, Simon, and Emma Widdis, eds. *National Identity in Russian Culture: An Introduction.* New York: Cambridge University Press, 2004.

Garshin, V. M. *From the Reminiscences of Private Ivanov and Other Stories.* Translated by Peter Henry. Chester Springs, Pa.: Dufour Editions, 1988.

Gasparov, B. M. *Poeticheskii iazyk Pushkina kak fakt istorii russkogo literaturnogo iazyka.* St. Petersburg: Akademicheskii proekt, 1999.

Gedeonov, S. A. "Otryvki iz issledovanii o variazhskom voprose." *Zapiski Imperatorskoi Akademii nauk* 1, supp. 3 (1862): 1–127; 2, supp. 3 (1862): 128 –239; 3, supp. 4 (1863): 241–74.

———. *Variagi i Rus': Istoricheskoe izsliedovanie.* 2 vols. St. Petersburg: Tipografiia Imperatorskoi Akademii nauk, 1876. 2nd ed., Moscow: Russkaia panorama, 2004.

Geraci, Robert. *Window on the East: National and Imperial Identities in Late Tsarist Russia.* Ithaca, N.Y.: Cornell University Press, 2001.

Gerasimov, Ilya, Serguei Glebov, Alexander Kaplunovskii, Marina Mogilner, and Alexander Semyonov. "In Search of New Imperial History." *Ab Imperio* 1 (2005): 33 –56.

———, eds. *Novaia imperskaia istoriia postsovetskogo prostranstva.* Kazan': Tsentr issledovanii natsionalizma i imperii, 2004.

Gerd, L. A. *Konstantinopol' i Peterburg: Tserkovnaia politika Rossii na pravoslavnom Vostoke.* Moscow: Indrik, 2006.

Gertsen, A. I. *Sobranie sochinenii*. 30 vols. Moscow: Izdatel'stvo Akademii nauk SSSR, 1954–66.

Geyer, Dietrich. *Russian Imperialism: The Interaction of Domestic and Foreign Policy, 1860–1914*. Translated by Bruce Little. New Haven, Conn.: Yale University Press, 1987.

Gil'ferding, A. F. "Chem podderzhivaetsia pravoslavnaia vera u iuzhnykh slavian." *Russkaia beseda* 2, no. 20 (1860): 1–46.

Gleason, Abbott. *Young Russia: The Genesis of Russian Radicalism in the 1860s*. New York: Viking, 1980.

Glinka, F. I. *Pis'ma russkogo ofitsera*. Moscow: Voennoe izdatel'stvo, 1987.

Goldfrank, David M. *The Origins of the Crimean War*. New York: Longman, 1994.

Golosa iz Rossii: Sborniki A. I. Gertsena i N. P. Ogareva. 4 vols. London, 1856–1860. Facsimile ed., Moscow: Nauka, 1974–75.

Gorizontov, L. E. "The 'Great Circle' of Interior Russia: Representations of the Imperial Center in the Nineteenth and Early Twentieth Centuries." In Burbank, von Hagen, and Remnev, *Russian Empire*, 67–93.

———. *Paradoksy imperskoi politiki: Poliaki v Rossii i russkie v Pol'she*. Moscow: Indrik, 1999.

———. "Pol'skii aspect podgotovki krest'ianskoi reformy v Rossii." In *Ivan Aleksandrovich Voronkov: Professor-slavist Moskovskogo universiteta; Materialy nauchnykh chtenii*, edited by G. F. Matveev, 96–114. Moscow: Izdatel'stvo Moskovskogo gorodskogo ob"edineniia arkhivov, 2001.

Gusev, N. N. *Lev Nikolaevich Tolstoy: Materialy k biografii s 1828 po 1855 god*. Moscow: Izdatel'stvo Akademii nauk SSSR, 1954.

Halberstam, Judith. "Technologies of Monstrosity: Bram Stoker's 'Dracula.'" *Victorian Studies* 36, no. 3 (1993): 333–52.

Hamburg, Gary M. *Boris Chicherin and Early Russian Liberalism, 1828–1866*. Stanford, Calif.: Stanford University Press, 1992.

Herzen, Aleksandr. *Byloe i dumy*. 2 vols. Moscow: Gosudarstvennoe izdatel'stvo khudozhestvennoi literatury, 1962.

Hobsbawm, E. J. *Nations and Nationalism since 1780: Programme, Myth, Reality*. 2nd ed. Cambridge: Cambridge University Press, 1992.

Hokanson, Katya. *Writing at Russia's Border*. Toronto: University of Toronto Press, 2008.

Hollingsworth, Christopher. *Poetics of Hive: The Insect Metaphor in Literature*. Iowa City: University of Iowa Press, 2001.

Hosking, Geoffrey. *Russia: People and Empire, 1552–1917*. Cambridge, Mass.: Harvard University Press, 1997.

Hosking, Geoffrey, and George Schopflin, eds. *Myths and Nationhood*. New York: Routledge, 1997.

Hosking, Geoffrey, and Robert Service, eds. *Russian Nationalism, Past and Present.* New York: St. Martin's, 1998.

Howard, Michael. "War and Nations." In *Nationalism,* edited by John Hutchinson and Anthony D. Smith, 254–57. Oxford: Oxford University Press, 1994.

Hroch, Miroslav. "Real and Constructed: The Nature of the Nation." In *The State of the Nation: Ernest Gellner and the Theory of Nationalism,* edited by John A. Hall, 91–106. New York: Cambridge University Press, 1998.

———. *Social Preconditions of National Revival in Europe: A Comparative Analysis of the Social Composition of Patriotic Groups among the Smaller European Nations.* Cambridge: Cambridge University Press, 1985.

Ilovaiskii, D. I. "O mnimom prizvanii variagov: Iz issledovanii o nachale Rusi." *Russkii vestnik* 96, no. 11 (1871): 5–50; no. 12 (1871): 371–414.

———. *Razyskaniia o nachale Rusi: Vmesto vvedeniia v Russkuiu istoriiu.* Moscow: Tipografiia Gracheva, 1876.

Innokentii, Archbishop of Kherson and Taurida [I. A. Borisov]. *Sochineniia Innokentiia, arkhiepiskopa Khersonskogo i Tavricheskogo.* 6 vols. St. Petersburg: Izdanie knigoprodavtsa I.L. Tuzova, 1908.

Iversen, Iu. B. *Medali v chest' russkikh gosudarstvennykh deiatelei i chastnykh lits.* St. Petersburg: Tipografiia Imperatorskoi Akademii nauk, 1877.

———. *Medali, vybitye v tsarstvovanie imperatora Aleksandra II.* St. Petersburg: Tipografiia Imperatorskoi Akademii nauk, 1880.

Izvol'skii, Sergei. *Slava vsevyshnemu Bogu! S nami Bog, spasshii dragotsennuiu zhizn' nashego gosudaria imperatora.* Moscow: M. A. Abramov, 1866.

Kappeler, Andreas. *The Russian Empire: A Multiethnic History.* Translated by Alfred Clayton. Harlow, England: Pearson Education, 2001. Originally published as *Russland als Vielvölkerreich: Entstehung, Geschichte, Zerfall* (Munich: Beck, 1992).

Karamzin, N. M. *Istoriia gosudarstva Rossiiskogo.* 4 vols. Moscow: Kniga, 1988–89.

Kaspe, Sviatoslav. "Imperial Political Culture and Modernization in the Second Half of the Nineteenth Century." In Burbank, von Hagen, and Remnev, *Russian Empire,* 455–93.

Katkov, M. N. *1863 god: Sobranie statei po pol'skomu voprosu, pomeshchavshikhsia v "Moskovskikh vedomostiakh," "Russkom vestnike" i "Sovremennoi letopisi."* 3 vols. Moscow: Universitetskaia tipografiia, 1887.

———. "Chto nam delat' s Pol'shei." *Russkii vestnik,* no. 3 (1863): 469–506.

———. *Sobranie peredovykh statei "Moskovskikh vedomostei": 1863-1887.* 25 vols. Moscow: Izdanie S. P. Katkovoi, 1897–99.

Katz, Martin. *Mikhail N. Katkov: A Political Biography, 1818-1887.* The Hague: Mouton, 1966.

Kel'siev, V. I., ed. *Sbornik pravitel'stvennykh svedenii o raskol'nikakh.* 4 vols. London: Trübner, 1860–62.

Khevrolina, V. M. *Rossiiskii diplomat graf Nikolai Pavlovich Ignatiev*. Moscow: Institut rossiiskoi istorii RAN, 2004.

Khlevov, A. A. *Normanskaia problema v otechestvennoi istoricheskoi nauke*. St. Petersburg: Izdatel'stvo S.-Peterburgskogo universiteta, 1997.

Khomiakov, A. S. *Polnoe sobranie sochinenii*. 8 vols. Moscow: Universitetskaia tipografiia, 1900.

Khristoforov, I. A. *"Aristokraticheskaia" oppozitsiia Velikim reformam (konets 1850–seredina 1870-kh gg.)*. Moscow: Russkoe slovo, 2002.

Kireevskii, P. V. "O drevnei russkoi istorii (Pis'mo k M. P. Pogodinu)." *Moskvitianin*, no. 3 (1845): 11–46.

Kiseleva, L. N. "Stanovlenie russkoi natsional'noi mifologii v nikolaevskuiu epokhu: Susaninskii siuzhet." In *Lotmanovskii sbornik*, 2:279–302. Moscow: OGI, 1997.

Klein, L. S. *Spor o variagakh: Istoriia protivostoianiia i argumenty storon*. Petersburg: Evraziia, 2009.

Kliuchevskii, V. O. *Sochineniia*. 9 vols. Moscow: Mysl', 1987–90.

Knight, Nathaniel. "Ethnicity, Nationality, and the Masses: *Narodnost'* and Modernity in Imperial Russia." In *Russian Modernity: Politics, Knowledge, Practices*, edited by David L. Hoffmann and Yanni Kotsonis, 41–64. New York: St. Martin's, 2000.

———. "Imperiia napokaz: Vserosiiskaia etnograficheskaia vystavka 1867." *Novoe literaturnoe obozrenie* 51, no. 5 (2001): 111–31.

Kohn, Hans. *Pan-Slavism: Its History and Ideology*. New York: Vintage Books, 1960.

Koialovich, M. O. "Vernopoddannichestvo poliakov Zapadnoi Rossii." In *Sbornik statei raz"iasniaiushchikh pol'skoe delo po otnosheniiu k Zapadnoi Rossii*, edited by S. V. Sholkovich, 1:359–62. Vilnius: Tip. A. G. Syrkina, 1885.

Kolokol: Gazeta A. I. Gertsena i N. P. Ogareva. 8 vols. London, 1857–67. Facsimile ed., Moscow: Izdatel'stvo Akademii nauk SSSR, 1960.

Kornblatt, Judith. *The Cossack Hero in Russian Literature: A Study in Cultural Mythology*. Madison: University of Wisconsin Press, 1992.

Kornilov, A. A. *Obshchestvennoe dvizhenie pri Aleksandre II*. Moscow: Tovarishchestvo tipografii A. I. Mamontova, 1909.

Koshelev, A. I. *Zapiski (1812–1883)*. Berlin: B. Behr's Verlag, 1884.

Kostomarov, N. I. *Avtobiografiia: Bunt Sten'ki Razina*. Kiev: Naukova dumka, 1992.

———. *Kazaki: Istoricheskie monografii i issledovaniia*. Moscow: Charli, 1995.

———. "Nachalo Rusi." *Sovremennik*, no. 1 (1860): 5–32.

———. *Raskol: Istoricheskie monografii i issledovaniia*. Moscow: Charli, 1994.

———. *Russkaia respublika*. Moscow: Charli, 1994.

Kotliarevskii, A. A. *Sochineniia*. 4 vols. Petersburg: Tipografiia Imperatorskoi Akademii nauk, 1889–95.

Kozelsky, Mara. "Ruins into Relics: The Monument to Saint Vladimir on the Excavations of Chersonesos, 1827–57." *Russian Review* 63 (October 2004): 655–72.

Kunik, A. "Zamechaniia [k "Otryvkam iz issledovanii o variazhskom voprose" S. Gedeonova]." *Zapiski Imperatorskoi Akademii nauk* 1, supp. 3 (1862): 121–27; 2, supp. 3 (1862): 207–39; 6, supp. 2 (1864): 53–84.

Kuz'min, A. G. "Ob etnicheskoi prirode variagov." In Gedeonov, *Variagi i Rus'* (2nd ed.), 576–620.

Layton, Susan. *Russian Literature and Empire: Conquest of the Caucasus from Pushkin to Tolstoy.* Cambridge: Cambridge University Press, 1994.

Leibov, Roman. *"Literaturnyi fragment" F. I. Tiutcheva: Zhanr i kontekst.* Tartu: Tartu Ülikooli Kirjastus, 2000.

Leont'ev, Konstantin. *Vostok, Rossiia i slavianstvo: Sbornik statei.* Osnabrück: Otto Zeller, 1966.

Leskov, N. S. "Bozhedomy: Povest' let vremennykh." In *Literaturnoe nasledstvo* 101 (*Neizdannyi Leskov*), edited by K. P. Bogaevskaia, O. E. Maiorova, and L. M. Rozenblium, 1:53–223. Moscow: Nasledie, 1977.

———. *Soboriane.* In *Sobranie sochinenii,* 4:5–319. Moscow: Khudozhestvennaia literatura, 1957.

Leslie, R. F. *Reform and Insurrection in Russian Poland, 1856–1865.* London: University of London, Athlone Press, 1963.

Levin, Sh. M. "Gertsen i Krymskaia voina." In *Istoricheskie zapiski,* 29:164–99. Moscow: Izdatel'stvo Akademii nauk SSSR, 1949.

———. *Ocherki po istorii russkoi obshchestvennoi mysli: Vtoraia polovina XIX–nachalo XX veka.* Leningrad: Nauka, 1974.

Lieven, Dominic. *Empire: The Russian Empire and Its Rivals.* New Haven, Conn.: Yale University Press, 2002.

Lincoln, W. Bruce. *The Great Reforms: Autocracy, Bureaucracy, and the Politics of Change in Imperial Russia.* DeKalb: Northern Illinois University Press, 1990.

Lohr, Eric. *Nationalizing the Russian Empire: The Campaign against Enemy Aliens during World War I.* Cambridge, Mass.: Harvard University Press, 2003.

Lomonosov, M. V. *Polnoe sobranie sochinenii.* 8 vols. Moscow: Izdatel'stvo Akademii nauk SSSR, 1951–59.

Love, Jeff. *The Overcoming of History in "War and Peace."* Amsterdam: Rodopi, 2004.

Lukashevich, Stephen. *Ivan Aksakov, 1823–1886: A Study in Russian Thought and Politics.* Cambridge, Mass.: Harvard University Press, 1965.

Lyttelton, Adrian. "The National Question in Italy." In *The National Question in Europe in Historical Context,* edited by Mikuláš Teich and Roy Porter, 63–105. Cambridge: Cambridge University Press, 1996.

MacMaster, Robert E. *Danilevsky: A Russian Totalitarian Philosopher.* Cambridge, Mass.: Harvard University Press, 1967.

Maikov, A. N. *Polnoe sobranie sochinenii.* 6th ed. 3 vols. St. Petersburg: Izdanie A. F. Marksa, 1893.

———. *Polnoe sobranie sochinenii*. 7th ed. 4 vols. St. Petersburg: Izdanie A. F. Marksa, 1901.

Maiorova, Olga. "Mitropolit Moskovskii Filaret v obshchestvennom soznanii kontsa 19 veka." In *Lotmanovskii sbornik*, edited by E. V. Permiakov, 2:615–38. Moscow: O.G.I., 1997.

———. "Obraz natsii i imperii v vernopoddanneishikh pis'makh k tsariu (1863–1864)." In *I vremia i mesto: Istoriko-filologicheskii sbornik k 60-letiiu Aleksandra L'vovicha Ospovata*, 357–69. Moscow: Novoe izdatel'stvo, 2008.

———. Review of *The Romanov Empire and Nationalism: Essays on the Methodology of Historical Research*, by Alexei Miller. *Nationalities Papers* 38, no. 1 (2010): 166–68.

———. "Tsarevich-samozvanets v sotsial'noi mifologii poreformennoi epokhi." *Rossia-Russia: Kul'turnye praktiki v ideologicheskoi perspective* 11, n.s., no. 3 (1999): 204–32.

Markova, Zina. *Bŭlgarkata ekzarkhiia: 1870–1879*. Sofia: Akademia na Naukite, 1989.

Martin, Alexander. *Romantics, Reformers, Reactionaries: Russian Conservative Thought and Politics in the Reign of Alexander I*. DeKalb: Northern Illinois University Press, 1997.

Martinsen, Deborah A. *Surprised by Shame: Dostoevsky's Liars and Narrative Exposure*. Columbus: Ohio State University Press, 2003.

Maslova, E. N. *Pamiatnik Tysiacheletiiu Rossii*. Leningrad: Lenizdat, 1977.

Materialy dlia istorii uprazdneniia krepostnogo sostoianiia pomeshchich'ikh krest'ian v Rossii v tsarstvovanie imperatora Aleksandra II. 3 vols. Berlin: F. Schneider, 1860–62.

Matsuzato, Kimitaka. "General-gubernatorstva v Rossiiskoi imperii: Ot etnicheskogo k prostranstvennomu podkhodu." In Gerasimov, Glebov, Kaplunovskii, Mogil'ner, and Semyonov, *Novaia imperskaia istoriia postsovetskogo prostranstva*, 427–58.

Mazur, N. N. "Iz istorii formirovaniia russkoi natsional'noi ideologii (Pervaia tret' 19 veka)." In *"Tsep' nepreryvnogo predaniia . . .": Sbornik statei pamiati A. G. Tartakovskogo*, edited by V. A. Milchina and A. L. Iurganov, 196–250. Moscow: RGGU, 2004.

Meininger, Thomas A. *Ignatiev and the Establishment of the Bulgarian Exarchate, 1864–1872: A Study in Personal Diplomacy*. Madison: University of Wisconsin Press, 1970.

Mel'gunov, N. A. "Mysli vslukh ob istekshem tridtsatiletii Rossii." *Golosa iz Rossii* 1 (1856): 62–151.

Miasoedova, N. Iu. "S. A. Gedeonov i imperatorskii Ermitazh." In *Peterburg i Moskva: Dve stolitsy Rossii v XVIII–XX vekakh*, edited by Iu. V. Krivosheeva, A. S. Fedotova, and M. V. Khodiakova, 62–69. Petersburg: Izdatel'stvo Peterburgskogo universiteta, 2001.

Mikeshin, M. O. "Vospominaniia khudozhnika." *Nieman*, no. 11 (1969): 127–66.

Miliukov, P. N. *Glavnye techeniia russkoi istoricheskoi mysli*. Moscow: I. N. Kushnerev, 1897.

Miliutin, D. A. *Vospominaniia: 1860–1862*. Moscow: Rossiiskii arkhiv, 1999.

Miller, Alexei. *The Romanov Empire and Nationalism: Essays in the Methodology of Historical Research*. Translated by Serguei Dobrynin. New York: Central European University Press, 2008. Originally published as *Imperiia Romanovykh i natsionalizm: Esse po metodologii istoricheskogo issledovaniia* (Moscow: Novoe literaturnoe obozrenie, 2006).

———. *"Ukrainskii vopros" v politike vlastei i russkom obshchestvennom mnenii (vtoraia polovina 19 veka)*. St. Petersburg: Aleteia, 2000. Translated by Olga Poato as *The Ukrainian Question: The Russian Empire and Nationalism in the Nineteenth Century* (New York: Central European University Press, 2003).

Milojković-Djurić, Elena. *Panslavism and National Identity in Russia and in the Balkans, 1830–1880: Images of the Self and Others*. Eastern European Monographs 394. Boulder, Colo.: East European Monographs, 1994.

Morson, Garry Saul. *Hidden in Plain View: Narrative and Creative Potentials in "War and Peace."* Stanford, Calif.: Stanford University Press, 1987.

Mosse, W. E. *Alexander II and the Modernization of Russia*. New York: Collier Books, 1962.

Na vziatie Varshavy: Tri stikhotvoreniia V. Zhukovskogo i A. Pushkina. St. Petersburg: Voennaia tipografiia, 1831.

Nardova, V. A. "Zakonodatel'nye dokumenty 60-kh godov XIX veka ob adresakh na vysochaishee imia." In *Vspomogatel'nye istoricheskie distsipliny*, 9:253–82. Leningrad: Nauka, 1978.

Nechaeva, V. S. *Zhurnal M. M. i F. M. Dostoevskikh "Vremia" 1861–1863*. Moscow: Nauka, 1972.

Nikitenko, A. V. *Dnevnik*. 3 vols. Moscow: Khudozhestvennaia literatura, 1955–56.

Nikitin, I. S. *Polnoe sobranie stikhotvorenii*. Biblioteka poeta. Moscow: Sovetskii pisatel', 1965.

Nikitin, S. A. *Slavianskie komitety v Rossii v 1858–1876 godakh*. Moscow: Izdatel'stvo Moskovskogo universiteta, 1960.

Norris, Stephen. *A War of Images: Russian Popular Prints, Wartime Culture, and National Identity, 1812–1945*. DeKalb: Northern Illinois University Press, 2006.

Novyi Susanin: Podrobnyi rasskaz o pokushenii na zhizn' ego imperatorskogo velichestva. . . . St. Petersburg: Tipografiia V. Spiridonova, 1866.

Obolenskii, D. A. *Zapiski: 1855–1879*. Petersburg: Nestor-Istoriia, 2005.

O chudesnom izbavlenii zhizni gosudaria imperatora ot zlodeiskoi ruki ubiitsy. St. Petersburg: Redaktsiia zhurnala "Mirskoi vestnik," 1866

Odoevskii, V. F. "Tekushchaia khronika i osobye proisshestviia." In *Literaturnoe nasledstvo* 22–24, 79–308. Moscow: Zhurnal'no-gazetnoe ob"edinenie, 1935.

"Opisanie pamiatnika tysiacheletiiu Rossii." In supplement to *Mesiatseslov na 1862 god*, 71–73. St. Petersburg: Imperatorskaia Akademiia nauk, 1861.

Orwin, Donna. "Tolstoy and Patriotism." In *Lev Tolstoy and the Concept of Brotherhood*, edited by Andrew Donskov and John Woodsworth, 51–70. New York: Legas, 1996.

———. *Tolstoy's Art and Thought, 1847–1880*. Princeton, N.J.: Princeton University Press, 1993.

Ospovat, A. L. "Elementy politicheskoi mifologii Tiutcheva: Kommentarii k stat'e 1844 goda." In *Tiutchevskii sbornik II*, edited by L. Kiseleva, R. Leibov, and A. Iunggren, 227–63. Tartu: Tartu Ülikooli Kirjastus, 1999.

———. "Pushkin, Tiutchev i pol'skoe vosstanie 1830–1831 godov." In *Pushkinskie chteniia v Tartu: Tezisy dokladov nauchnoi konferentsii 13–14 noiabria 1987 goda*, 49–52. Tallinn: Tartuskii gosudarstvennyi universitet, 1987.

Ostrovskii, A. N. *Polnoe sobranie sochinenii*. 16 vols. Moscow: Khudozhestvennaia literatura, 1949–53.

Otto, N., and I. Kupriianov. *Biograficheskie ocherki lits, izobrazhennykh na pamiatnike tysiacheletiia Rossii, vozdvignutom v gorode Novgorode*. Novgorod: Tipografiia M. Sukhova, 1862.

Paperno, Irina. "The Liberation of the Serfs as a Cultural Symbol." *Russian Review* 50 (October 1991): 417–36.

Pavlov, P. V. "Tysiacheletie Rossii." In supplement to *Mesiatseslov na 1862 god*, 3–70. St. Petersburg: Imperatorskaia Akademiia nauk, 1861.

Petrovich, Michael. *The Emergence of Russian Panslavism: 1856–1870*. New York: Columbia University Press, 1956.

———. "Russian Pan-Slavists and the Polish Uprising of 1863." *Harvard Slavic Studies* 1 (1953): 219–47.

Pick, Daniel. *War Machine: The Rationalization of Slaughter in the Modern Age*. New Haven, Conn.: Yale University Press, 1993.

Pis'ma dukhovnykh i svetskikh lits k mitropolitu Moskovskomu Filaretu. St. Petersburg: Tip. A. P. Lopukhina, 1900.

Plokhy, Serhii. "The City of Glory: Sevastopol in Russian Historical Mythology." *Journal of Contemporary History* 35, no. 3 (July 2000): 369–83.

Pobedonostsev, K. P., and I. K. Babst. *Pis'ma o puteshestvii gosudaria naslednika tsesarevicha po Rossii ot Peterburga do Kryma*. Moscow: Tipografiia Gracheva, 1864.

Pogodin, M. P. "Chtenie poslednego manifesta po prikhodskim tserkvam v Moskve sego dekabria 25 chisla, 1854 goda." In Barsukov, *Zhizn' i trudy M. P. Pogodina*, 13:198–203.

———. "Gedeonov i ego sistema o proiskhozhdenii variagov i Rusi." *Zapiski Imperatorskoi Akademii nauk* 6, supp. 2 (1864): 1–48.

———. *Istoriko-kriticheskie otryvki.* 2 vols. Moscow: Tipografiia Avgusta Semena, 1846–67.

———. "Kogda Russkomu gosudarstvu ispolnitsia tysiacha let?" *Moskvitianin*, no. 2 (1852): 53–60.

———. *K slavianam.* Moscow, 1862.

———. "Otvet P. V. Kireevskomu." *Moskvitianin*, no. 3 (1845): 47–58.

———. *Pol'skii vopros: Sobranie rassuzhdenii, zapisok i zamechanii; 1831–1867.* Moscow: Tipografiia gazety "Russkii," 1868.

———. *Sobranie statei, pisem i rechei po povodu slavianskogo voprosa.* Moscow: Tipografiia D. M. Pogodina, 1878.

———. *Sochineniia.* 5 vols. Moscow: Sinodal'naia tipografiia, 1872–76.

———. "Sviatye Kirill i Mefodii—slaviane, a ne greki." *Pravoslavnoe obozrenie* 14, no. 5 (1864): 1–9.

Polunov, A. Iu. "Konstantin Petrovich Pobedonostsev—chelovek i politik." *Otechestvennaia istoriia*, no. 1 (1998): 42–55.

Popov, N. A. *Po povodu vosstanovleniia bolgarskogo ekzarkhata.* Moscow: Redaktsiia "Pravoslavnogo obozreniia," 1872.

[Popov, N. A.]. *Vserossiiskaia etnograficheskaia vystavka i slavianskii s"ezd v Moskve v mae 1867 goda.* Moscow: Tipografiia Moskovskogo universiteta, 1867.

Porter, Brian. *When Nationalism Began to Hate: Imagining Modern Politics in Nineteenth-Century Poland.* New York: Oxford University Press, 2000.

Prymak, Thomas. "Mykola Kostomarov as a Historian." In *Historiography of Imperial Russia: The Profession and Writing of History in a Multinational State*, edited by Thomas Sanders, 332–43. Armonk, N.Y.: M. E. Sharpe, 1999.

Pushkin, A. S. *Dnevniki: Zapiski.* St. Petersburg: Nauka, 1995.

Ransel, David L., and Bozena Shallcross, eds. *Polish Encounters, Russian Identity.* Bloomington: Indiana University Press, 2005.

Rebekkini, D. "Russkie istoricheskie romany 1830-kh godov XIX veka (Bibliograficheskii ukazatel')." *Novoe literaturnoe obozrenie* 34 (1998): 416–33.

Renner, Andreas. "Defining a Russian Nation: Mikhail Katkov and the 'Invention' of National Politics." *Slavonic and East European Review* 81, no. 4 (October 2003): 659–82.

———. *Russischer Nationalismus und Öffentlichkeit im Zarenreich: 1855–1875.* Cologne: Böhlau, 2000.

Revunenkov, V. G. *Pol'skoe vosstanie 1863 goda i evropeiskaia diplomatiia.* Leningrad: Izdatel'stvo Leningradskogo universiteta, 1957.

Reyfman, I. V. "Zametki A. N. Radishcheva po russkoi istorii." In *Istoriia filosofii kak filosofiia*, edited by T. V. Artem'eva and M. I. Mikeshin, 2:227–34. St. Petersburg: Sankt-Peterburgskii tsentr istorii idei, 2003.

Riasanovsky, Alexander V. "Ideological and Political Extensions of the 'Norman'

Controversy." In *Nation and Ideology: Essays in Honor of Wayne S. Vucinich*, edited by Ivo Banac, John G. Ackerman, and Roman Szporluk, 335–50. Boulder, Colo.: East European Monographs, 1981.

Riasanovsky, Nicholas V. *Nicholas I and Official Nationality in Russia, 1825–1855*. Berkeley: University of California Press, 1967.

———. *Russia and the West in the Teaching of the Slavophiles: A Study of Romantic Ideology*. Gloucester, Mass.: P. Smith, 1965.

Riasanovsky, Valentin A. *Obzor russkoi kul'tury*. 2 vols. New York: L. Rausen, 1947–48.

Rieber, Alfred J. "Interest-Group Politics in the Era of the Great Reforms." In *Russia's Great Reforms, 1855–1881*, edited by Ben Eklof, John Bushnell, and Larissa Zakharova, 58–83. Bloomington: Indiana University Press, 1994.

Rowley, D. G. "Imperial versus National Discourse: The Case of Russia." *Nations and Nationalism* 6, no. 1 (2000): 23–42.

Rubinshtein, N. L. *Russkaia istoriografiia*. Moscow: Gospolitizdat, 1941.

Saltykov-Shchedrin, M. E. *Sobranie sochinenii*. 20 vols. Moscow: Khudozhestvennaia literatura, 1965–77.

Samarin, Iu. F. *Sochineniia*. 12 vols. Moscow: Izdanie D. Samarina, 1877–1911.

Sanborn, Joshua. *Drafting the Russian Nation: Military Conscription, Total War, and Mass Politics, 1905–1925*. DeKalb: Northern Illinois University Press, 2003.

Saunders, David. "Mikhail Katkov and Mykola Kostomarov: A Note on Petr A. Valuev's Anti-Ukrainian Edict of 1863." *Harvard Ukrainian Studies* 17, no. 3–4 (1993): 365–83.

Sbornik postanovlenii po Ministerstvu narodnogo prosveshcheniia. Vol. 2, *Tsarstvovanie Imperatora Nikolaia I, 1825–1855*, pt. 2, *1840–1855*. 2nd ed. St. Petersburg: Tipografiia V. S. Balasheva, 1876.

Semenovskii, A. I. *Pamiatnik tysiacheletiiu Rossii, vozdvignutyi v Novgorode 8 sentiabria 1862g. po poveleniiu Imperatora Aleksandra II-go*. St. Petersburg: Tipografiia Peterburgskoi tiur'my, 1908.

Seton-Watson, R. W. *The Rise of Nationality in the Balkans*. New York: Howard Fertig, 1966.

Shilov, A. A. *Karakozov i pokushenie 4 aprelia 1866 goda*. Petrograd: Gosudarstvennoe izdatel'stvo, 1919.

Shklovskii, V. B. "M. I. Kutuzov i Platon Karataev v romane 'Voina i mir.'" *Znamia* 5 (1948): 137–45.

Shtakenshneider, Elena A. *Dnevnik i zapiski: 1854–1886*. Moscow, 1934. Reprint with new foreword, Newtonville, Mass.: Oriental Research Partners, 1980.

Smith, Anthony D. *Chosen Peoples: Sacred Sources of National Identity*. Oxford: Oxford University Press, 2003.

———. "The 'Golden Age' and National Renewal." In Hosking and Schopflin, *Myths and Nationhood*, 36–59.

———. *Myths and Memories of the Nation.* Oxford: Oxford University Press, 1999.

———. *National Identity.* Reno: University of Nevada Press, 1991.

———. *Nationalism: Theory, Ideology, History.* Malden, Mass.: Blackwell, 2003.

———. "War and Ethnicity: The Role of Warfare in the Formation, Self-Images and Cohesion of Ethnic Communities." *Ethnic and Racial Studies* 4, no. 4 (October 1981): 375–97.

Smolich, I. K. *Istoriia russkoi tserkvi: 1700–1917.* 2 vols. Moscow: Izdatel'stvo Spaso-Preobrazhenskogo Valaamskogo monastyria, 1996–97.

Solov'ev, S. M. *Istoriia Rossii s drevneishikh vremen.* 29 vols. Moscow: Universitetskaia tipografiia, 1851–79.

———. *Sochineniia.* 18 vols. Moscow: Mysl', 1988–95.

———. *Zapiski.* Petrograd: Prometei, 1914.

Sreznevskii, I. I. "Zamechaniia o knige S. A. Gedeonova *Variagi i Rus'.*" In *Otchet o dvadtsatom prisuzhdenii nagrad grafa Uvarova* (supplement to *Zapiski Imperatorskoi Akademii nauk* 33 [1879]), 666–700. St. Petersburg: Tipografiia Imperatorskoi Akademii nauk, 1878.

Staliunas, Darius. *Making Russians: Meaning and Practice of Russification in Lithuania and Belarus after 1863.* New York: Rodopi, 2007.

Strakhov, Nikolai. *Bor'ba s Zapadom v nashei literature: Istoricheskie i kriticheskie ocherki.* 3 vols. Kiev: Tip. I. I. Chokolova, 1897. Reprint, The Hague: Mouton, 1969.

———. "*Voina i mir*: Sochinenie grafa Tolstogo." *Zaria*, no. 1 (1870): 108–42.

Suny, Ronald. "The Empire Strikes Out: Imperial Russia, National Identity, and Theories of Empire." In *A State of Nations: Empire and Nation-Making in the Age of Lenin and Stalin,* edited by Ronald Suny and Terry Martin, 23–66. Oxford: Oxford University Press, 2001.

Tarle, E. V. *Krymskaia voina.* 2nd ed. Moscow: Izdatel'stvo Akademii nauk SSSR, 1950.

Tartakovskii, A. G. *1812 god i russkaia memuaristika: Opyt istochnikovedcheskogo izucheniia.* Moscow: Nauka, 1980.

Tatishchev, S. S. *Imperator Aleksandr Vtoroi: Ego zhizn' i tsarstvovanie.* 2 vols. Moscow: Algoritm, Charli, 1996.

Teplov, V. A. *Greko-bolgarskii tserkovnyi vopros po neizdannym istochnikam.* St. Petersburg: Tipografiia V. S. Balashova, 1889.

Thaden, Edward C. *Conservative Nationalism in Nineteenth-Century Russia.* Seattle: University of Washington Press, 1964.

———. *Russia's Western Borderlands, 1710–1870.* Princeton, N.J.: Princeton University Press, 1984.

———. *Russification in the Baltic Provinces and Finland, 1855–1914.* Princeton, N.J.: Princeton University Press, 1981.

Thompson, Ewa M. *Imperial Knowledge: Russian Literature and Colonialism.* Westport, Conn.: Greenwood Press, 2000.

Titov, G. *Krestovye pokhody i Vostochnyi vopros.* St. Petersburg: Voennaia tipografiia, 1854.

Tiutchev, F. I. "Pis'ma k moskovskim publitsistam." In *Literaturnoe nasledstvo 97 (Fedor Ivanovich Tiutchev)*, edited by S. A. Makashin, K. V. Pigarev, and T. G. Dinesman, 1:258–430. Moscow: Nauka, 1988.

———. "Pis'ma k rodnym." In *Literaturnoe nasledstvo 97 (Fedor Ivanovich Tiutchev)*, edited by S. A. Makashin, K. V. Pigarev, and T. G. Dinesman, 1:431–96. Moscow: Nauka, 1988.

———. "Pis'mo doktoru Gustavu Kol'bu, redaktoru *Vseobshchei gazety*." In *Tiutchevskii sbornik II*, edited by L. Kiseleva, R. Leibov, and A. Iunggren, 202–26. Tartu: Tartu Ülikooli Kirjastus, 1999.

———. *Polnoe sobranie stikhotvorenii.* Biblioteka poeta. Leningrad: Sovetskii pisatel', 1987.

Tiutcheva, A. F. *Pri dvore dvukh imperatorov: Vospominaniia, dnevnik.* 2 vols. Moscow: Izdanie M. i S. Sabashnikovykh, 1928–29. Reprint with new foreword, Cambridge, Mass.: Oriental Research Partners, 1975.

Todes, Daniel P. *Darwin without Malthus: The Struggle for Existence in Russian Evolutionary Thought.* New York: Oxford University Press, 1989.

Todorova, Maria. "The Ottoman Legacy in the Balkans." In *Imperial Legacy: The Ottoman Imprint on the Balkans and the Middle East*, edited by L. Carl Brown, 45–77. New York: Columbia University Press, 1996.

Tolstoi, A. K. *Sobranie sochinenii.* 4 vols. Moscow: Khudozhestvennaia literatura, 1963.

Tolstoi, D. N. "Zapiski." *Russkii arkhiv* 2, no. 5 (1885): 5–70.

Tolstoy, L. N. *Kazaki.* Moscow: Izdatel'stvo Akademii nauk, 1963.

———. *Polnoe sobranie sochinenii.* 90 vols. Moscow: Khudozhestvennaia literatura, 1928–58.

Tolz, Vera. *Russia.* New York: Oxford University Press, 2001.

Tsimbaev, N. I. *I. S. Aksakov v obshchestvennoi zhizni poreformennoi Rossii.* Moscow: Izdatel'stvo Moskovskogo universiteta, 1978.

———. *Slavianofil'stvo: Iz istorii russkoi obshchestvenno-politicheskoi mysli XIX veka.* Moscow: Izdatel'stvo Moskovskogo universiteta, 1986.

"Tsirkuliar ministerstva vnutrennikh del." *Golosa iz Rossii* 2 (1856): 31–45.

Turgenev, I. S. *Polnoe sobranie sochinenii i pisem: Pis'ma.* 13 vols. Moscow: Izdatel'stvo Akademii nauk SSSR, 1961–68.

———. *Polnoe sobranie sochinenii i pisem: Sochineniia.* 15 vols. Moscow: Izdatel'stvo Akademii nauk SSSR, 1960–68.

Tvardovskaia, V. A. *Ideologiia poreformennogo samoderzhaviia: M. N. Katkov i ego izdaniia.* Moscow: Nauka, 1978.

Ungurianu, Dan. *Plotting History: The Russian Historical Novel in the Imperial Age.* Madison: University of Wisconsin Press, 2007.

Ustrialov, N. G. "Zapiska." In *Sbornik postanovlenii po Ministerstvu narodnogo prosveshcheniia*, vol. 2, pt. 2, col. 1389 – 96.

Valuev, P. A. *Dnevnik P. A. Valueva, ministra vnutrennikh del*. 2 vols. Moscow: Izdatel'stvo Akademii nauk SSSR, 1961.

———. "Duma russkogo vo vtoroi polovine 1855 goda." *Russkaia starina* 79, no. 9 (1893): 503 –14.

[Valuev, P. A.]. "8-e sentiabria 1862 goda: Iz vospominanii sovremennika." *Russkaia starina* 57, no. 1 (1888): 1–16.

Verdery, Katherine. *The Political Lives of Dead Bodies: Reburial and Postsocialist Change*. New York: Columbia University Press, 1999.

Verhoeven, Claudia. *The Odd Man Karakozov: Imperial Russia, Modernity, and the Birth of Terrorism*. Ithaca, N.Y.: Cornell University Press, 2009.

Viroli, Maurizio. *For Love of Country: An Essay on Patriotism and Nationalism*. Oxford: Clarendon, 1995.

Vucinich, Alexander. *Darwin in Russian Thought*. Berkeley: University of California Press, 1988.

Walicki, Andrzej. *The Slavophile Controversy: History of a Conservative Utopia in Nineteenth-Century Russian Thought*. Oxford: Clarendon, 1975.

———. "The Slavophile Thinkers and the Polish Question in 1863." In Ransel and Shallcross, *Polish Encounters, Russian Identity*, 89 – 99.

Weeks, Theodore R. "Monuments and Memory: Immortalizing Count M. N. Murav'ev in Vilna, 1898." *Nationalities Papers* 27, no. 4 (1999): 551– 64.

———. *Nation and State in Late Imperial Russia: Nationalism and Russification on the Western Frontier, 1863–1914*. DeKalb: Northern Illinois University Press, 1996.

———. "Official and Popular Nationalism: Imperial Russia 1863 –1912." In *Nationalismen in Europa: West- und Osteuropa im Vergleich*, edited by U. von Hirschhausen and J. Leonhard, 410–32. Göttingen: Wallstein, 2001.

———. "Religion and Russification: Russian Language in the Catholic Churches of the 'North-West Provinces' after 1863." *Kritika: Explorations in Russian and Eurasian History* 2, no. 1 (2001): 87 –110.

———. "Russification and the Lithuanians, 1863 –1905." *Slavic Review* 60, no. 1 (2001): 96 –114.

———. "Slavdom, Civilization, Russification: Comments on Russia's World-Historical Mission, 1861–1878." *Ab Imperio* 2 (2002): 223 – 48.

Werth, Paul. "Changing Conceptions of Difference, Assimilation, and Faith in the Volga-Kama Region, 1740–1870." In Burbank, von Hagen, and Remnev, *Russian Empire*, 169 – 95.

———. "Georgian Autocephaly and the Ethnic Fragmentation of Orthodoxy." *Acta Slavica Iaponica* 23 (2006): 74 –100.

Whittaker, Cynthia Hyla. "The Idea of Autocracy among Eighteenth-Century

Russian Historians." In *Imperial Russia: New Histories for the Empire*, edited by Jane Burbank and David L. Ransel, 32–59. Bloomington: Indiana University Press, 1998.

Widdis, Emma. "Russia as Space." In Franklin and Widdis, *National Identity in Russian Culture*, 30–49.

Wortman, Richard. "Natsionalizm, narodnost' i rossiiskoe gosudarstvo." *Neprikos-novennyi zapas* 3, no. 17 (2001): 100–105.

———. *Scenarios of Power: Myth and Ceremony in Russian Monarchy*. 2 vols. Princeton, N.J.: Princeton University Press, 1995–2000.

———. "Simvoly imperii: Ekzoticheskie narody i tseremonii koronatsii rossiiskikh imperatorov." In Gerasimov, Glebov, Kaplunovskii, Mogil'ner, and Semyonov, *Novaia imperskaia istoriia postsovetskogo prostranstva*, 409–26.

Zakharenko, A. E. "Istoriia sooruzheniia pamiatnika 'Tysiacheletiiu Rossii' v Novgorode." *Uchenye zapiski Novgorodskogo gosudarstvennogo pedagogicheskogo insti-tuta*, 2, no. 2 (1956): 51–82.

Zarubezhnye slaviane i Rossiia: Dokumenty arkhiva M. F. Raevskogo; 40–80 gody XIX veka. Moscow: Nauka, 1975.

Zorin, Andrei. *Kormia dvuglavogo orla: Literatura i gosudarstvennaia ideologiia v Rossii v poslednei treti XVIII–pervoi treti XIX veka*. Moscow: Novoe literaturnoe obozrenie, 2001.

Index

Page numbers in italics refer to illustrations.

economic issues, 6, 15; backwardness and, 7; nationalism and, 186; Old Believers and, 49; Varangian legend and, 58, 93
Editing Commission, 16
Eikhenbaum, B. M., 36
England: Crimean War and, 26, 30, 199n8; literary representations of war and, 132–33, 139; origin myths and, 55; Polish uprising and, 103; Russian national self-perception and, 5, 14, 16, 86, 90; Varangian legend and, 55
Estland, 106
Estonians, 88–89, 186–87
ethnographic exhibition, 162–64
evolution, 85, 95, 185–89
expansionism, 23, 164, 170

"The Fatal Question" (Strakhov), 100
Filaret (V. M. Drozdov): Crimean War and, 40, 204n60; myth of spiritual descent and, 160–61, 233n23; Varangian legend and, 67, 210n57; war memories and, 223n86
Filippov, Tertii, 178, 180
Finnish, 33, 56–60, 81, 186–87
Fonvizin, D. I., 67
France: Crimean War and, 26, 29–30, 50, 199n8; legacy of reform-era nationalism and, 187; literary representations of war and, 132–34, 139, 227n13; Napoleon I and, 22, 27–35, 38–40, 51, 101–2, 108, 111–16, 139, 144–45, 148, 189, 201n26, 218n30, 218n32, 219n36, 223n94, 224n97; Napoleon III and, 16, 29–30, 113, 115; Polish uprising and, 97–98, 103, 113–16; Russian national self-perception and, 5, 14, 16, 90; Second Empire of, 29; Varangian legend and, 55
freedom of speech, 6, 9
freedom of the press, 9. See also censorship
French Revolution, 3

Garshin, Vsevolod, 126
Gedeonov, S. A.: empire-nation nexus and, 81–87, 89; Norman theory and, 75–76; Varangian legend and, 82–90, 93, 213n99, 213n104, 214nn113–14, 215n137; vision of the nation and, 8–9, 16, 82–90, 93
General History of Civilization in Europe, The (Guizot), 56–57
Georgian kings, 88–89
Germany: Bismarck and, 174; growing power of, 171; legacy of reform-era nationalism and, 185–89; myth of spiritual descent and, 170–74; Polish uprising and, 105–6, 113–14; Prussia and, 159; superiority of German language and, 90; unification of, 8, 159, 170; Varangian legend and, 54, 74, 82–85, 88–92, 213n104, 214n114, 215n128
Geyer, Dietrich, 99
Gil'ferding, A. F., 160–61
Glinka, F. I., 125, 218n32, 230n61
Glinka, M. I., 67
Gnedich, A. S., 67
Gogol, Nikolai, 46, 67, 67, 105, 206n85, 210n55
Golos (The Voice; newspaper), 163
Golosa iz Rossii (Voices from Russia; journal), 9
Gorchakov, A. M., 131, 172
Gorchakov, M. N., 34
Gospels, 23, 134–35
Grand Armée, 3, 29, 139
Grazhdanin (The Citizen; newspaper), 178
Great Reforms: Crimean War and, 26–52; legacy of, 183–91; myth of spiritual descent and, 155–82; Polish uprising and, 94–127; visions of the nation and, 3–25; Varangian legend and, 53–93; war memories and, 128–54
Great Russians, 10, 75, 78, 105–6, 111, 118
Greben community, 42–49, 205n66, 206n75